DUAL PROCESS THEORY 2.0

Dual Process Theory 2.0 provides a comprehensive overview of the new directions in which dual process research is heading. Human thinking is often characterized as an interplay between intuition and deliberation, and this two-headed, dual process view of human thinking has been very influential in the cognitive sciences and popular media. However, despite the popularity of the dual process framework, it faces multiple challenges.

Recent advances indicate that there is a strong need to re-think some of the fundamental assumptions of the original dual process model. With chapters written by leading scholars who have been actively involved in the development of an upgraded 'Dual Process Theory 2.0', this edited volume presents an accessible overview of the latest empirical findings and theoretical ideas.

With cutting-edge insights on the interaction between intuition and deliberation, *Dual Process Theory 2.0* will be of interest to psychologists, philosophers, and economists who are using dual process models.

Wim De Neys is a Research Director at the French National Centre for Scientific Research (CNRS) and is affiliated with the LaPsyDE lab at the Sorbonne Paris Cité University, Paris, France.

Current Issues in Thinking and Reasoning
Series Editor: Linden Ball

Current Issues in Thinking and Reasoning is a series of edited books which will reflect the state of the art in areas of current and emerging interest in the psychological study of thinking processes.

Each volume will be tightly focussed on a particular topic and will consist of from seven to ten chapters contributed by international experts. The editors of individual volumes will be leading figures in their areas and will provide an introductory overview.

Example topics include thinking and working memory, visual imagery in problem solving, evolutionary approaches to thinking, cognitive processes in planning, creative thinking, decision making processes, pathologies of thinking, individual differences, neuropsychological approaches and applications of thinking research.

Emotion and Reasoning
Edited by Isabelle Blanchette

New Approaches in Reasoning Research
Edited by Wim De Neys and Magda Osman

The Developmental Psychology of Reasoning and Decision-Making
Edited by Henry Markovits

Aberrant Beliefs and Reasoning
Edited by Niall Galbraith

Reasoning as Memory
Edited by Aidan Feeney and Valerie A. Thompson

Individual Differences in Judgement and Decision making
Edited by Maggie E. Toplak and Joshua Weller

Moral Inferences
Edited by Jean-François Bonnefon & Bastien Trémolière

Dual Process Theory 2.0
Edited by Wim De Neys

The New Reflectionism in Cognitive Psychology
Edited by Gordon Pennycook

Insight and Creativity in Problem Solving
Edited by Kenneth J. Gilhooly, Linden J. Ball and Laura Macchi

DUAL PROCESS THEORY 2.0

Edited by Wim De Neys

Routledge
Taylor & Francis Group
LONDON AND NEW YORK

First published 2018
by Routledge
2 Park Square, Milton Park, Abingdon, Oxon OX14 4RN

and by Routledge
711 Third Avenue, New York, NY 10017

Routledge is an imprint of the Taylor & Francis Group, an informa business

© 2018 selection and editorial matter, Wim De Neys; individual chapters, the contributors

The right of the editor to be identified as the author of the editorial material, and of the authors for their individual chapters, has been asserted in accordance with sections 77 and 78 of the Copyright, Designs and Patents Act 1988.

All rights reserved. No part of this book may be reprinted or reproduced or utilised in any form or by any electronic, mechanical, or other means, now known or hereafter invented, including photocopying and recording, or in any information storage or retrieval system, without permission in writing from the publishers.

Trademark notice: Product or corporate names may be trademarks or registered trademarks, and are used only for identification and explanation without intent to infringe.

British Library Cataloguing-in-Publication Data
A catalogue record for this book is available from the British Library

Library of Congress Cataloging-in-Publication Data
A catalog record for this book has been requested

ISBN: 978-1-138-70062-8 (hbk)
ISBN: 978-1-138-70064-2 (pbk)
ISBN: 978-1-315-20455-0 (ebk)

Typeset in Bembo
by Apex CoVantage, LLC

CONTENTS

Contributors — vii

1 Dual process theory 2.0: an introduction — 1
  Wim De Neys

2 A perspective on the theoretical foundation of dual process models — 5
  Gordon Pennycook

3 The parallel processing model of belief bias: review and extensions — 28
  Dries Trippas and Simon J. Handley

4 Bias, conflict, and fast logic: towards a hybrid dual process future? — 47
  Wim De Neys

5 Comparing dual process theories: evidence from event-related potentials — 66
  Adrian P. Banks

6 The fuzzy-trace dual process model — 82
  Valerie F. Reyna, Shahin Rahimi-Golkhandan, David M. N. Garavito, and Rebecca K. Helm

7 Conflict and dual process theory: the case of belief bias 100
Linden J. Ball, Valerie A. Thompson and Edward J. N. Stupple

8 Logical intuitions and other conundra for dual process theories 121
Valerie A. Thompson and Ian R. Newman

9 Dual process theory: perspectives and problems 137
Jonathan St B. T. Evans

Index *157*

CONTRIBUTORS

Linden J. Ball, School of Psychology, University of Central Lancashire, Preston, United Kingdom

Adrian P. Banks, School of Psychology, AD Building, University of Surrey, Guildford, Surrey, United Kingdom

Wim De Neys, LaPsyDE, Université Paris Sorbonne Cité, Sorbonne – Labo A. Binet, Paris, France

Jonathan St B. T. Evans, Emeritus Professor, School of Psychology, Portland Square, Plymouth, United Kingdom

David M. N. Garavito, Human Neuroscience Institute, Cornell University, Ithaca, New York

Simon J. Handley, Macquarie University, Faculty of Human Sciences, North Ryde, Australia

Rebecca K. Helm, Human Neuroscience Institute, Cornell University, Ithaca, New York

Ian R. Newman, Department of Psychology, University of Saskatchewan, Saskatoon, Canada

Gordon Pennycook, Yale University, Department of Psychology, New Haven, Connecticut

Shahin Rahimi-Golkhandan, Human Neuroscience Institute, Cornell University, Ithaca, New York

Valerie F. Reyna, Human Neuroscience Institute, Cornell University, Ithaca, New York

Edward J. N. Stupple, Centre for Psychological Research, University of Derby, United Kingdom

Valerie A. Thompson, Department of Psychology, University of Saskatchewan, Saskatoon, Canada

Dries Trippas, Center for Adaptive Rationality, Max Planck Institute for Human Development, Berlin, Germany

1
DUAL PROCESS THEORY 2.0

An introduction

Wim De Neys

Background

Human thinking is often characterized as an interplay between intuition and deliberation. Sometimes a solution to a problem pops up in our minds without any effort. At other times, arriving at a sound conclusion will take time and laborious inferencing. These types of reasoning are often referred to as intuitive and deliberate thinking. Intuitive thinking is effortless and fast. It provides us with problem solutions in the blink of an eye. Deliberative thinking is slower and burdens our cognitive resources, but will sometimes be indispensable to correct the output of our intuitions. Indeed, many cases of biased decision-making – from bad financial investments to racial or gender-based discrimination in job hiring – have been attributed to a failure to switch from intuitive to deliberate thinking. This two-headed, dual process view of human thinking has been very influential in the cognitive sciences and popular media. Examples range from the Nobel Prize–winning work of Daniel Kahneman to the best-selling popular science writing of Malcolm Gladwell.

However, despite the popularity of the dual process framework, it faces multiple challenges. A key issue that has long bothered dual process theorists is that the precise interaction between intuitive and deliberate thought processes (or System 1 and System 2, as they are often referred to) is not well understood. There is little dispute that sometimes intuitions can be helpful and sometimes deliberation is required to arrive at a conclusion. But how does our reasoning engine decide which route to take? Are both processes activated simultaneously from the start, or do we initially rely on the intuitive system and switch to deliberate processing when it is needed? But how do we know whether deliberation is needed and determine whether merely relying on our intuitions is warranted or not? What mechanism signals the need for more deliberate reflection?

In recent years empirical work has started to address these outstanding issues. This has resulted in theoretical advances that indicate that there is a need to re-think fundamental assumptions of the original dual process model. The aim of this edited *Dual Process 2.0* volume is to give the reader a comprehensive overview of these new directions in which dual process research is heading.

Book structure

The book consists of nine chapters. The seven chapters that follow this brief introduction are all written by leading experts who have been actively involved in the experimental testing and development of the dual process framework in the last years. The chapters present an accessible overview of their main findings, the theoretical modifications they propose, and discussion of pressing issues and challenges. In the closing chapter, Jonathan Evans presents a reflection on the evolutions that are highlighted in the book.

Chapter overview

Chapter 2

A perspective on the theoretical foundation of dual process models
Gordon Pennycook (Yale University, USA)

In his thought-provoking chapter Pennycook lays out what he views to be the core theoretical groundwork for future dual process models. He draws on these foundations and parallels them with the executive functioning literature to outline an updated framework.

Chapter 3

The parallel processing model of belief bias: review and extensions
Dries Trippas (Max Planck Institute for Human Development, Germany) and Simon J. Handley (Macquarie University, Australia)

In their chapter Trippas and Handley describe how the classic Stroop effect inspired them to introduce a new reasoning paradigm in which participants have to switch between belief-based and logic-based thinking. They clarify how this led them to present a new dual process model in which multiple problem features are processed simultaneously from the start. The chapter presents a comprehensive overview of the core assumptions and critical empirical tests.

Chapter 4

Bias, conflict, and fast logic: towards a hybrid dual process future?
Wim De Neys (CNRS & Université Sorbonne Paris Cité, France)

In my personal chapter contribution, I present the basic dual process model that I believe to be supported by my own empirical findings and the work of many of the contributors to this volume. I review critical findings from my team and discuss outstanding questions and issues.

Chapter 5

Comparing dual process theories: evidence from event-related potentials
Adrian P. Banks (University of Surrey, UK)

Banks and his collaborators have pioneered the use of event-related potentials (ERP) to test dual process theories of reasoning. ERP research has the potential to tap fast intuitive processes that can be difficult to investigate using behavioural paradigms. In his chapter Banks reviews the relevant ERP literature and shows how his findings favour a model in which logic and belief are processed in parallel by fast System 1 processes.

Chapter 6

The fuzzy-trace dual process model
Valerie F. Reyna, Shahin Rahimi-Golkhandan, David M. N. Garavito, and Rebecca K. Helm (Cornell University, USA)

Reyna and collaborators present an overview of their fuzzy-trace dual process framework. The unique cornerstone of the fuzzy-trace approach lies in the distinction – inspired by classic psycholinguistics – between verbatim and gist-based representations of presented information. Within this framework, intuitive gist-based processing is placed at the apex of advanced thinking. Reyna et al. present an extensive overview of the wide range of studies that tested the fuzzy-trace predictions.

Chapter 7

Conflict and dual process theory: the case of belief bias
Linden J. Ball (University of Central Lancashire, UK),
Valerie A. Thompson (University of Saskatchewan, Canada),
and Edward J. N. Stupple (University of Derby, UK)

Traditional dual process theories were heavily inspired by research on the belief bias effect in syllogistic reasoning. Ball et al. present an overview of this literature and recent challenges to the traditional dual process model of belief bias. They sketch the core tenets of an attempt to reconcile the traditional framework with the contradictory challenges.

Chapter 8

Logical intuitions and other conundra for dual process theories
Valerie A. Thompson and Ian R. Newman
(University of Saskatchewan, Canada)

Thompson and Newman review how recent findings have challenged three pillars of the traditional dual process framework with respect to the speed, sequence, and cognitive capacity dependency of intuitive and deliberate processing. They discuss key implications and questions for the future of dual process research.

Chapter 9

Dual process theory: perspectives and problems
Jonathan St B. T. Evans (Plymouth University, UK)

As an editor, I am very grateful that Jonathan Evans agreed to write the closing chapter to this volume. Jonathan is widely considered the godfather of the standard dual process model that has come to dominate the field. Various contributors to this book indicate that there is a need to revise key features of this model and re-think our conceptualization of the way intuition and deliberation interact. Although Jonathan is now officially retired, he agreed to use the chapter to comment on these new developments. He points to possible misconceptions and ways to integrate the recent findings in the default-interventionist model that he favours.

In closing

Taken together, I believe that the book presents an excellent overview of the state of the art of the dual process field. My hope is that the volume will help to familiarize the wide range of psychologists, philosophers, and economists who have grown an interest in dual process models with the latest insights and discussions. At the same time, the book should also make it clear that the field is still in full development and the last word on key debates has not been said. More work is definitely needed. I hope that the book will stimulate at least some readers to join in this exciting journey.

2
A PERSPECTIVE ON THE THEORETICAL FOUNDATION OF DUAL PROCESS MODELS

Gordon Pennycook

Overview

> *Educating the mind without educating the heart is no education at all.*
> — Aristotle (384–322 BCE)

> *Where the senses fail us, reason must step in.*
> — Galileo Galilei (1564–1642 ACE)

> *The heart has its reasons of which reason knows nothing.*
> — Blaise Pascal (1623–1662 ACE)

> *Faith consists in believing when it is beyond the power of reason to believe.*
> — Voltaire (1694–1778 ACE)

> *Reason is, and ought only to be the slave of the passions, and can never pretend to any other office than to serve and obey them.*
> — David Hume (1711–1776 ACE)

Dual process theories formalize a salient feature of human cognition: we have the capacity to rapidly formulate answers to questions, but we sometimes engage in deliberate reasoning processes before responding. It does not require deliberative thought to respond to the question "what is your name." It did, however, require some thinking to write this paragraph (perhaps not enough). We have, in other words, two minds that might influence what we decide to do (Evans, 2003; Evans & Frankish, 2009). Although this distinction is acceptable (and, as I'll argue, essentially irrefutable), it poses serious challenges for our understanding of cognitive architecture. In this chapter, I will outline what I view to be important theoretical groundwork for future dual process models. I will start with two core premises that

I take to be foundational: 1) dual process theory is irrefutable, but falsifiable; and 2) analytic thought has to be triggered by something. I will then use these premises to outline my perspective on what I consider the most substantial challenge for dual process theorists: we don't (yet) know what makes us think.

Introduction

The distinction between intuition (heart, senses, passion, faith) and reflection (mind, reason, analytic thinking) dates, at least, to antiquity and has been the object of philosophical musing for centuries (as evidenced by the opening quotations). It is perhaps unsurprising, then, that dual process theories are popular in many domains of psychology (see Evans, 2008 for a review), such as reasoning (Evans, 1989; Sloman, 1996; Stanovich & West, 2000), decision making (Barbey & Sloman, 2007; Kahneman, 2011; Kahneman & Frederick, 2005), social cognition (Chaiken & Trope, 1999; Epstein, Pacini, Denes-Raj, & Heier, 1996), cognitive development (Barrouillet, 2011; Brainerd & Reyna, 2001; Klaczynski, 2001), clinical psychology (Beevers, 2005; Pyszczynski, Greenberg, & Solomon, 1999), and cognitive neuroscience (Goel, 2007; Greene, Sommerville, Nystrom, Darley, & Cohen, 2001; Lieberman, 2007). Indeed, as evidenced by Figure 2.1, dual process theories in psychology have proliferated (see Frankish & Evans, 2009 for an historical overview).

Naturally, contemporary dual process theories go well beyond the musings of philosophers like Aristotle and Voltaire (see De Neys, this volume). The proliferation of dual process theories evidenced in Figure 2.1 corresponds with a proliferation of characteristics that have been used to distinguish the two types of processes. Intuitive (or 'Type 1', or 'System 1') processes have been considered autonomous, fast, domain specific, evolutionarily old, unconscious, high capacity, and associative (among others), whereas analytic (or 'Type 2' or 'System 2') processing has

FIGURE 2.1 Number of journal articles using the terms "dual process theory," "dual process theory," or "dual processes" in the field of psychology since 1970. Search completed on November 25, 2016.

been considered deliberative, slow, domain general, evolutionarily young, conscious, capacity limited, and rule-based (among others). Recently, Evans and Stanovich (2013a) noted that most of these are merely *correlated* features of intuition and reflection and that a few characteristics can be isolated as *defining* features of Type 1 and Type 2 processes. Specifically, they argued that Type 1 processes operate autonomously and do not require working memory, whereas Type 2 processes require working memory and allow for cognitive decoupling and mental simulation.

Evans and Stanovich's (2013a) new synthesis represents a crucial step forward for dual process theories insofar as they have provided a framework that can be used to organize and guide future theorization. This work corresponds with previous attempts to delineate and eliminate common fallacies in dual process theorizing (Evans, 2012), such as the claim that intuition always leads to errors, whereas reflection always produces normatively correct responses. Nonetheless, there is still much work to be done (hence the necessity of this volume). The goal of this chapter is to discuss what I think is the most crucial problem facing dual process theories: we have a good sense of what intuitive and analytic processes *are*, but we do not have a good sense of how they *operate*. That is, dual process theories have not sufficiently modelled analytic engagement.

My goal with this chapter is to lay out what I take to be the core theoretical foundations that should guide the pursuit of a better understanding of analytic engagement. I will then use these foundations to briefly outline an updated dual process theory – the three-stage dual process model (Pennycook, Fugelsang, & Koehler, 2015b) – as a way to formalize and (begin to) address the crucial question: "What makes us think?" (i.e., What triggers Type 2 processing?).

Prior to outlining the three-stage dual process model, which I view as largely a synthesis of previous models (with a few added components), I will explicate the two key premises that form the motivation for the model and by which the model is built. The premises are as follows:

Premise 1: Dual process theory is irrefutable, but falsifiable.
Premise 2: Analytic thought has to be triggered by something.

These premises will provide the organization for the first half of this chapter.

Premise 1: dual process theory is irrefutable, but falsifiable

Evans and Stanovich (2013a) isolated both autonomy and working memory as defining features of dual process theories. However, it is only necessary for a single dimension to distinguish intuitive and reflective processes for the theory to be based on an acceptable proposition. Indeed, Thompson (2013) has argued that autonomy is the only feature needed to distinguish the two types of processes – an argument that I agree with. Thus, to understand why dual process theory, at its most basic level, is irrefutable,[1] the concept of autonomy needs to be explained.

Plainly, some cognitive outputs are engendered directly as a result of stimulus–response pairings. One cannot help but think of their name when asked "what is your name," Autonomous processes initiate and complete outside of deliberate control, and there is little doubt that this is something that actually occurs in the mind (Stanovich, 2009).[2] However, there is also little doubt that humans are capable of reasoning in the absence of an immediate autonomous response. Consider the following arithmetic problems (c/o Thompson, 2013): [$2 \times 0 = ?$] and [$2217 \times 72 = ?$]. The former cues an autonomous response (assuming a basic level of mathematics education), whereas a response to the latter can only be generated with some effort. This highlights an important aspect of analytic processing: the reasoner can decide whether to carry out (or continue carrying out) a mental operation. That is, humans are able to decide about deciding. Crucially, this can occur even in cases where an intuitive response is evident. Imagine, for example, if you were told to perform addition when the symbol for multiplication was present. The problem [$2 \times 0 = ?$] would still engender the initial response ('0'), but (under normal conditions) you would be able to stop yourself from answering '0' in lieu of the alternative analytic response ('2'). Naturally, one could also choose to not bother with the addition operation. Note in this case, the actual operation of adding 2 and 0 does not require analytic thought. Rather, replacing multiplication with addition is what requires analytic thought.

It is important to note that this is a falsifiable claim. It needn't be the case that people are capable of autonomous processing – 2×0 does not have to automatically equal 0.[3] Similarly, it needn't be the case that people must be able to purposefully deliberate. Bechara, Damasio, Damasio, and Anderson (1994) famously observed that patients with damage to the ventromedial prefrontal cortex are insensitive to the future consequences of decisions. Moreover, analytic thinking increases during adolescent development (Kokis, Macpherson, Toplak, West, & Stanovich, 2002). That most adult humans are capable of generating both intuitive and reflective answers to questions is merely an empirical observation. Dual process theory – or, at least, the basic claim that individual dual process theories all assume – is irrefutable. The very act of arguing against this proposition would require deliberative processes (following, perhaps, an autonomous visceral reaction to the polemical use of the term 'irrefutable').

The observation that the distinction between intuition and reflection is irrefutable is foundational because it means that dual process models should not be concerned with justifying this claim. That is, dual process models must take this distinction as a given and build from there. If we know with a reasonable degree of certainty that the mind has this capacity for two different types of processes (autonomous and non-autonomous), where do we go from there?

Premise 2: analytic thought has to be triggered by something

The irrefutability of dual process theory does not bear on its usefulness. Indeed, the true test of a good theory is whether it can be applied successfully to problems and generate hypotheses (see Evans & Stanovich, 2013a for a discussion of this issue in the context of dual process theory). Thus, the mere distinction between intuition and reflection based on autonomy is sufficient for the claim that dual process theory is irrefutable, but not sufficient for the claim that the theory is worth anyone's time. What is needed, then, is a discussion of the ways that the distinction bears on further cognitive processing. This can then be used to generate further hypotheses.

Focusing on autonomy as the defining feature that distinguishes intuitive and analytic processing is beneficial for more reasons than that it offers an irrefutable foundation for the theory. Namely, the concept of autonomy naturally leads to questions about the potential *source* of the cognitive output. For an autonomous intuitive response, the answer to the question is straightforward: the (proximal[4]) source of the response is the stimulus–response pairing(s). There is a direct and uninterrupted mapping between the stimulus and the intuitive output. This may be either external, such as when someone asks your name, or internal, such as through associative processes (e.g., thinking about one's name could automatically prime aspects of self-concept).

But what is the source of an analytic response? Put differently, when analytic processing is used to engage in some way with representation content (e.g., via hypothetical thought; Evans, 2007), what causes the process to initiate? Although there may be many answers to this question, it is important to note that some are more central to our understanding of cognitive architecture. For example, one way to force participants to initiate analytic thought is to simply instruct them to do so (Evans, Handley, Neilens, Bacon, & Over, 2010). There are also situations in which individuals should intuitively recognize when analytic thought is necessary. When an individual is handed an entrance exam, it is no mystery why they spend a lot of time pondering the questions contained therein. Regardless, even within these contexts there may be things that trigger increased analytic processing – such as a particularly difficult problem on an intelligence test. Moreover, there are many situations in which there is little obvious incentive to spend time thinking analytically, but at least some people nonetheless think analytically (at least some of the time). Thus, the task is to determine what causes individuals to engage analytic processing in the absence of some obvious situational or instructional cue (Pennycook, Fugelsang, & Koehler, 2015b).

To illustrate the phenomena of interest, consider the following problem (Frederick, 2005):

> A bat and ball cost $1.10 in total. The bat costs $1.00 more than the ball. How much does the ball cost?

This problem, now famous, is one of three from the original Cognitive Reflection Test (CRT). The majority of participants answer $0.10 to this problem (e.g., 64.9% among Canadian undergraduate students; Pennycook, Cheyne, Koehler, & Fugelsang, 2016) although a cursory double-check shows that the ball cannot cost $0.10 as it would mean the bat would have to cost $1.10 (totalling $1.20). Performance is surprisingly poor on the bat-and-ball problem because 10 cents comes to mind quickly and fluently – it is an autonomous intuitive response.

Still, some people do successfully solve the bat-and-ball problem (e.g., 30.3% in Pennycook et al., 2016; very few give an answer other than $0.10 or $0.05). Moreover, accuracy on the CRT has been shown to correlate with a wide range of measures of psychological interest (see Pennycook, 2015a for a review). Indeed, one only needs the single bat-and-ball problem to predict an impressive range of beliefs and behaviours. To demonstrate, I re-analyzed the studies that my research group published in the period between 2012 and 2016 (the duration of my PhD) with the goal of demonstrating the predictive power of the single bat-and-ball problem. For simplicity, I did not include redundant measures (i.e., religious belief was included in various studies, but only the largest and most recent sample is shown in Table 2.1). Those who give the correct answer to the bat-and-ball problem differ on a wide range of measures, ranging from religious belief to morality to creativity to technology use to distress following sleep paralysis episodes. There is very strong evidence that the CRT (and the bat-and-ball problem) measures something that is of some importance for human psychology. It should also be noted that cognitive ability or intelligence rarely explain these correlations (see Pennycook et al., 2015a). A wide range of other potential third variables have been explored in some cases as well (most substantively in the case of religious belief, see Pennycook, 2014).

The question, then, is what does the bat-and-ball question measure? Perhaps the most common argument is that the presence of the intuitive response means that one must be willing to think analytically to solve the problem (e.g., Pennycook & Ross, 2016). That is, the CRT is thought to measure one's propensity to engage in deliberative processing and override the incorrect intuitive response (Campitelli & Gerrans, 2014; Toplak, West, & Stanovich, 2014; Toplak, West, & Stanovich, 2011). This stance follows directly from Stanovich's (Stanovich, 1999, 2005; Stanovich & West, 2000; Stanovich & West, 1998; Stanovich, 2012) influential work distinguishing analytic thinking disposition from standard intelligence or cognitive ability. The argument, in short, is that both the *willingness* and *ability* to engage analytic reasoning are important components of human rationality.

This is a largely acceptable account of CRT performance, but a significant question remains: How does the analytic person know to engage in analytic processing? Perhaps the answer is simply that analytic individuals are cautious when given reasoning problems. This may be an acceptable account when it comes to the bat-and-ball problem, but what of the wide variety of things with which the bat-and-ball problem correlate (Table 2.1)? The presumption here is that the bat-and-ball problem is predictive because the propensity to think analytically is applied not only to reasoning problems in psychology studies, but also in people's everyday lives (Pennycook et al., 2015a). The idea that analytic people are simply cautious when given reasoning problems in the lab cannot explain why these people are also, evidently, more likely to think analytically about religious and paranormal claims, or how they use technology, or their sleep paralysis experiences, etc. There has to be something that spontaneously *triggers* analytic thought, and the cues that cause

TABLE 2.1 Various correlates of the bat-and-ball problem. Participants were put into one of three groups based on their answer. Means are of dependent variables (DV) converted to z-scores.

Source	Dependent Variable	Intuitive ($0.10)	Other (e.g., $1.05)	Correct ($0.05)	ANOVA
Pennycook, Ross, Koehler, and Fugelsang (2016) – Studies 1–4	Religious Belief	0.13 (629)	0.10 (40)	−0.21 (394)	$F(2, 1060) = 14.97^{***}$
Barr, Pennycook, Stolz, and Fugelsang (2015) – Study 3	Online Smartphone Use	0.15 (144)	0.20 (10)	−0.32 (73)	$F(2, 224) = 5.77^{**}$
Pennycook, Cheyne, Barr, Koehler, and Fugelsang (2015) – Study 1	Bullshit Receptivity	0.18 (170)	0.14 (16)	−0.36 (93)	$F(2, 276) = 9.33^{***}$
	Ontological Confusions	0.20 (170)	−0.08 (16)	−0.35 (93)	$F(2, 276) = 9.67^{***}$
Pennycook, Cheyne, Barr, Koehler, and Fugelsang (2014b)	Moral Judgment (Disgust-Based Dilemmas)	0.24 (280)	−0.54 (16)	−0.29 (204)	$F(2, 497) = 21.03^{***}$
	Traditional Moral Values	0.20 (282)	−0.07 (16)	−0.27 (207)	$F(2, 502) = 13.58^{***}$
	Social Conservatism	0.14 (281)	−0.37 (16)	−0.17 (207)	$F(2, 501) = 7.14^{**}$
	Fiscal Conservatism	0.10 (281)	−0.37 (16)	−0.11 (207)	$F(2, 501) = 3.88^{*}$
Barr et al. (2015)	Cross-Domain Analogy (Accuracy)	−0.22 (60)	– (3)	0.37 (38)	$F(1, 96) = 8.82^{**}$
	Remote Associates Test (Accuracy)	−0.15 (60)	– (3)	0.27 (38)	$F(1, 96) = 4.17^{*}$
Cheyne and Pennycook (2013)	Sleep Paralysis Post-Episode Distress	0.09 (210)	−0.10 (12)	−0.24 (76)	$F(2, 295) = 3.09^{*}$
Pennycook, Cheyne, Seli, Koehler, and Fugelsang (2012) – Study 2	Paranormal Belief	0.11 (196)	−0.11 (11)	−0.27 (76)	$F(2, 280) = 4.10^{*}$

See sources for more information on DVs.

*** $p < .001$
** $p < .01$
* $p < .05$. N's listed in subscript

people to think analytically in all of these cases surely differ. What this means is that dual process theories require a mechanism to explain how the mind detects when analytic processing is necessary. Unfortunately, this problem has not received the attention it deserves by dual process theorists. Fortunately, there are some clues from related literatures.

Understanding what makes us think: parallels between dual processing and executive functioning

There is a very clear parallel between the foregoing and a diverse range of theorizing in the executive functioning literature. Indeed, the concepts used to explain dual processes in reasoning are very similar to those used to explain cognitive control. The primary difference has to do with scope: dual process theorists are concerned with high-level reasoning tasks (often with response times [RTs] of 15 to 30 seconds), whereas the cognitive control literature grapples with relatively low-level tasks (e.g., the Stroop task) with millisecond RTs. Moreover, the cognitive control literature is characterized by a stronger focus on neuroscientific (Mars, Sallet, Rushworth, & Yeung, 2011) and computational (Botvinick & Cohen, 2014) models. Nonetheless, a key question for cognitive control has to do with determining what causes our cognitive system to engage in controlled processing (Botvinick, Cohen, & Carter, 2004; Carter et al., 1998; Shenhav, Botvinick, & Cohen, 2013). Parsimony suggests that the low-level mechanism that triggers controlled processing also triggers analytic processing. Moreover, the difference between 'controlled' and 'analytic' processing may merely be one of scope.[5]

According to Botvinick and Braver (2015) cognitive control refers to

> that set of superordinate functions that encode and maintain a representation of the current task – i.e., contextually relevant stimulus-response associations, action-outcome contingencies, and target states or goals – marshaling to that task subordinate functions including working, semantic, and episodic memory; perceptual attention; and action selection and inhibition.
>
> (p. 85)

The Stroop task, where conflict between colour words and colour names causes increases in RT, is a classic example of a cognitive control task (MacLeod, 1991).

In parallel with the bat-and-ball example, part of the reason why people engage in cognitive control on Stroop-like tasks is obvious: they were given a task to do and are simply completing it. Nonetheless, the reason why the Stroop task is interesting is because there are trials in which participants engage in more controlled processing (as indexed by increased RT). People spend more time when the colour word and name conflict than when they correspond. Moreover, incentives enhance cognitive control (as indexed by RTs on the Stroop task; Padmala & Pessoa, 2010). Thus, as with the explanation of the bat-and-ball problem, some aspect of cognitive

TABLE 2.2 Comparison of a classic cognitive control task (Stroop, 1935) with a classic reasoning and decision-making task (Kahneman & Tversky, 1973)

A trial from the Stroop task		A trial from a base-rate neglect task	
What colour is the word? **WHITE**		In a study 1,000 people were tested. Among the participants there were 995 nurses and 5 doctors. Paul is a randomly chosen participant of this study.	
		Paul is 34 years old. He lives in a beautiful home in a posh suburb. He is well spoken and very interested in politics. He invests a lot of time in his career.	
		What is most likely?	
		(a) Paul is a nurse.	
		(b) Paul is a doctor.	
Prepotent response: White	Correct answer: Black	Prepotent response: Doctor	Correct answer: Nurse

control is discretionary. The question, then, is how does the cognitive system know when further processing is necessary?

Consider the comparison offered in Table 2.2. Verily, the Stroop task does not appear at all similar to the reasoning task (in this case, a base-rate neglect problem; De Neys & Glumicic, 2008). Nonetheless, in both cases there is a strong prepotent response. It has long been noted in the Stroop literature that reading the colour word ('WHITE') interferes with naming the word colour (black) (MacLeod, 1991). The cognitive control literature has therefore focused largely on response conflict as an initiator of controlled processing (see Botvinick & Cohen, 2014 for a historical overview). According to Botvinick and Cohen (2014), for example, "circumstances that demand control are typically characterized by the presence of processing conflict" (see also Berlyne, 1957) and "conflict is quantified as the coactivation of competing representations" (p. 1257). The monitoring of conflict is thought to occur in the anterior cingulate cortex, which then leads to controlled processing in the dorsolateral prefrontal cortex (e.g., Botvinick et al., 2004; Carter & van Veen, 2007; Shenhav et al., 2013).

In parallel with the cognitive control literature, conflict has also been an important component of dual process theorizing (Evans, 2007; Sloman, 1996). In fact, there are functional magnetic resonance imaging (fMRI) studies that report patterns of activation in the prefrontal cortex that correspond nicely to that reported in the cognitive control literature (e.g., Goel, Buchel, Frith, & Dolan, 2000; Goel & Dolan, 2004; Stollstorff, Vartanian, & Goel, 2012). Moreover, the congruence–sequence effect (Egner, 2007) – a crucial finding in the cognitive control literature wherein the effect of conflict on Stroop-like tasks is smaller after incongruent (conflict) relative to congruent (non-conflict trials) – has recently been reported in the context of a decision-making paradigm (Aczel &

Palfi, 2017). This indicates parallel modulation of control following conflict processing in quite different paradigms.

In the case of the base-rate task, there is a strong tendency for people to respond according to the intuitive stereotypical information presented in the personality description despite the presence of objective and contradictory base-rate information about the sample (this is the "representativeness heuristic"; [Kahneman & Tversky, 1973; see Pennycook & Thompson, 2016 for a review]). A core finding is that people tend to take longer and are less confident when given "conflict" versions of this task (as seen in Table 2.2) relative to "non-conflict" versions (e.g., if the base rates were reversed in the Table 2.2 example), even in cases when the stereotypical response is given (De Neys, Cromheeke, & Osman, 2011; De Neys & Glumicic, 2008). This indicates that the conflict between base rate and stereotype has an effect on later reasoning.

Notably, De Neys, Vartanian, and Goel (2008) found increased activation in the anterior cingulate cortex when participants gave stereotypical responses to incongruent (conflict) versions of base-rate problems relative to congruent (non-conflict) baseline. De Neys et al. also reported increased activation in the right lateral prefrontal cortex when participants overrode the intuitive stereotypical response in lieu of the alternative base-rate response. This directly parallels neuroimaging experiments in the cognitive control literature – a remarkable convergence given the difference between the tasks (as illustrated in Table 2.2; see also Simon, Lubin, Houdé, & De Neys, 2015).

The foregoing indicates a strong convergence between two very different literatures. There is, however, one key difference in terms of theorizing: cognitive control theorists have grappled with "disarming the homunculus" (Botvinick & Cohen, 2014) – that is, a source of intelligence used to fill theoretical gaps – more seriously and substantially than have dual process theorists. The conflict monitoring hypothesis (e.g., Botvinick et al., 2004) requires only the coactivation of competing responses to explain what initiates control. Modeling work illustrates how cognitive control can be adjusted based on "local computations" (basically, comparisons of coactivated response outputs; see Botvinick & Cohen, 2014).

As has been argued elsewhere (Pennycook et al., 2015b), the most common assumption among dual process theorists is that Type 2/System 2 (analytic) processing is responsible for monitoring the output of Type 1/System 1 (intuitive) processes (Evans, 2006; Kahneman & Frederick, 2005; Stanovich, 1999). When considered in light of the question "what makes us think" and alongside research on cognitive control, it is clear that this assumption is untenable. Type 2 processing cannot be responsible for monitoring Type 1 processing because Type 2 processing would therefore have to be responsible for its own initiation. Type 2 processing would have to cause itself. This indicates that a third process is necessary to explain how Type 1 and Type 2 processes interact (Thompson et al., 2013; Thompson, Prowse Turner, & Pennycook, 2011; Thompson, 2009; Thompson & Morsanyi, 2012).

An important downstream consequence of the foregoing assumption is that conflict in reasoning tasks has most commonly been considered a conflict *between*

Type 1 and Type 2 processes (De Neys & Glumicic, 2008; Evans, 2007; Sloman, 1996). This is also an untenable position: if it's the conflict between Type 1 and Type 2 responses that initiates Type 2 processing, how was the initial Type 2 response generated? The only possible answer that I can see is that the Type 2 response was generated as a direct result of the stimulus, which then presumes that it was generated autonomously. This violates the key component of the first premise (that Type 1 and 2 processes are distinguished by autonomy) and would therefore mean that dual process theory is not only refutable, but easily so.

Two conclusions emerge from this line of reasoning: 1) in keeping with the cognitive control literature, conflict during reasoning should be considered a result of the coactivation of competing Type 1 responses; and 2) considering the reasoning process in stages may help delineate what is causing what. I will conclude by discussing these in the context of two recent dual process models.

The logical intuition model

As outlined elsewhere in this volume, evidence that people are capable of detecting conflicts between reasoning outputs has been mounting (De Neys, 2012, 2014). Evidence from RT, confidence, and neuroimaging experiments in the context of base-rate neglect has already been discussed. However, there is also good evidence for successful detection of conflict between logic and belief in the context of syllogistic reasoning (De Neys & Franssens, 2009; Handley, Newstead, & Trippas, 2011; Handley & Trippas, 2015; Trippas, Handley, Verde, & Morsanyi, 2016). There is even evidence for conflict detection (via confidence measures) in the context of the bat-and-ball problem that was introduced earlier in this chapter (De Neys, Rossi, & Houdé, 2013; Johnson, Tubau, & De Neys, 2016; but see Travers, Rolison, & Feeney, 2016).[6] A wide range of additional dependent variables has been employed, including memory recall (De Neys & Franssens, 2009; De Neys & Glumicic, 2008), skin conductance response (De Neys, Moyens, & Vansteenwegen, 2010), liking ratings (Morsanyi & Handley, 2012; Trippas et al., 2016), eye tracking (Ball, Phillips, Wade, & Quayle, 2006), and event-related potential (Banks & Hope, 2014; De Neys, Novitskiy, Ramautar, & Wagemans, 2010).

The tension that these results revealed for dual process models was evident from the outset. If two types of processes are capable of producing different answers, what process determines if those answers correspond? De Neys and Glumicic (2008) used "shallow analytic monitoring" (SHAM) to explain how a type of Type 2 processing could accomplish this. However, the SHAM was clearly patchwork – it was thought to "always accompany" heuristic (intuitive) processing, but also is not "full-fledged" analytic thinking (p. 1278). It is not clear what makes this monitoring process "analytic", apart from the fact that it held the function that was typically attributed to analytic processing (an untenable attribution, as I have outlined earlier). From what I can tell, SHAM was only referred to directly in one subsequent publication (Pennycook & Thompson, 2012), although it was discussed indirectly by Bonner and Newell (2010).

Logical intuition model

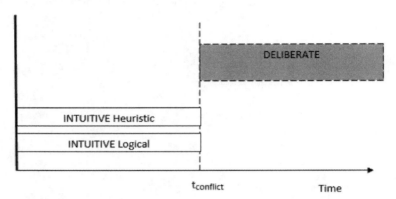

FIGURE 2.2 Updated logical intuition model (De Neys, personal communication). Analytic (deliberate, Type 2) processing is represented by the gray bar, and intuitive (Type 1) processing by the white bars. The horizontal axis represents time. Deliberate processing is triggered by conflict ($t_{conflict}$) between intuitive 'heuristic' and intuitive 'logical' processing. The dashed lines represent the "optional nature of the triggered deliberate processing" (De Neys, personal communication).

The core theoretical insight that emerged from this line of work was that conflict detection effects can be parsimoniously explained by appealing to a conflict between intuitions (De Neys, 2012; Pennycook & Thompson, 2012). De Neys' logical intuition model formalized this argument (De Neys, 2012, 2014; De Neys & Bonnefon, 2013; see Figure 2.2). The term "logical intuition" refers to the observation that, in the context of the reasoning paradigms that have been employed, conflict detection relies upon the presence of some sort of intuition that emerges from more logical considerations or principles.

The logical intuition model (Figure 2.2) was, in my view, an important step forward for the dual process literature (for another important perspective, see Handley & Trippas, 2015, Trippas & Handley, this volume). Nonetheless, there are elements that I disagree with. First, and most pedantically, I view the term "logical intuition" to be unnecessarily specific. It is perfectly possible (and perhaps more common) for *illogical* intuitions to conflict and lead to analytic processing. That intuitions have the appearance of logicality in some situations does not mean that this is necessary for Type 1–Type 1 conflict to initiate Type 2 processing. Indeed, one of the things that I think will be important for future theorizing is a broader view of intuitions.

Second, and more substantively, the logical intuition model assumes perfectly efficient (De Neys, 2012) – or, at least, highly efficient (De Neys, 2014, Figure 2.2) – conflict detection. One of the key arguments is that even particularly biased individuals detect conflicts (De Neys & Bonnefon, 2013). This is a crucial issue because it tells us about the source of bias. Namely, if biased individuals successfully detect conflicts, bias cannot be the result of lax conflict monitoring and must therefore be the result of faulty Type 2 processing (e.g., through inhibition failures). This has been the context through which the logical intuition model has been largely framed.

There are, however, reasons to believe that conflict detection is not highly efficient in terms of initiating analytic thinking. Pennycook, Fugelsang, and Koehler (2012) found that subtle manipulations to prior probabilities in base-rate neglect problems were sufficient to abolish the increase in RT for stereotypical responses. Specifically, there was consistent evidence for conflict detection when base rates are extreme (e.g., 995 lawyers, 5 engineers), but no evidence when base rates were implicit (e.g., by using natural base rates, such as between the low number of statistics majors and high number of psychology majors at the University of Waterloo) or moderate (e.g., 70 lawyers, 30 engineers). Later work with a larger set of base-rate problems that produce shorter and more reliable RTs (i.e., a more sensitive measure) successfully found a conflict detection effect using moderate base rates (Pennycook, Fugelsang, & Koehler, 2015b). However, this effect was driven primarily by a small number of individuals who were particularly *un*biased (that is, they did not fall prey to the stereotypes as consistently as most). In other words, conflict detection was evident among those who demonstrated a propensity to override the intuitive stereotypes – presumably because conflict detection leads to analytic thinking, which increases the likelihood of analytic overriding of stereotypical responses. There was little to no evidence of conflict detection among those who primarily gave stereotypical responses (the particularly 'biased' individuals). This negative correspondence between bias and conflict detection has been reported elsewhere as well (Mevel et al., 2015). This indicates that conflict detection errors do occur and are an important component of biased responding.

One possibility, discussed by Pennycook et al. (2015b), is that conflict *detection* is efficient in the sense that the signal in the anterior cingulate cortex is usually present, but that some people are not *responsive* to conflict. Indeed, there is evidence that people with an intuitive thinking disposition have smaller conflict detection effects (RT differences for base-rate problems; Pennycook et al., 2014a; Pennycook et al., 2015b). Regardless, in the context of the dual process models, conflict detection that does not cue a meaningful (detectable) increase in analytic processing should not, in my opinion, be considered "efficient." That is to say, it is important to include this aspect of conflict detection in our dual process models. This leads me to the three-stage model.

The three-stage model

The evidence for conflict detection inefficiency complicates the picture offered by the fairly straightforward logical intuition model. Most directly, if conflicts are sometimes not detected, what determines the likelihood of conflict detection? Given that, in accordance with the cognitive control literature (as discussed earlier), conflict detection can be viewed as a key determinant of analytic thinking, the underlying processes that influence conflict detection can be considered a window into the key question of 'what makes us think'. This is the context within which the three-stage model (Figure 2.3) was developed. I will focus on the components of the three-stage model that bear on the current issue ('what makes us think') for present purposes. For further discussion of the third stage of the model and, in particular, the distinction between rationalization and decoupling, see the full explication of the model in Pennycook et al. (2015b).

Given the foundational claim that intuitive processing is autonomous (as argued earlier), it must also therefore be the case that more than one intuition (IR) can come to mind in parallel. That is, autonomous processes are the result of activated stimulus–response pairings and more than one stimulus–response pairing is always possible (if not probable). Moreover, as discussed earlier, evidence for parallel processing has been mounting (Bago & Neys, 2017; Handley et al., 2011; Pennycook, Trippas, Handley, & Thompson, 2014; Trippas et al., 2016; Trippas, Thompson, & Handley, 2016). Thus, in the first stage of the model, problems/cues/stimuli may automatically lead to the generation of more than one initial response (IR). These

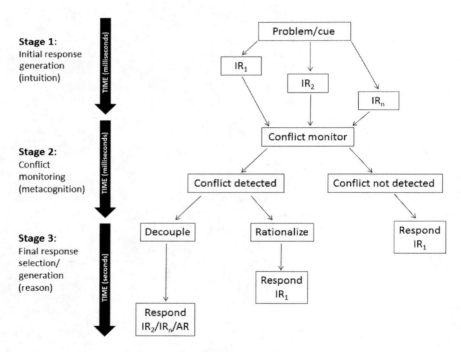

FIGURE 2.3 Three-stage dual process model of analytic engagement

Adapted from Pennycook et al., 2015b.

IR = initial response. IRs are numbered to reflect alternative speeds of generation – it is the difference between generation speeds (answer fluency) that determines the likelihood of conflict detection. IR_1 is the most salient and fluent possible response. IR_n refers to the possibility of multiple, potentially competing, initial responses. AR = alternative response. IR_n refers to the possibility of an alternative response that is grounded in an initial response.

are intuitive or heuristic responses, although the labels are generic, as the model need not apply only to the sorts of responses typically associated with "intuition". That is, the first initial response (IR_1) could very well refer to the output of the colour reading process in the Stroop task (and, likewise, IR_2 would refer to the output of the colour naming process).

As argued by Thompson et al. (2013) (see also, Pennycook, Trippas, et al., 2014; Thompson & Johnson, 2014), some intuitive responses should reasonably be expected to come to mind faster than others – a concept referred to as answer fluency. This aspect of autonomous output generation is not a component of the logical intuition model (Figure 2.2, but see De Neys, 2014). However, in the three-stage model, answer fluency is displayed as the length of arrow between the problem and the IR (short arrows indicate a very fast and fluent answer). Crucially, it is the association between the answer fluencies of the initial responses that determines the likelihood of successful conflict detection. That is, two IRs that come to mind in close succession (both could be fast and fluent or relatively slow and disfluent) are likely to be recognized as conflicting (it should be noted that IRs may actually coincide, in which case conflict would not be detected). This admittedly abstract discussion of conflict monitoring accords with neurocomputational models of cognitive control which, as quoted earlier, quantify "conflict" as the "coactivation of competing representations" (Botvinick & Cohen, 2014).

The question, then, is what evidence is there that the difference in processing fluencies of initial responses determines the likelihood of conflict detection. The answer is, unfortunately, very little. It is possible that moderate (as opposed to extreme) base rates lead to less fluent (or less consistently fluent) intuitive responses, thereby explaining why moderate base rates apparently decrease the likelihood of conflict detection (Pennycook et al., 2015b). However, this is more of an explanation of a known effect using the three-stage framework than evidence for the framework itself.

Limitations and future directions

As is often the case, the *explanans* gained from conflict detection experiments has created a new *explanandum*. If conflict detection causes analytic thinking, what determines the success of conflict detection? Here I've furthered the proposal (from Pennycook et al., 2015b) that the difference in processing fluencies of initial (intuitive) responses determines the likelihood of successful conflict detection. I believe that this is a solid proposal because it follows from the following premises:

1) More than one autonomous response is always possible.
2) It is unlikely that autonomous responses are equally fluent. That is, stimulus–response pairings are sometimes strong and sometimes weak. Moreover, some responses (such as stereotypical responses) are strongly favored over others (such as base-rate responses).
3) Conflict monitoring relies on the coactivation of competing responses.

If these premises are sound, as I believe them to be, it follows that fluency differences should result in differential coactivation and, in turn, differential likelihood of conflict detection. Nonetheless, future research is required to test this idea directly.

Another issue for the three-stage model is that it is vague in terms of metacognitive processes. Consider, for example, recent findings from experiments using the two-response paradigm (Thompson et al., 2011). In these studies (see Thompson & Newman, this volume), participants are asked to a) quickly give the first response that comes to mind, b) indicate how "right" that response "feels", and c) give a second response (a "final answer") over free time. A crucial finding from this paradigm is that less fluent initial responses (i.e., slower IRs) are positively associated with lower feelings of rightness, which is positively associated with time spent giving the final answer (Bago & De Neys, 2017; Thompson & Johnson, 2014; Thompson et al., 2013; Thompson, Evans, & Campbell, 2013; Thompson et al., 2011). Importantly, the presence of conflict decreases feelings of rightness in these experiments as well. Bago and De Neys (2017) recently found that confidence was lower for the initial response (implying a higher degree of experienced conflict) when participants ultimately changed their answer relative to when the first and final answer stayed the same (see also Thompson & Johnson, 2014). This pattern of results indicates subtle (and early) changes in confidence levels as a function of conflict. Thus, in keeping with the three-stage model, Bago and De Neys argued that this pattern of results could be explained by activation differences between alternative intuitive (logical and heuristic) responses. Again, however, these results do not offer direct evidence that differential response fluencies determine the likelihood of conflict detection. This is an important area for future research.

Conclusion

The capacity to reason is arguably the feature that most saliently sets humans apart from other animals (Stanovich, 2005). The dual process framework is a solid theoretical[7] approach to understanding human reasoning and decision making. Indeed, as I've argued, the foundation of dual process theory – that is, the assumption of autonomous processing – is essentially irrefutable (but falsifiable). However, as evidenced by this volume, there are notable gaps in the dual process theory literature. One of the most important gaps is the lack of solid explanation of how analytic thinking is actually triggered. I have reviewed the background of this problem and offered my own perspective. Specifically, there is now considerable evidence that conflict monitoring is a key determinant of analytic thinking. This parsimoniously accords with evidence and theorizing from the parallel cognitive control literature. Nonetheless, this has merely pushed the explanation of what causes us to think back a level. There is still much work to be done, and my goal for the present chapter was to facilitate this progress. My stance is that the three-stage model is certainly incorrect, but it may be correct enough to be useful. This is also my stance on the current chapter.

Acknowledgements

This work was supported by a Banting Postdoctoral Fellowship from the Social Sciences and Humanities Research Council of Canada. I would like to thank Nathaniel Barr and Jonathan Fugelsang for their constructive comments on an earlier version of this chapter. Correspondence regarding this manuscript should be addressed to Gordon Pennycook, Department of Psychology, Yale University, 2 Hillhouse Ave, New Haven, CT, USA, 06520–8205 or by email: gordon.pennycook@yale.edu.

Notes

1. A more accurate but clunky way to phrase this is: "the central claim on which dual process theories rest is essentially irrefutable."
2. This is a simplification, as it is possible that autonomy occurs on a continuum. Regardless, just because autonomous things differ on a continuum does not mean that some things are not best considered not autonomous. The reading of that sentence, for example.
3. Even more complicated multiplication problems can be automatic and working memory independent (Ashcraft, Donley, Halas, & Vakali, 1992; Tronsky, 2005).
4. Delineating the ultimate source requires evolutionary theorizing, which is a separate topic.
5. Although I think that theorists who are interested in executive functioning would benefit from a greater understanding of phenomena in the reasoning literature, delineating how this might be achieved is beyond the scope of this chapter.
6. Although I must admit that it is unclear to me what is conflicting with what in this problem. It is clear that the correct answer is not being computed intuitively; otherwise, accuracy would be much higher. Speculatively, it may be that participants pick up on the mismatch between the (apparent) ease of the problem and the fact that a psychologist deemed it necessary to administer the problem.
7. Or, perhaps, metatheoretical (Evans & Stanovich, 2013b).

References

Aczel, B., & Palfi, B. (2017). Studying the role of cognitive control in reasoning: Evidence for the congruency sequence effect in the ratio-bias task. *Thinking & Reasoning*. Retrieved from doi:10.1080/13546783.2016.1220424

Ashcraft, M., Donley, R., Halas, M., & Vakali, M. (1992). Working memory, automaticity, and problem difficulty. *Advances in Psychology*. Retrieved from www.sciencedirect.com/science/article/pii/S0166411508608900

Bago, B., & De Neys, W. (2017). Fast logic? Examining the time course assumption of dual process theory. *Cognition*, 158, 90–109. doi:10.1016/j.cognition.2016.10.014

Ball, L. J., Phillips, P., Wade, C. N., & Quayle, J. D. (2006). Effects of belief and logic on syllogistic reasoning: Eye-movement evidence for selective processing models. *Experimental Psychology*, 53(1), 77–86. doi:10.1027/1618-3169.53.1.77

Banks, A. P., & Hope, C. (2014). Heuristic and analytic processes in reasoning: An event-related potential study of belief bias. *Psychophysiology*, 51(3), 290–297. doi:10.1111/psyp.12169

Barbey, A. K., & Sloman, S. A. (2007). Base-rate respect : From ecological rationality to dual processes, *Behavioral and Brain Sciences*, 30, 241–297.

Barr, N., Pennycook, G., Stolz, J. A., & Fugelsang, J. A. (2015a). The brain in your pocket: Evidence that Smartphones are used to supplant thinking. *Computers in Human Behavior*, 48, 473–480. doi:10.1016/j.chb.2015.02.029

Barr, N., Pennycook, G., Stolz, J. A., & Fugelsang, J. A. (2015b). Reasoned connections: A dual-process perspective on creative thought. *Thinking and Reasoning, 21*(1), 61–75. doi:10.1080/13546783.2014.895915

Barrouillet, P. (2011). Dual-process theories and cognitive development: Advances and challenges. *Developmental Review, 31*(2–3), 79–85. doi:10.1016/j.dr.2011.07.002

Bechara, A., Damasio, A., Damasio, H., & Anderson, S. (1994). Insensitivity to future consequences following damage to human prefrontal cortex. *Cognition*. Retrieved from www.sciencedirect.com/science/article/pii/0010027794900183

Beevers, C. (2005). Cognitive vulnerability to depression: A dual process model. *Clinical Psychology Review*. Retrieved from www.sciencedirect.com/science/article/pii/S0272735805000267

Berlyne, D. (1957). Uncertainty and conflict: A point of contact between information-theory and behavior-theory concepts. *Psychological Review*. Retrieved from psycnet.apa.org/psycinfo/1959-03696-001

Bonner, C., & Newell, B. R. (2010). In conflict with ourselves? An investigation of heuristic and analytic processes in decision making. *Memory & Cognition, 38*(2), 186–196. doi:10.3758/MC.38.2.186

Botvinick, M. M., & Braver, T. (2015). Motivation and cognitive control: From behavior to neural mechanism. *Annual Review of Psychology, 66*, 83–113. doi:10.1146/annurev-psych-010814-015044

Botvinick, M. M., & Cohen, J. D. (2014). The computational and neural basis of cognitive control: Charted territory and new frontiers. *Cognitive Science, 38*(6), 1249–1285. doi:10.1111/cogs.12126

Botvinick, M. M., Cohen, J. D., & Carter, C. S. (2004). Conflict monitoring and anterior cingulate cortex: An update. *Trends in Cognitive Sciences, 8*(12), 539–546. doi:10.1016/j.tics.2004.10.003

Brainerd, C., & Reyna, V. (2001). Fuzzy-trace theory: Dual processes in memory, reasoning, and cognitive neuroscience. *Advances in child development*. Retrieved from idml.medicine.arizona.edu/Articles/Fuzzy traceTheoryDualProcessesinMemoryReasoningandCo.pdf

Campitelli, G., & Gerrans, P. (2014). Does the cognitive reflection test measure cognitive reflection? A mathematical modeling approach. *Memory & Cognition, 42*(3), 434–447. doi:10.3758/s13421-013-0367-9

Carter, C. S., Braver, T. S., Barch, D. M., Botvinick, M. M., Noll, D., & Cohen, J. D. (1998). Anterior cingulate cortex, error detection, and the online monitoring of performance. *Science, 280*(5364), 747–749. doi:10.1126/science.280.5364.747

Carter, C. S., & van Veen, V. (2007). Anterior cingulate cortex and conflict detection: An update of theory and data. *Cognitive, Affective & Behavioral Neuroscience, 7*(4), 367–379. doi:10.3758/cabn.7.4.367

Chaiken, S., & Trope, Y. (1999). *Dual-process theories in social psychology*. Retrieved from books.google.ca/books?hl=en&lr=&id=5X_auIBx99EC&oi=fnd&pg=PA3&dq=chaiken+trope&ots=OIUS_R4dpi&sig=IiM_NXY00rARlPXlirUdjz8S_Gw

Cheyne, J. A., & Pennycook, G. (2013). Sleep paralysis postepisode distress: Modeling potential effects of episode characteristics, general psychological distress, beliefs, and cognitive style. *Clinical Psychological Science, 1*(2), 135–148. doi:10.1177/2167702612466656

De Neys, W. (2012). Bias and conflict: A case for logical intuitions. *Perspectives on Psychological Science, 7*(1), 28–38. doi:10.1177/1745691611429354

De Neys, W. (2014). Conflict detection, dual processes, and logical intuitions: Some clarifications. *Thinking & Reasoning, 20*(2), 169–187. doi:10.1080/13546783.2013.854725

De Neys, W., & Bonnefon, J. F. (2013). The "whys" and "whens" of individual differences in thinking biases. *Trends in Cognitive Sciences, 17*(4), 172. doi:10.1016/j.tics.2013.02.001

De Neys, W., Cromheeke, S., & Osman, M. (2011). Biased but in doubt: Conflict and decision confidence. *PLoS One*, *6*(1), e15954. doi:10.1371/journal.pone.0015954

De Neys, W., & Franssens, S. (2009). Belief inhibition during thinking: Not always winning but at least taking part. *Cognition*, *113*(1), 45–61. doi:10.1016/j.cognition.2009.07.009

De Neys, W., & Glumicic, T. (2008). Conflict monitoring in dual process theories of thinking. *Cognition*, *106*(3), 1248–1299. doi:10.1016/j.cognition.2007.06.002

De Neys, W., Moyens, E., & Vansteenwegen, D. (2010). Feeling we're biased: Autonomic arousal and reasoning conflict. *Cognitive, Affective & Behavioral Neuroscience*, *10*(2), 208–216. doi:10.3758/CABN.10.2.208

De Neys, W., Novitskiy, N., Ramautar, J., & Wagemans, J. (2010). What Makes a Good Reasoner? Brain Potentials and Heuristic Bias Susceptibility. *Proceedings of the 32nd Annual Meeting of the Cognitive Science Society*, Portland, Oregon, 1020–1025.

De Neys, W., Rossi, S., & Houdé, O. (2013). Bats, balls, and substitution sensitivity: Cognitive misers are no happy fools. *Psychonomic Bulletin & Review*, *20*(2), 269–273. doi:10.3758/s13423-013-0384-5

De Neys, W., Vartanian, O., & Goel, V. (2008). Smarter than we think. *Psychological Science*, *19*(5), 483–489.

Egner, T. (2007). Congruency sequence effects and cognitive control. *Cognitive, Affective, & Behavioral Neuroscience*. Retrieved from link.springer.com/article/10.3758/CABN.7.4.380

Epstein, S., Pacini, R., Denes-Raj, V., & Heier, H. (1996). Individual differences in intuitive-experiential and analytical-rational thinking styles. *Journal of Personality and Social Psychology*, *71*(2), 390–405. doi:10.1037/0022-3514.71.2.390

Evans, J. (1989). *Bias in human reasoning: Causes and consequences*. Retrieved from psycnet.apa.org/psycinfo/1989-98394-000

Evans, J. (2007). *Hypothetical thinking: Dual processes in reasoning and judgement*. Retrieved from books.google.ca/books?hl=en&lr=&id=UcR4AgAAQBAJ&oi=fnd&pg=PP1&dq=evans+hypothetical+thinking&ots=eynH0n7mnu&sig=kMBJUMjOOiq22avtgZgdo1BZ0HU

Evans, J. (2012). Dual process theories of deductive reasoning: Facts and fallacies. *The Oxford handbook of thinking and reasoning*. Retrieved from books.google.ca/books?hl=en&lr=&id=BNdBAgAAQBAJ&oi=fnd&pg=PA115&dq=Dual-process+theories+of+reasoning:+facts+and+fallacies.&ots=-TgSCSLemE&sig=0mf7m-4YOxR1raJB1uzdTnqqI00

Evans, J., & Frankish, K. (2009). *In two minds: Dual processes and beyond*. Retrieved from psycnet.apa.org/psycinfo/2009-05881-000

Evans, J., Handley, S., Neilens, H., Bacon, A., & Over, D. (2010). The influence of cognitive ability and instructional set on causal conditional inference. *The Quarterly Journal of Experimental Psychology*, *63*, 892–909. Retrieved from www.tandfonline.com/doi/abs/10.1080/17470210903111821

Evans, J. St B. T. (2003). In two minds: Dual-process accounts of reasoning. *Trends in Cognitive Sciences*, *7*(10), 454–459. doi:10.1016/j.tics.2003.08.012

Evans, J. St B. T. (2006). The heuristic-analytic theory of reasoning: Extension and evaluation. *Psychonomic Bulletin & Review*, *13*(3), 378–395. doi:10.3758/BF03193858

Evans, J. St B. T. (2008). Dual-processing accounts of reasoning, judgment, and social cognition. *Annual Review of Psychology*, *59*, 255–278. doi:10.1146/annurev.psych.59.103006.093629

Evans, J. St B. T., & Stanovich, K. E. (2013a). Dual-process theories of higher cognition: Advancing the debate. *Perspectives on Psychological Science*, *8*(3), 223–241. doi:10.1177/1745691612460685

Evans, J. St B. T., & Stanovich, K. E. (2013b). Theory and metatheory in the study of dual processing: Reply to comments. *Perspectives on Psychological Science, 8*(3), 263–271. doi:10.1177/1745691613483774

Frankish, K., & Evans, J. (2009). The duality of mind: An historical perspective. In *In two minds: Dual processes and beyond*. Retrieved from citeseerx.ist.psu.edu/viewdoc/download?doi=10.1.1.521.2151&rep=rep1&type=pdf

Frederick, S. (2005). Cognitive reflection and decision making. *Journal of Economic Perspectives, 19*(4), 25–42. doi:10.1257/089533005775196732

Goel, V. (2007). Anatomy of deductive reasoning. *Trends in Cognitive Sciences, 11*(10), 435–441. doi:10.1016/j.tics.2007.09.003

Goel, V., Buchel, C., Frith, C., & Dolan, R. J. (2000). Dissociation of mechanisms underlying syllogistic reasoning. *NeuroImage, 12*(5), 504–514. doi:10.1006/nimg.2000.0636

Goel, V., & Dolan, R. J. (2004). Differential involvement of left prefrontal cortexin inductive and deductive reasoning. *Cognition, 93*(3), 109–121. doi:10.1016/j.cognition.2004.03.001

Greene, J. D., Sommerville, R. B., Nystrom, L. E., Darley, J. M., & Cohen, J. D. (2001). An fMRI investigation of emotional engagement in moral judgment. *Science (New York, N.Y.), 293*(5537), 2105–2108. doi:10.1126/science.1062872

Handley, S. J., Newstead, S. E., & Trippas, D. (2011). Logic, beliefs, and instruction: A test of the default interventionist account of belief bias. *Journal of Experimental Psychology: Learning, Memory, & Cognition, 37*(1), 28–43. doi:10.1037/a0021098

Handley, S. J., & Trippas, D. (2015). Dual processes and the interplay between knowledge and structure: A new parallel processing model. *Psychology of Learning and Motivation – Advances in Research and Theory, 62*, 33–58. doi:10.1016/bs.plm.2014.09.002

Johnson, E. D., Tubau, E., & De Neys, W. (2016). The doubting system 1: Evidence for automatic substitution sensitivity. *Acta Psychologica, 164*, 56–64. doi:10.1016/j.actpsy.2015.12.008

Kahneman, D. (2011). *Thinking, fast and slow*. New York, NY: Farrar, Straus and Giroux.

Kahneman, D., & Frederick, S. (2005). A model of heuristic judgment. In K Holyoak, R. G, Morrison, (Eds.), *The Cambridge handbook of thinking and reasoning* (pp. 267–294). doi:10.1111/cogs.12119

Kahneman, D., & Tversky, A. (1973). On the psychology of prediction. *Psychological Review*. Retrieved from psycnet.apa.org/journals/rev/80/4/237/

Klaczynski, P. (2001). Analytic and heuristic processing influences on adolescent reasoning and decision-making. *Child Development*. doi:10.1111/1467-8624.00319/full

Kokis, J. V., Macpherson, R., Toplak, M. E., West, R. F., & Stanovich, K. E. (2002). Heuristic and analytic processing: Age trends and associations with cognitive ability and cognitive styles. *Journal of Experimental Child Psychology, 83*(1), 26–52. doi:10.1016/S0022-0965(02)00121-2

Lieberman, M. (2007). Social cognitive neuroscience: A review of core processes. *Annual Review of Psychology*. doi:10.1146/annurev.psych.58.110405.085654

MacLeod, C. (1991). Half a century of research on the Stroop effect: An integrative review. *Psychological Bulletin*. Retrieved from psycnet.apa.org/journals/bul/109/2/163/

Mars, R., Sallet, J., Rushworth, M., & Yeung, N. (Eds.). (2011). *Neural basis of motivational and cognitive control*. Cambridge, MA: MIT Press. Retrieved from books.google.ca/books?hl=en&lr=&id=A_eoYgtLmFMC&oi=fnd&pg=PR5&dq=Neural+Basis+of+Motivational+and+Cognitive+Control&ots=YdrMFRZmMV&sig=y79S3I4he46p1_11DslsY-BLp_s

Mevel, K., Poirel, N., Rossi, S., Cassotti, M., Simon, G., Houdé, O., & De Neys, W. (2015). Bias detection: Response confidence evidence for conflict sensitivity in the ratio bias task. *Journal of Cognitive Psychology, 27*(2), 227–237. doi:10.1080/20445911.2014.986487

Morsanyi, K., & Handley, S. J. (2012). Logic feels so good – I like it! Evidence for intuitive detection of logicality in syllogistic reasoning. *Journal of Experimental Psychology: Learning, Memory, and Cognition, 38*(3), 596–616. doi:10.1037/a0026099

Padmala, S., & Pessoa, L. (2010). Interactions between cognition and motivation during response inhibition. *Neuropsychologia*. Retrieved from www.sciencedirect.com/science/article/pii/S0028393209004205

Pennycook, G. (2014). Evidence that analytic cognitive style influences religious belief: Comment on Razmyar and Reeve (2013). *Intelligence, 43*(1), 21–26. doi:10.1016/j.intell.2013.12.005

Pennycook, G., Cheyne, J. A., Barr, N., Koehler, D. J., & Fugelsang, J. A. (2014a). Cognitive style and religiosity: The role of conflict detection. *Memory and Cognition, 42*(1), 1–10. doi:10.3758/s13421-013-0340-7

Pennycook, G., Cheyne, J. A., Barr, N., Koehler, D. J., & Fugelsang, J. A. (2014b). The role of analytic thinking in moral judgements and values. *Thinking & Reasoning, 20*(2), 188–214. doi:10.1080/13546783.2013.865000

Pennycook, G., Cheyne, J. A., Barr, N., Koehler, D. J., & Fugelsang, J. A. (2015). On the reception and detection of pseudo-profound bullshit. *Judgment and Decision Making, 10*(6), 549–563. doi:10.3389/fpsyg.2013.00279

Pennycook, G., Cheyne, J. A., Koehler, D. J., & Fugelsang, J. A. (2016). Is the cognitive reflection test a measure of both reflection and intuition? *Behavior Research Methods, 48*(1), 341–348. doi:10.3758/s13428-015-0576-1

Pennycook, G., Cheyne, J. A., Seli, P., Koehler, D. J., & Fugelsang, J. A. (2012). Analytic cognitive style predicts religious and paranormal belief. *Cognition, 123*(3), 335–346. doi:10.1016/j.cognition.2012.03.003

Pennycook, G., Fugelsang, J. A., & Koehler, D. J. (2012). Are we good at detecting conflict during reasoning? *Cognition, 124*(1), 101–106. doi:10.1016/j.cognition.2012.04.004

Pennycook, G., Fugelsang, J. A., & Koehler, D. J. (2015a). Everyday consequences of analytic thinking. *Current Directions in Psychological Science, 24*(6), 425–432. doi:10.1177/0963721415604610

Pennycook, G., Fugelsang, J. A., & Koehler, D. J. (2015b). What makes us think? A three-stage dual-process model of analytic engagement. *Cognitive Psychology, 80*, 34–72. doi:10.1016/j.cogpsych.2015.05.001

Pennycook, G., & Ross, R. M. (2016). Commentary on: Cognitive reflection vs. calculation in decision making. *Frontiers in Psychology, 7*, 9. doi:10.3389/fpsyg.2015.00532

Pennycook, G., Ross, R. M., Koehler, D. J., & Fugelsang, J. A. (2016). Atheists and agnostics are more reflective than religious believers: Four empirical studies and a meta-analysis. *PLoS One, 11*(4), e0153039. doi:10.1371/journal.pone.0153039

Pennycook, G., & Thompson, V. A. (2012). Reasoning with base rates is routine, relatively effortless, and context dependent. *Psychonomic Bulletin & Review, 19*(3), 528–534. doi:10.3758/s13423-012-0249-3

Pennycook, G., & Thompson, V. A. (2016). Base rate neglect. In R. F. Pohl (Ed.), *Cognitive illusions* (pp. 44–61). London: Routledge. Retrieved from books.google.ca/books?hl=en&lr=&id=0Ge3DAAAQBAJ&oi=fnd&pg=PA44&dq=Base+rate+neglect+gordon+pennycook+valerie+thompson&ots=ibCDvspUlE&sig=2sk5KsbSWBXddL0-zTbQAdsHxns

Pennycook, G., Trippas, D., Handley, S. J., & Thompson, V. A. (2014). Base rates: Both neglected and intuitive. *Journal of Experimental Psychology: Learning Memory and Cognition*, *40*(2), 544–554. doi:10.1037/a0034887

Pyszczynski, T., Greenberg, J., & Solomon, S. (1999). A dual-process model of defense against conscious and unconscious death-related thoughts: An extension of terror management theory. *Psychological Review*. Retrieved from psycnet.apa.org/journals/rev/106/4/835/

Shenhav, A., Botvinick, M., & Cohen, J. (2013). The expected value of control: An integrative theory of anterior cingulate cortex function. *Neuron*, *79*(2), 217–240. doi:10.1016/j.neuron.2013.07.007

Simon, G., Lubin, A., Houdé, O., & De Neys, W. (2015). Anterior cingulate cortex and intuitive bias detection during number conservation. *Cognitive Neuroscience*, (July), 6, 158–168. doi:10.1080/17588928.2015.1036847

Sloman, S. A. (1996). The empirical case for two systems of reasoning. *Psychological Bulletin*, *119*(1), 3–22. doi:10.1037/0033-2909.119.1.3

Stanovich, K. E. (1999). *Who is rational? Studies of individual differences in reasoning*. Retrieved from books.google.ca/books?hl=en&lr=&id=-C15AgAAQBAJ&oi=fnd&pg=PP1&dq=stanovich+1999&ots=Qw9eewWfVY&sig=q4fM4iDb1joycLUpAiKyzrQKc0o

Stanovich, K. E. (2005). *The robot's rebellion: Finding meaning in the age of Darwin*. Retrieved from books.google.ca/books?hl=en&lr=&id=gib3SwqcH8AC&oi=fnd&pg=PR7&dq=stanovich+robots+rebellion&ots=usG0dwta65&sig=D2sBjunrZeFstrynz60tWlHUN7U

Stanovich, K. E. (2009). Distinguishing the reflective, algorithmic, and autonomous minds: Is it time for a tri-process theory. In *In two minds: Dual processes and beyond*. Retrieved from keithstanovich.com/Site/Research_on_Reasoning_files/Stanovich_Two_MInds.pdf

Stanovich, K. E. (2012). On the distinction between rationality and intelligence: Implications for understanding individual differences in reasoning. In In K. Holyoak & R. Morrison (Eds.), *The Oxford handbook of thinking and reasoning* (pp. 433–455). New York, NY: Oxford University Press.

Stanovich, K. E., & West, R. F. (1998). Individual differences in rational thought. *Journal of Experimental Psychology: General*, *127*(2), 161–188. doi:10.1037/0096-3445.127.2.161

Stanovich, K. E., & West, R. F. (2000). Individual differences in reasoning: Implications for the rationality debate? *The Behavioral and Brain Sciences*, *23*(5), 645–665. doi:10.1017/S0140525X00003435

Stollstorff, M., Vartanian, O., & Goel, V. (2012). Levels of conflict in reasoning modulate right lateral prefrontal cortex. *Brain Research*, *1428*, 24–32. doi:10.1016/j.brainres.2011.05.045

Stroop, J. (1935). Studies of interference in serial verbal reactions. *Journal of Experimental Psychology*. Retrieved from psycnet.apa.org/journals/xge/18/6/643/

Thompson, V. A. (2009). Dual process theories: A metacognitive perspective. In *Two minds: Dual processes and beyond*. Oxford. Retrieved from faculty.weber.edu/eamsel/ResearchGroups/DualPRocessResearch/NewPapers/Thomson(2009).pdf

Thompson, V. A. (2013). Why it matters: The implications of autonomous processes for dual process theories: Commentary on Evans & Stanovich (2013). *Perspectives on Psychological Science*, *8*, 253–256. doi:10.1177/1745691613483476

Thompson, V. A., Ackerman, R., Sidi, Y., Ball, L. J., Pennycook, G., & Prowse Turner, J. A. (2013). The role of answer fluency and perceptual fluency in the monitoring and control of reasoning: Reply to Alter, Oppenheimer, and Epley (2013). *Cognition*, *128*(2), 256–258. doi:10.1016/j.cognition.2013.03.003

Thompson, V. A., Evans, J. St B. T., & Campbell, J. I. D. (2013). Matching bias on the selection task: It's fast and feels good. *Thinking & Reasoning*, *19*(3–4), 431–452. doi:10.1080/13546783.2013.820220

Thompson, V. A., & Johnson, S. C. (2014). Conflict, metacognition, and analytic thinking. *Thinking & Reasoning, 20*(January 2015), 215–244. doi:10.1080/13546783.2013.869763

Thompson, V. A., & Morsanyi, K. (2012). Analytic thinking: Do you feel like it? *Mind and Society, 11*(1), 93–105. doi:10.1007/s11299-012-0100-6

Thompson, V. A., Prowse Turner, J. A., & Pennycook, G. (2011). Intuition, reason, and metacognition. *Cognitive Psychology, 63*(3), 107–140. doi:10.1016/j.cogpsych.2011.06.001

Thompson, V. A., Turner, J. A. P., Pennycook, G., Ball, L. J., Brack, H., Ophir, Y., & Ackerman, R. (2013). The role of answer fluency and perceptual fluency as metacognitive cues for initiating analytic thinking. *Cognition, 128*(2), 237–251. doi:10.1016/j.cognition.2012.09.012

Toplak, M. E., West, R. F., & Stanovich, K. E. (2011). The cognitive reflection test as a predictor of performance on heuristics-and-biases tasks. *Memory & Cognition, 39*(7), 1275–1289. doi:10.3758/s13421-011-0104-1

Toplak, M. E., West, R. F., & Stanovich, K. E. (2014). Assessing miserly information processing: An expansion of the cognitive reflection test. *Thinking & Reasoning, 20*(2), 147–168. doi:10.1080/13546783.2013.844729

Travers, E., Rolison, J. J., & Feeney, A. (2016). The time course of conflict on the cognitive reflection test. *Cognition, 150*, 109–118. doi:10.1016/j.cognition.2016.01.015

Trippas, D., Handley, S., Verde, M., & Morsanyi, K. (2016). Logic brightens my day: Evidence for implicit sensitivity to logical validity. Retrieved from psycnet.apa.org/psycinfo/2016-08774-001/

Trippas, D., Thompson, V., & Handley, S. (2016). When fast logic meets slow belief: Evidence for a parallel-processing model of belief bias. *Memory & Cognition*. Retrieved from link.springer.com/article/10.3758/s13421-016-0680-1

Tronsky, L. (2005). Strategy use, the development of automaticity, and working memory involvement in complex multiplication. *Memory & Cognition*. Retrieved from link.springer.com/article/10.3758/BF03193086

3
THE PARALLEL PROCESSING MODEL OF BELIEF BIAS
Review and extensions

Dries Trippas and Simon J. Handley

Introduction

The idea that human behaviour is often influenced by competing processes that support unique responses is pervasive in psychological science. Its early origins can be found in Sigmund Freud's belief that personality and behaviour derive from the constant interaction of conflicting conscious and unconscious psychological influences (see Frankish & Evans, 2009, for a comprehensive review of these ideas stretching all the way back to Plato). In modern psychology, such dual process theories have been developed to explain a whole range of psychological phenomena, including the operation of human memory (Jacoby, Toth, & Yonelinas, 1993), perceptual category learning (Ashby & Maddox, 2005), person perception (Chaiken & Trope, 1999), judgment and decision making (Epstein, 1994; Kahneman, 2011; Sloman, 1996), and reasoning (Evans & Over, 1996; Stanovich, 1999). In all cases, the presence of a conflict between competing responses is seen as diagnostic of dual processes at work.

The Stroop (1935) task is probably the most famous demonstration of how behavioural experiments can provide insights into the nature of cognitive processing (for a comprehensive review, see MacLeod, 1991). A typical Stroop task looks like this: participants are presented with words (e.g., "green") in a no-conflict fashion (the word "green" printed in green font) or in a conflict fashion (the word "green" printed in red font). The canonical finding is that the conflict between the semantics of the word and the actual colour of the word interferes more with the ability to name the colour of the word than with the ability to read the word. Simply put, the conflict makes responses less accurate and slower when it comes to colour naming, but not word reading.

For some of Stroop's contemporaries, this particular result was not ground-breaking. Indeed, as Cattell (1886) and others had demonstrated before, word reading was generally found to be quicker than object naming. One popular explanation for these findings was that word reading was automatic, in contrast to object naming, which was presumed to be more effortful (James, 1890). This is an elegant and straightforward interpretation, were it not for the fact that Stroop (1935) also reported an additional experiment in which he demonstrated that his effect could be *reversed*. By providing an elaborate training phase, he managed to make the semantic–colour conflict affect word reading more than colour naming. More recent research has even demonstrated that mere suggestions could reduce the Stroop effect (Raz, Kirsch, Pollard, & Nitkin-Kaner, 2006). These findings are clearly inconsistent with the idea that reading is fully automatic and that the object naming is fundamentally effortful. At the very least, these findings suggested that the simple association of automaticity with reading versus effort with object naming was too simple. A more recent interpretation of the Stroop effect is that it is best understood in terms of a parallel architecture (Rumelhart, Hinton, & McClelland, 1986). We argue that research on dual process theories of thinking and reasoning has recently traversed a similar trajectory by relying on experimental designs inspired by Stroop's method.

Dual process theory: the classic perspective

According to dual process theories of reasoning (Evans & Over, 1996; Evans & Stanovich, 2013; Stanovich, 1999) and judgment (Epstein, 1994; Kahneman, 2011; Sloman, 1996) human cognition is best captured in terms of two qualitatively distinct types of processing. Have you ever had a song stuck in your head that just would not go away? This is an example of Type 1 processing, the defining characteristic of which is that it is autonomous – once the process has started, it will run to completion. Have you ever had to think long and hard about which gifts to buy for your loved ones for Christmas? This is an example of Type 2 processing, the defining characteristic of which is that it requires working memory engagement (Evans & Stanovich, 2013). A more formal characterization of Type 1 and Type 2 processing in the context of reasoning can be made by considering the following statement as an example:

> *Assume that snow is either white or black, but not both.*
> *Assume further that the snow which fell yesterday is not black.*
> *Does it necessarily follow that the snow is white?*

The solution to the problem seems obvious and trivial. Assuming the premises are true, the conclusion necessarily follows. A different way of saying this is that the disjunctive syllogism presented here is logically valid. However, this conclusion may become less obvious if we shuffle some terms around while keeping the structure of the syllogism constant:

> *Assume that snow is either* black *or* white, *but not both.*
> *Assume further that the snow which fell yesterday is not* white.
> *Does it necessarily follow that the snow is* black?

Research has shown that people are less likely to accept this second conclusion as logically valid. Although it may seem reasonable from a pragmatic perspective to accept the former conclusion and to reject the latter, it is a bias according to the rules of deductive logic (Evans, 2002).

The influence of prior knowledge on deductive reasoning is well established (Evans, Barston, & Pollard, 1983; Wilkins, 1929). The most influential interpretation of this finding is in terms of a default-interventionist account (Evans, 2007). According to the default-interventionist account, belief bias occurs because belief-based responses are driven by Type 1 processing, in contrast to logic-based responses, which require Type 2 processing (Evans & Stanovich, 2013). Belief-based responding is assumed to be effortless, presumably because people judge the believability of statements dozens of times per day, making the retrieval of facts from memory a well-practiced and nearly automatic process. Logical analysis via deduction – that is, assuming a series of premises are true and then judging whether a conclusion necessarily follows according to some rules of logic – is effortful by its very definition. Deduction requires several mental representations of the premises to be kept in working memory simultaneously such that they can be combined and evaluated.

Experimental evidence consistent with the characterization of belief-based and logic-based responding in terms of Type 1 and Type 2 processing is backed up by a study in which a response-time limit was shown to increase belief-based responding and decrease logic-based responding (Evans & Curtis-Holmes, 2005). Further evidence in the same vein was provided by a study which showed that the presence of a working memory load during reasoning increased belief-based responding and reduced logic-based judgments (De Neys, 2006). In sum, much like James' (1890) conclusion that word reading was effortless (or a Type 1 process in modern-day parlance) and that colour naming was effortful (Type 2), researchers of thinking and reasoning concluded that there was a similar mapping between Type 1 processing and beliefs, on the one hand, and Type 2 processing and logic, on the other. Thus, the default-interventionist account appears to be the supreme candidate for explaining the interplay between beliefs and logic.

A parallel processing model of belief bias

For all its elegance and intuitive appeal, a number of findings in the literature seem incompatible with the default-interventionist view, which regards belief-based responding as an exclusive Type 1 process and logical reasoning as exclusively based on Type 2 processing. For instance, imposing a response-time limit on a causal conditional reasoning task did not seem to increase belief bias (Evans, Handley, & Bacon, 2009). Similarly, a developmental study on the origin of belief bias suggested that as children get older, they showed *more* rather than less belief bias – and this was particularly pronounced for children with higher levels of cognitive ability (Morsanyi & Handley, 2008; though see also Toplak, West, & Stanovich, 2014). One study demonstrated that people were able to make logically correct transitive inferences implicitly, suggesting they were reasoning in accordance to the normative principle of transitivity without explicit awareness of doing so (Leo & Greene, 2008). A host of findings from the text-comprehension literature similarly suggested that people apparently readily draw logical inferences while reading, without being explicitly instructed to reason logically (Lea, 1995; Rader & Sloutsky, 2002). Perhaps the association between Type 1 processing and beliefs and Type 2 processing and logic is not quite as clear-cut as the default interventionist account presumes?

Inspired by these and other findings, Handley and Trippas (2015) proposed a parallel processing model which no longer assumes that beliefs are cued as a default by Type 1 processing and that a Type 2–based logical analysis can intervene only if enough effort is expended (for examples of alternative characterizations of parallel processing models in related domains, see: Chaiken & Trope, 1999; Sloman, 1996). Instead, the parallel processing model rests on the following principles:

(1) *Problem features and processing type are not mapped one to one.*
(2) *Multiple instantiations of Type 1 and Type 2 processes can operate in parallel. Each fork of the process has the ability to process a particular feature of the problem. These features may be structural, perceptual, semantic, etc.*
(3) *Multiple Type 1 processes running in parallel are cued at the problem onset. After an implicit conflict has been detected between problem features, or after a self-imposed deadline has been exceeded, multiple Type 2 processes are engaged.*[1]
(4) *Depending on a set of determinants, Type 2 processes will override the outputs of Type 1 processes which focused on irrelevant features, provide additional scrutiny for the outputs of Type 1 processes which focus on relevant problem features, or integrate the resulting outputs prior to producing a response.*

In the context of belief bias, Principle 1 entails that the parallel processing model no longer assumes that belief-based judgments are necessarily a product of Type 1 processing. The model also assumes that correct logic-based responses are not necessarily driven by Type 2 processing. The model acknowledges that it takes effort to operate on the basis of knowledge sometimes (e.g., is it true that some humans are not reptiles?) and that structure-based responses may occasionally be pretty effortless (e.g., if p then q; p; therefore q?). Note that this assumption is shared with a recently revised version of the default-interventionist account (Evans & Stanovich, 2013).

Principle 2 builds on the first principle by assuming that *both* Type 1 and Type 2 processes can process several relevant aspects of the problem at the same time. Applied to belief bias, this means that one strand of Type 1 processing may be engaged in accessing the relevant knowledge and beliefs required to comprehend a given conclusion, whereas a different strand of Type 1 processing is simultaneously engaged to extract structural regularities which may be correlated with logical validity (structure based).

The third principle entails that Type 2 processing will be added into the mix after an initial period of Type 1 processing. Type 2 processing may be engaged because an implicit conflict is detected between the various problem features. For instance, one strand of Type 1 processing may be accumulating evidence towards a "reject" response, whereas the other strand's evidence accumulation is converging to an "accept" response. Importantly, the model acknowledges that for all intents and purposes, *every* response which is made in a reasoning task – with the exception perhaps of simply randomly pressing a button as fast as you can – will require some degree of Type 2 engagement. Thus, it is perfectly possible that Type 2 processing is engaged even if no conflict is detected.

Principle 4 addresses the important question of which response will ultimately be reported by the person according to the model. The answer lies in the fact that one crucial aim of Type 2 processing is to arbitrate between a set of possible answers. Exactly how this all plays out depends on a number of task-specific and person-specific determinants such as the instructional set, the relative complexity of the problem features, the amount of processing resources available, and individual characteristics of the person, such as motivational and cognitive traits. Finally, there are several ways in which Type 2 processing can achieve the aim, for instance, by inhibiting a structure-based response if the task specifications require a knowledge-based response, or by consciously applying the rules of logic if a counterfactual conclusion was reached.

In the next section we review a series of recent experimental tests of the model which were conducted by our colleagues and us, before moving on to an oft-ignored topic in research on dual process theories of thinking and reasoning: the integration of, rather than competition between, structure and knowledge.

A series of critical tests

The first piece of evidence for the parallel processing model of belief bias was presented by Handley, Newstead, and Trippas (2011), who actually set out to conduct a critical test of the default-interventionist account (Evans, 2007). The default-interventionist account of belief bias assumes that beliefs interfere with the assessment of logical validity in a deduction task (Evans, 2002) because beliefs are cued as a default response by Type 1 processing. Correct responses on the basis of logic can only be produced if Type 2 processing is engaged to stage a successful intervention. Handley and colleagues modified the traditional deduction paradigm, where participants are instructed to respond exclusively on the basis of logic by turning it into a Stroop-like extension of the deduction paradigm.

Instructional set

In this Stroop deduction task, participants were asked to respond on the basis of logic in some instances, but to respond on the basis of *beliefs* in others. Furthermore, each problem featured some combination of logical validity and conclusion believability, such that two types of conflict problems were created (a valid argument with an unbelievable conclusion and an invalid argument with a believable conclusion), as well as two types of no-conflict problems (a valid argument with a believable conclusion and an invalid argument with an unbelievable conclusion). Consider the following example of a conflict problem:

If a child is crying, then it is happy.
Suppose a child is crying.
Does it follow that the child is happy?

The correct response to this problem on the basis of logic is "yes", because the conclusion necessarily follows assuming the premises are true. However, on the basis of beliefs, the correct response is "no", as it is unbelievable that a child who is crying is also happy. Now consider this no-conflict problem:

If a child is crying, then it is sad.
Suppose a child is crying.
Does it follow that the child is sad?

In this case, the correct response on the basis of both logic and beliefs is "yes": the conclusion is valid and believable. Based on this extended experimental paradigm, a set of divergent predictions for the default-interventionist and the parallel processing model could be made. Specifically, according to the default-interventionist account, given that Type 1 processes are less effortful than Type 2 processes, people should be less accurate when reasoning on the basis of logic than when reasoning on the basis of beliefs. Furthermore, given that Type 1 processes are often faster than Type 2 processes, people should also be quicker to respond correctly under belief instructions than under logic instructions. Finally, for the reasons outlined earlier, the conflict between logic and belief should affect accuracy and response time most when operating under the instructions to respond on the basis of logic.

The parallel processing model makes qualitatively different predictions. First, given the assumed disconnect between processing type and problem features embodied by Principle 1, the model does not straightforwardly predict that responses on the basis of beliefs should be more accurate or quicker than responses on the basis of logic. Indeed, Principle 4 suggests that to make predictions, we need to assess the various determinants of the problems, such as the relative complexity of the problem features. A quick inspection of the problems given as examples earlier suggests that the logical structure underlying these problems – in this case, the conditional inference known as "modus ponens" – may be relatively simple.

The predictions from the default-interventionist model were pitted against those of the parallel processing model in a series of five experiments. Across all of these experiments, almost without exception, it was found that people were more accurate when they were instructed to respond on the basis of logic than on the basis of beliefs. It was also found that they were quicker when they were instructed to respond on the basis of logic than on the basis of beliefs. Finally, the experiments unequivocally demonstrated that belief–logic conflict interfered more with belief judgments than with logic judgments. Importantly, these five experiments featured a wide array of methods and arguments, ensuring that the findings were not a product of idiosyncrasies in the design. For instance, although most experiments relied on a full within-subjects treatment, some featured a blocked design, allowing for between-subjects comparisons. Similarly, although the majority of the experiments focused on the modus ponens argument form (if p then q; p; therefore q), others used disjunctive syllogisms (p or q but not both; not p; therefore q) and universal syllogisms (all p are q; r is a p; therefore r is a q). In fact, although not directly related to belief bias in deductive reasoning, recent work has conceptually replicated these findings in a base-rate neglect task often used in research on judgment and decision making (Pennycook, Trippas, Handley, & Thompson, 2014).

But why were people all of a sudden better at logical reasoning than at responding on the basis of their presumably well-practiced knowledge of the world? Based on the parallel processing model, one straightforward explanation is that the relative complexity of the problem features was responsible for the unexpected results. Specifically, given the relative ease with which the employed arguments can be solved when compared to the ease with which various facts can be retrieved, in this particular case a situation was created in which logical responding trumped belief-based responding. This generates an interesting prediction that argument complexity should moderate these effects. We tested exactly this prediction in a recent study.

Relative complexity

Trippas, Thompson, and Handley (2017) tested the parallel processing model's prediction that argument complexity is a crucial determinant of whether logic-based responding is more efficient than belief-based responding or vice versa in a series of two experiments. In the first experiment, participants were presented with two types of arguments in the Stroop deduction paradigm: modus ponens (if p, then q, p, therefore q; as shown earlier) and modus tollens (if p then q, not q, therefore not p). Several decades of reasoning research has established that modus tollens is a more complex inference to draw than modus ponens (see, for example, Evans, Newstead, & Byrne, 1993). The prediction was that increasing the complexity of the argument structure would put the difficulty of making logic judgments on par with the difficulty of making belief judgments, thus equating the conflict. Notably, the parallel processing model would still predict that there should be *some* form of conflict-driven interference, if it is indeed implicitly detected, but that it is no longer providing an advantage to logic judgments in the case of modus tollens. Consistent with these predictions, Experiment 1 demonstrated that there was mutual interference between logic and belief judgments for the modus tollens problems, in contrast to modus ponens problems, which replicated the results reported by Handley et al. (2011) that belief–logic conflict interfered more with logic judgments than belief judgments.

In the second experiment Trippas and colleagues tested an even more extreme prediction of the parallel processing model: if the relative complexity of the argument form is increased even further, a *reversal* of the result reported by Handley et al. (2011)

should be found. In other words, if the logical structure of the arguments is substantially more complex than the processes required to judge the conclusion's believability, then the parallel processing model predicts that belief–logic conflict should interfere more with logic judgments than with belief judgments. This prediction was tested by asking people to reason about three-term categorical syllogisms of the type typically studied in research on belief bias in the classic deduction paradigm (Evans et al., 1983). For example:

No boats are mips
Some yachts are mips
Some yachts are not boats

It is clear to see that these types of arguments are substantially more complex than the conditional inferences and the disjunctive syllogisms we relied on thus far. Confirming the parallel processing model's prediction, the results indicated that for these types of problems, logic judgments were affected more by conflict than belief judgments, but that there was still an effect of conflict on the ability to make belief judgments – suggesting that even here both the structural and knowledge-based problem features were being processed by Type 1 processing from the problem outset.

Of course, an experimental task features more critical elements than the complexity of its stimuli and instructional sets alone. In fact, a criticism of the evidence we presented so far might be that we are forgetting about the reasoner in our study of reasoning. To counter this response, we present a series of studies focusing on more person-centric traits and features to further test the parallel processing model.

Cognitive resources

Howarth, Handley, and Walsh (2016) set out to investigate another determinant predicted to influence response outcomes according to the parallel processing model: working memory. In a series of three experiments, Howarth and colleagues investigated the role of a working memory load on the ability to make logic- and belief-based judgments in the Stroop deduction paradigm. One of the main features of the parallel processing model is that there is no straightforward mapping between belief-based and logic-based judgments, on the one hand, and Type 1 processing and Type 2 processing, on the other. More specifically, the model also suggests that *both* belief- and logic-based responding require cognitive resources to some degree. Thus, it should follow that the imposition of a load on working memory should affect both types of responses to some extent. For comparison, note that the classic default-interventionist account would predict that Type 1 processing is unaffected by working memory, and thus that a secondary task load should have no effect on the ability to make belief-based judgments.

In a series of three experiments Howarth and colleagues demonstrated that imposing a working memory load by instructing people to generate random numbers whilst reasoning about the logical validity and believability of problems was detrimental for their performance. The working memory load interfered with judgments under both belief and logic instructions to the same degree, consistent with predictions from the parallel processing model. We should also note that these findings were replicated across a number of distinct argument forms (modus ponens conditionals and disjunctive syllogisms) and even held in a blocked between-subjects design. This latter finding is of particular interest as it counteracts the potential criticism that these findings are merely linked to the task-switching component inherent to the paradigm (i.e., responding on the basis of logic on one trial but on the basis of believability on the next). Indeed, a replication using this type of blocked design further strengthens our confidence that the results reflect genuine aspects of cognitive processing.

In two of their experiments, Howarth et al. also collected individual differences data by administering the Cognitive Reflection Test (CRT) (Frederick, 2005), a short questionnaire which has proven to be pretty good at distinguishing between people who are more inclined to think harder (so-called analytic reasoners) and people who are happy to go with their gut (so-called intuitive reasoners; Pennycook, Cheyne, Koehler, & Fugelsang, 2016). This trait is often referred to as analytic cognitive style, and it has been shown to predict a wide range of real-world beliefs and behaviours (e.g., religious belief, paranormal belief, etc.; for a review, see Pennycook, Fugelsang, & Koehler, 2015). Interestingly, Howarth et al.'s administration of the CRT revealed that more analytic reasoners were particularly affected in their ability to make belief-based judgments when faced with a belief–logic conflict – a finding which, yet again, directly counters the default-interventionist proposal that belief-based reasoning is predominantly driven by Type 1 processing (if this was the case, these more able reasoners would have been less, rather than more, affected). But could it also be the case that not all logical reasoning requires Type 2 processing?

In the next section, we assess one final broad strand of indirect evidence consistent with one of the key principles of the parallel processing model (Handley & Trippas, 2015): the possibility that responses in accord to logical validity are to some extent driven by implicit, nondeliberative (i.e., Type 1) processing.

Implicit logic

Although perhaps the most controversial strand of evidence consistent with some of the main principles of the parallel processing model, we believe the evidence is suggestive enough to warrant discussion. One of the key principles which defines the parallel processing model and distinguishes it from the default-interventionist account is the assumption that not all correct responses on the basis of logic necessarily require effortful processing. This proposal was first put to the test by Morsanyi and Handley (2012) in a paper entitled: "Logic feels so good – I like it!" In a series of four experiments designed to draw on the link between fluency, affect, and intuition (Topolinski & Strack, 2009), Morsanyi and Handley set out to test the possibility that people exhibit a modest amount of sensitivity to logical validity based purely on Type 1 processing. People were presented with categorical syllogisms, but instead of asking people to judge whether they were valid or not, the participants had to indicate simply how much they liked the conclusion.

Surprisingly, people indicated that they liked logically valid conclusions more than logically invalid conclusions. Of course, it is perfectly possible that people simply performed an effortful Type 2 analysis and indicated they liked the valid problems more than the invalid ones (what's not to like?). However, in a follow-up study Morsanyi and Handley provided evidence consistent with the idea that the sensitivity was driven by affect-based, Type 1 processing. When participants performed the liking task while listening to a piece of music which they were told can generate feelings of affect, the effect of logic on liking was attenuated, suggesting people were attributing their affective feelings to the music rather than relying on them as logic-driven intuitions. This finding that some sources of logical responding may be seemingly intuitive was certainly incompatible with the idea of a strict mapping of Type 1 and Type 2 processing to belief- and logic-based responding, as proposed by the default-interventionist account. However, the work was not without its critics.

In a number of follow-up studies, Klauer and Singmann (2013) (see also Singmann, Klauer, & Kellen, 2014) investigated the alternative possibility that various aspects of the stimuli used were partially responsible for some of the effects and found evidence consistent with their proposal. In two out of the four studies featuring the most complex syllogistic structures, the evidence for an effect of logic on liking seemed challenging to replicate.

Following up on this debate, Trippas, Handley, Verde, and Morsanyi (2016) attempted to replicate and extend Morsanyi and Handley's logic-liking effect while addressing the issues pointed out by Klauer and colleagues. In a first experiment, they replicated the finding that participants liked valid arguments more than invalid arguments, using a wide range of argument structures, including modus ponens and modus tollens conditional inferences, affirmation and denial disjunctive syllogisms, and categorical three-term syllogisms. However, as argued before, it may well be the case that the effect of logic on liking was simply driven by a conscious decision to prefer logically valid arguments – suggesting that the actual source of the liking judgment may not necessarily have been rooted in Type 1 processing. To counter this alternative explanation, in a follow-up experiment, we asked people to judge the physical brightness (i.e., text-to-background contrast) of the sentences which made up the argument. Importantly, in these studies there was an objective criterion for accuracy – that is, the actual contrast of the text, which was manipulated to vary (though the manipulation was subtle). Why would we possibly expect a high-level concept such as logical validity to interfere with the fairly low-level process of contrast discrimination? Following Morsanyi and Handley (2012), the prediction draws on the concepts of processing fluency and misattribution. The idea is that a statement which follows logically from a series of previously presented statements is processed more fluently, thus giving rise to a vague, implicit evidence signal. If our assertion that various Type 1 responses are cued autonomously holds, then this implicit validity-driven evidence signal could, in some cases, be misinterpreted as an increase in physical brightness. Our findings confirmed, consistent with this prediction, that there was a small but reliable effect of logic on brightness judgments, such that people perceived logically valid problems to be brighter than logically invalid ones – occasionally going against the objectively correct response of the physical contrast level. Taken together, these findings are, at the very least, suggestive of the idea that a non-negligible component of logical responding is based on an implicit, Type 1–driven evaluation of structural features correlated with logical validity (cf., Chater & Oaksford, 1999) – consistent with the principles of the parallel processing model.

On the integration of knowledge and structure

In our discussion so far we have focused mainly on a large set of studies suggesting that the parallel processing model provides a better account of belief bias in reasoning than the default-interventionist account. One thing which binds all of these studies is that they were designed with a focus on eliciting conflict between the two relevant problem features – logical validity (structure) and conclusion believability (knowledge). However, one of the key findings in the study of belief bias in syllogistic reasoning is not captured well in terms of the interplay between logic and beliefs as a competitive conflict: the effect of beliefs on the ability to reason logically.

Evans et al. (1983) conducted three experiments on the belief bias effect in syllogistic reasoning. Their study was seminal because it was the first to account for potential alternative explanations of the belief bias effect such as illicit conversion or atmosphere (Begg & Denny, 1969; Dickstein, 1981; Woodworth & Sells, 1935) by instantiating the proper experimental controls. Participants were presented with valid and invalid syllogisms, half of which had believable conclusions and half of which had unbelievable conclusions. However, Evans and colleagues did not analyze their experiments in terms of the now-common conflict versus no-conflict framing, but instead analyzed the full 2 (logic: valid vs. invalid) ×2 (belief: believable vs. unbelievable) design of the study. A consistent pattern of three effects emerged: people accepted valid arguments more than invalid arguments, suggesting they were sensitive to logical validity to an extent greater than chance. People also accepted arguments with believable conclusions more than arguments with unbelievable conclusions – the standard belief bias effect which most dual process accounts of belief bias set out to explain. However, the majority of the experiments also demonstrated that people were more competent at discriminating between valid and invalid arguments when these arguments had unbelievable conclusions as opposed to when they had believable conclusions. We refer to this reasoning facilitation in the face of unbelievable conclusions as *motivated reasoning* to underscore its analogical similarity to other findings across a range of domains (e.g., attitude polarization: Lord, Ross, & Lepper, 1979).

Measuring motivated reasoning

Recent research has cast some doubt on the veracity of the motivated reasoning component of belief bias based on concerns related to measurement (Dube, Rotello, & Heit, 2010; Heit & Rotello, 2014). Dube and colleagues essentially demonstrated that most of the research on the motivated reasoning component of belief bias had inappropriately relied on the class of linear models (such as ANOVA and multiple regression), where generalized linear models (such as signal detection theory and logistic regression) would have been more appropriate. Importantly, Dube and colleagues showed that this reliance on inappropriate measurement models overstated the statistical evidence for the motivated reasoning component of belief bias. Based on their experiments and modeling, they argued that belief bias could be traced back mainly to the response stage of cognition, rather than the reasoning stage.

Inspired by their findings, we conducted a series of belief bias experiments in which we relied on one of these alternative measurement models. Trippas, Handley, and Verde (2013) demonstrated in their first experiment that there was in fact still statistical evidence consistent with motivated reasoning even when the appropriate measurement models were used. Surprised by this contradictory result, in a second study we traced back this finding to an important individual differences component: apparently, reasoners of higher cognitive capacity showed the motivated reasoning bias, whereas lower cognitive capacity reasoners did not. After replicating this finding several times using alternative methods (Trippas, Handley, & Verde, 2014; Trippas, Verde, & Handley, 2014), we ultimately traced it back to the influence of analytic cognitive style on reasoning (Trippas, Pennycook, Verde, & Handley, 2015). Our findings demonstrated that analytic reasoners were *more* likely to show the motivated reasoning bias – although we hasten to add that they were less likely to show the belief bias effect in the response stage. By contrast, the more intuitive reasoners were not at all likely to engage in motivated reasoning: they responded almost exclusively on the basis of conclusion believability. Why? We argue that this finding is understood best in terms of the parallel processing model.

Motivated reasoning: a parallel processing interpretation

As we highlighted before, most of the research that we have focused on in our discussion of the parallel processing model of belief bias has examined cases where knowledge and structure provide competing cues for a response. For instance, all of our studies featured problems for which the structure of the argument implied a certain logical status (e.g., valid), but for which the presented conclusion was actually inconsistent with that logical status based on what we know is true from experience (e.g., unbelievable). Perhaps this opposition – although a good starting point – is too much of a simplification when the aim is to construct a more comprehensive account of thinking and reasoning. In our opinion, the human mind is set up in such a way that integration is the norm, whereas conflict, and hence failure to integrate, is unusual. Indeed, it could be argued that much of our everyday thinking benefits from drawing upon multiple cues – perceptual, structural, knowledge based, among others – each of which may provide relevant evidence in support of a particular decision, problem solution, or course of action. Framed otherwise, the truly critical task in this context then becomes to discriminate between relevant and irrelevant cues. In some senses the belief bias task illustrates this requirement within a toy domain, where the relevance of cues is externally determined through the instructions that the experimenter provides (i.e., to respond on the basis of logic on some trials but on the basis of beliefs on others as in the Stroop deduction task). But what happens if no such external guidance is provided and if multiple cues may in fact be relevant to some degree? In real-world situations where this is the case, successful thinking about complex problems often depends upon the integration of several relevant but distinct cues. We would argue that the parallel processing model, with its emphasis on the simultaneous processing of distinct problem features, naturally supports an integration process in circumstances where the various cues each provide some relevant information that supports the solution of the problem. But how does this apply to motivated reasoning?

The key insight in this respect is that the integration of information in working memory is a Type 2 process. As entailed in principle 4, people vary in their capacity and propensity to do so successfully. A good example in the reasoning literature is the use of counterexamples in conditional reasoning where the availability of alternative antecedents determines rates of drawing invalid inferences such as acceptance of the consequent (if p then q; q; therefore p) and denial of the antecedent (if p then q; not p; therefore not q). Interestingly, participants with greater cognitive capacity are more able to retrieve and selectively use counterexample knowledge (said alternative antecedents) in rejecting invalid inferences, but they do not rely on disablers to the same degree, as these would block perfectly valid inferences (De Neys, Schaeken, & d'Ydewalle, 2005; Verschueren, Schaeken, & d'Ydewalle, 2005). This suggests that the integration of relevant counterexamples with logical structure is an effortful process that depends upon Type 2 resources.

Applying these principles to the concept of motivated reasoning, we would argue that it is a product of the effortful process of integrating beliefs into the representational construction process. Specifically, motivated reasoners rely on Type 2 processing to construct a mental representation of the argument that allows them to reject an unbelievable conclusion – in this case the representational construction is being guided by their beliefs, resulting in an increased ability to reject invalid problems. By contrast, when the conclusion is believable, these reasoners seek a representation that supports it. Given that multiple supportive representations are typically available (e.g., some cats are furry logically entails anything from "somewhere, out there, there is a cat which is furry" up to and including the possibility that "all cats which exist are furry"), invalid problems are much less likely to be rejected when they have believable conclusions. This proposal is perhaps most clearly embedded within the selective processing model of belief bias (Evans, Handley, & Harper, 2001; Klauer, Musch, & Naumer, 2000; Stupple, Ball, Evans, & Kamal-Smith, 2011). However, one issue with the selective processing theory – essentially couched within the default-interventionist framework – is that it makes no explicit prediction as to why a non-negligible subset of participants does not routinely engage in motivated reasoning. The parallel processing model predicts that only more analytical reasoners are able (or willing) to engage in integration processes that are guided by relevant knowledge in the way outlined earlier. Less analytical reasoners may also try to do so, but do not have the resources to do so successfully (or equivalently, they may simply not be willing to perform this type of routine integration). The end result is that these people will be much more likely to base their response on problem features which takes comparatively less effort to process – in this case, believability.

One potential criticism of the parallel processing account of motivated reasoning we just outlined is that it is fairly post hoc. We agree; however, we note that our model also allows for two predictions. First, recall that the parallel processing model draws heavily on the concept of relative complexity (Trippas et al., 2017). Specifically, motivated reasoning is thought to occur exclusively when sufficiently analytical people reason about arguments for which the structural features (e.g., syllogistic form) require more complex processing than the knowledge-based problem aspects (e.g., conclusion believability). When this is not the case – for instance, because the structural and knowledge-based features require relatively shallow depths of processing – then no motivated reasoning is predicted to occur, regardless of the reasoner's tendency to respond analytically. Simply put, the parallel processing model predicts that motivated reasoning should not occur for simple syllogisms. This prediction is consistent with the vast majority of the empirical data (Evans, Newstead, Allen, & Pollard, 1994; Klauer et al., 2000; Trippas et al., 2013). A second prediction also draws on the parallel processing model's assumption that unbelievable conclusions will give rise to additional structure-based Type 2 processing for analytic reasoners via the search for an inconsistent representation of the premises – but only if the structural features entail more complex processing than the knowledge-based problem cue. This implies that if we could somehow make the knowledge-based judgment dependent on *more* complex processes than the associated argument structure – still keeping both sufficiently complex to ensure that multiple mental representations can be constructed – then we should find a facilitation of *belief-based* responding (i.e., an increased ability to discriminate between believable and unbelievable conclusions when the task is to do so) for invalid arguments compared to valid arguments. We would consider such an experiment a strong test of the parallel processing model of motivated reasoning. It goes without saying that this study will require further development of the Stroop deduction paradigm.

Concluding thoughts

In this chapter we drew an analogy between the progress made in cognitive science using the Stroop task methodology over the past century and the recent progress in the study of dual process theories of thinking and reasoning. Using the Stroop deduction paradigm developed by Handley et al., (2011), substantial progress toward a fuller understanding of human thinking and reasoning has been achieved. The experimental paradigm has spurred on the testing of predictions from established models and in doing so it has supported the development of a new model of thinking and reasoning: the parallel processing model of belief bias. In turn, the parallel processing model has exposed (or rather, allowed us to make sense of) a series of unintuitive effects, such as the apparently implicit sensitivity to structural features associated with logical validity and the fact that more analytic people are more prone to motivated reasoning.

The parallel processing model is our humble attempt at trying to make sense of the large corpus of studies on thinking and reasoning in general, and belief bias in particular. By drawing on methods, models, and techniques from other domains, we arrived at our account, which is but one of the many models to build on the impressive default-interventionist instantiation of dual process theory (see De Neys and Pennycook, both in this volume). Going forward, we think that more progress will be achieved by fully exploiting the research practices which have led to the proposal of the parallel processing model. Two practices stand out in this respect. First, we argue that it is important to stay open to ideas and methods which come out of left field. Two decades ago, the idea that under some circumstances logical reasoning could be more accurate than belief-based reasoning, or that motivated reasoning (in some senses a bias) could be more prevalent in more capable reasoners would be considered utterly bizarre in most circles. Although still the topic of vigorous debate, we believe progress has been made by accepting these ideas into the set of possibilities, allowing them to be formally tested and modeled.

Second, it seems wise to continue borrowing ideas from our neighbouring fields in psychological science – such as perception and memory – for potentially interesting experimental paradigms and models which can be applied to better understand research on reasoning. An example of the former can be traced back directly to the Stroop deduction paradigm, which took a very well-known method from research on perception and applied it to the study of deductive reasoning. An example of the latter can be found in the application of signal detection theory to the study of belief bias in deductive reasoning (Dube et al., 2010). One particularly interesting avenue for future research of the latter variety is the application of sequential sampling models of response time, such as the drift diffusion model (Ratcliff, 1978) or the linear ballistic accumulator (Brown & Heathcote, 2005), to research on thinking and reasoning. In fact, recent work has already made substantial progress in this direction (Alós-Ferrer, 2016; Hawkins, Hayes, & Heit, 2016). Given the heavy emphasis dual process theorists put on the interplay between response time and response accuracy, applying sequential sampling models which model both these variables simultaneously to the study of belief bias seems like the logical next step.

We conclude this chapter by acknowledging that dual process theory has had its critics (Keren & Schul, 2009; Kruglanski & Gigerenzer, 2011; Osman, 2004). However, we believe that as a meta-theory, dual process theory is matched by no other account of reasoning and judgment in two respects. First, dual process theory is a great way to generate novel and testable predictions, facilitating the framing of scientific debates, something which we have hopefully demonstrated in this chapter. Second, the willingness of dual process researchers such as Jonathan Evans to update their theories in light of new experimental evidence is particularly admirable. Indeed, if the trajectory traversed by Evans and colleagues from Evans and Over (1996) to Evans and Stanovich (2013) is even just partially indicative of the things yet to come, we think it is fair to say that dual process theory will be alive and kicking for at least a few more decades.

Note

1 Although the assumption is that sufficiently motivated individuals will routinely rely on some form of Type 2 processing, be it to analyze or rationalize, we cannot exclude the possibility that certain individuals rely exclusively on Type 1 processing – for instance, when they repeatedly choose response options at random.

References

Alós-Ferrer, C. (2016). A dual-process diffusion model. *Journal of Behavioral Decision Making*. doi:10.1002/bdm.1960

Ashby, F. G., & Maddox, W. T. (2005). Human category learning. *Annual Review of Psychology*, *56*, 149–178. doi:10.1146/annurev.psych.56.091103.070217

Begg, I., & Denny, P. J. (1969). Empirical reconcilliation of atmosphere and conversion interpretations of syllogistic reasoning errors. *Journal of Experimental Psychology*, *81*, 351–354. doi:10.1037/h0027770

Brown, S., & Heathcote, A. (2005). A ballistic model of choice response time. *Psychological Review*, *112*, 117–128. doi:10.1037/0033-295X.112.1.117

Cattell, J. M. (1886). The time it takes to see and name objects. *Mind*, *11*, 63–65.

Chaiken, S., & Trope, Y. (Eds.). (1999). *Dual-process theories in social psychology*. New York, NY: Guilford Press.

Chater, N., & Oaksford, M. (1999). The probability heuristics model of syllogistic reasoning. *Cognitive Psychology*, *38*, 191–258. doi:10.1006/cogp.1998.0696

De Neys, W. (2006). Dual processing in reasoning: Two systems but one reasoner. *Psychological Science*, *17*, 428–433. doi:10.1111/j.1467-9280.2006.01723.x

De Neys, W., Schaeken, W., & d'Ydewalle, G. (2005). Working memory and everyday conditional reasoning: Retrieval and inhibition of stored counterexamples. *Thinking & Reasoning*, *11*, 349–381. doi:10.1080/13546780442000222

Dickstein, L. S. (1981). Conversion and possibility in syllogistic reasoning. *Bulletin of the Psychonomic Society*, *18*, 229–232. doi:10.3758/BF03333612

Dube, C., Rotello, C. M., & Heit, E. (2010). Assessing the belief bias effect with ROCs: It's a response bias effect. *Psychological Review*, *117*, 831–863. doi:10.1037/a0019634

Epstein, S. (1994). Integration of the cognitive and the psychodynamic unconscious. *American Psychologist*, *49*, 709–724. doi:10.1037/0003-066X.49.8.709

Evans, J. St B. T. (2002). Logic and human reasoning: An assessment of the deduction paradigm. *Psychological Bulletin*, *128*, 978–996. doi:10.1037/0033-2909.128.6.978

Evans, J. St B. T. (2007). On the resolution of conflict in dual process theories of reasoning. *Thinking & Reasoning*, *13*, 321–339. doi:10.1080/13546780601008825

Evans, J. St B. T., Barston, J. L., & Pollard, P. (1983). On the conflict between logic and belief in syllogistic reasoning. *Memory & Cognition*, *11*, 295–306. doi:10.3758/BF03196976

Evans, J. St B. T., & Curtis-Holmes, J. (2005). Rapid responding increases belief bias: Evidence for the dual-process theory of reasoning. *Thinking & Reasoning*, *11*, 382–389. doi:10.1080/13546780542000005

Evans, J. St B. T., Handley, S. J., & Bacon, A. M. (2009). Reasoning under time pressure. *Experimental Psychology, 56*, 77–83. doi:10.1027/1618-3169.56.2.77

Evans, J. St B. T., Handley, S. J., & Harper, C. N. J. (2001). Necessity, possibility and belief: A study of syllogistic reasoning. *The Quarterly Journal of Experimental Psychology Section A, 54*, 935–958. doi:10.1080/713755983

Evans, J. St B. T., Newstead, S. E., Allen, J. L., & Pollard, P. (1994). Debiasing by instruction: The case of belief bias. *European Journal of Cognitive Psychology, 6*, 263–285. doi:10.1080/09541449408520148

Evans, J. St B. T., Newstead, S. E., & Byrne, R. R. M. J. (1993). *Human reasoning: The psychology of deduction*. Hillsdale, NJ: Erlbaum.

Evans, J. St B. T., & Over, D. E. (1996). *Rationality and reasoning*. Hove, England: Psychology Press.

Evans, J. St B. T., & Stanovich, K. E. (2013). Dual-process theories of higher cognition: Advancing the debate. *Perspectives on Psychological Science, 8*, 223–241. doi:10.1177/1745691612460685

Frankish, K., & Evans, J. St B. T. (2009). The duality of mind: An historical perspective. In K. Frankish & J. St B. T. Evans (Eds.), *In two minds: Dual processes and beyond* (pp. 1–29). New York, NY: Oxford University Press.

Frederick, S. (2005). Cognitive reflection and decision making. *The Journal of Economic Perspectives, 19*, 25–42. doi:10.1257/089533005775196732

Handley, S. J., Newstead, S. E., & Trippas, D. (2011). Logic, beliefs, and instruction: A test of the default interventionist account of belief bias. *Journal of Experimental Psychology: Learning, Memory, and Cognition, 37*, 28–43. doi:10.1037/a0021098

Handley, S. J., & Trippas, D. (2015). Dual processes and the interplay between knowledge and structure: A new parallel processing model. In B. H. Ross (Ed.), *Psychology of learning and motivation* (Vol. 62, pp. 33–58). Academic Press. Retrieved from www.sciencedirect.com/science/article/pii/S0079742114000036

Hawkins, G. E., Hayes, B. K., & Heit, E. (2016). A dynamic model of reasoning and memory. *Journal of Experimental Psychology: General, 145*, 155–180. doi:10.1037/xge0000113

Heit, E., & Rotello, C. M. (2014). Traditional difference-score analyses of reasoning are flawed. *Cognition, 131*, 75–91. doi:10.1016/j.cognition.2013.12.003

Howarth, S., Handley, S. J., & Walsh, C. (2016). The logic-bias effect: The role of effortful processing in the resolution of belief – logic conflict. *Memory & Cognition, 44*, 330–349. doi:10.3758/s13421-015-0555-x

Jacoby, L. L., Toth, J. P., & Yonelinas, A. P. (1993). Separating conscious and unconscious influences of memory: Measuring recollection. *Journal of Experimental Psychology: General, 122*, 139–154. doi:10.1037/0096-3445.122.2.139

James, W. (1890). *The principles of psychology*. New York, NY: Holt.

Kahneman, D. (2011). *Thinking, fast and slow*. New York, NY: Macmillan.

Keren, G., & Schul, Y. (2009). Two is not always better than one: A critical evaluation of two-system theories. *Perspectives on Psychological Science, 4*, 533–550. doi:10.1111/j.1745-6924.2009.01164.x

Klauer, K. C., Musch, J., & Naumer, B. (2000). On belief bias in syllogistic reasoning. *Psychological Review, 107*, 852–884. doi:10.1037/0033-295X.107.4.852

Klauer, K. C., & Singmann, H. (2013). Does logic feel good? Testing for intuitive detection of logicality in syllogistic reasoning. *Journal of Experimental Psychology: Learning, Memory, and Cognition, 39*, 1265–1273. doi:10.1037/a0030530

Kruglanski, A. W., & Gigerenzer, G. (2011). Intuitive and deliberate judgments are based on common principles. *Psychological Review, 118*, 97–109. doi:10.1037/a0020762

Lea, R. B. (1995). On-line evidence for elaborative logical inferences in text. *Journal of Experimental Psychology: Learning, Memory, and Cognition, 21*, 1469–1482. doi:10.1037/0278-7393.21.6.1469

Leo, P. D., & Greene, A. J. (2008). Is awareness necessary for true inference? *Memory & Cognition, 36*, 1079–1086. doi:10.3758/MC.36.6.1079

Lord, C. G., Ross, L., & Lepper, M. R. (1979). Biased assimilation and attitude polarization: The effects of prior theories on subsequently considered evidence. *Journal of Personality and Social Psychology, 37*, 2098–2109. doi:10.1037/0022-3514.37.11.2098

MacLeod, C. M. (1991). Half a century of research on the Stroop effect: An integrative review. *Psychological Bulletin, 109*, 163–203. doi:10.1037/0033-2909.109.2.163

Morsanyi, K., & Handley, S. J. (2008). How smart do you need to be to get it wrong? The role of cognitive capacity in the development of heuristic-based judgment. *Journal of Experimental Child Psychology, 99*, 18–36. doi:10.1016/j.jecp.2007.08.003

Morsanyi, K., & Handley, S. J. (2012). Logic feels so good – I like it! Evidence for intuitive detection of logicality in syllogistic reasoning. *Journal of Experimental Psychology: Learning, Memory, and Cognition, 38*, 596–616. doi:10.1037/a0026099

Osman, M. (2004). An evaluation of dual process theories of reasoning. *Psychonomic Bulletin & Review, 11*, 988–1010. doi:10.3758/BF03196730

Pennycook, G., Cheyne, J. A., Koehler, D. J., & Fugelsang, J. A. (2016). Is the cognitive reflection test a measure of both reflection and intuition? *Behavior Research Methods, 48*, 341–348. doi:10.3758/s13428-015-0576-1

Pennycook, G., Fugelsang, J. A., & Koehler, D. J. (2015). Everyday consequences of analytic thinking. *Current Directions in Psychological Science. 24*, 425–432. doi:10.1177/0963721415604610

Pennycook, G., Trippas, D., Handley, S. J., & Thompson, V. A. (2014). Base rates: Both neglected and intuitive. *Journal of Experimental Psychology: Learning, Memory, and Cognition, 40*, 544–554. doi:10.1037/a0034887

Rader, A. W., & Sloutsky, V. M. (2002). Processing of logically valid and logically invalid conditional inferences in discourse comprehension. *Journal of Experimental Psychology: Learning, Memory, and Cognition, 28*, 59–68. doi:10.1037/0278-7393.28.1.59

Ratcliff, R. (1978). A theory of memory retrieval. *Psychological Review, 85*, 59–108. doi:10.1037/0033-295X.85.2.59

Raz, A., Kirsch, I., Pollard, J., & Nitkin-Kaner, Y. (2006). Suggestion reduces the Stroop effect. *Psychological Science, 17*, 91–95. doi:10.1111/j.1467-9280.2006.01669.x

Rumelhart, D. E., Hinton, G. E., & McClelland, J. L. (1986). A general framework for parallel distributed processing. In David E. Rumelhart, James L. McClelland and PDP Research Group (Eds.), *Parallel distributed processing: Explorations in the microstructure of cognition* (Vol. 1, pp. 45–76). Cambridge, MA: MIT Press.

Singmann, H., Klauer, K. C., & Kellen, D. (2014). Intuitive logic revisited: New data and a Bayesian mixed model meta-analysis. *PLoS One, 9*, e94223. doi:10.1371/journal.pone.0094223

Sloman, S. A. (1996). The empirical case for two systems of reasoning. *Psychological Bulletin, 119*, 3–22. doi:10.1037/0033-2909.119.1.3

Stanovich, K. E. (1999). *Who is rational? Studies of individual differences in reasoning.* Hove, England: Erlbaum.

Stroop, R. J. (1935). Studies of interference in serial verbal reactions. *Journal of Experimental Psychology, 18*, 643–662.

Stupple, E. J. N., Ball, L. J., Evans, J. St B. T., & Kamal-Smith, E. (2011). When logic and belief collide: Individual differences in reasoning times support a selective processing model. *Journal of Cognitive Psychology, 23,* 931–941. doi:10.1080/20445911.2011.589381

Toplak, M. E., West, R. F., & Stanovich, K. E. (2014). Rational thinking and cognitive sophistication: Development, cognitive abilities, and thinking dispositions. *Developmental Psychology, 50,* 1037. doi:10.1037/a0034910

Topolinski, S., & Strack, F. (2009). The architecture of intuition: Fluency and affect determine intuitive judgments of semantic and visual coherence and judgments of grammaticality in artificial grammar learning. *Journal of Experimental Psychology: General, 138,* 39–63. doi:10.1037/a0014678

Trippas, D., Handley, S. J., & Verde, M. F. (2013). The SDT model of belief bias: Complexity, time, and cognitive ability mediate the effects of believability. *Journal of Experimental Psychology: Learning, Memory, and Cognition, 39,* 1393–1402. doi:10.1037/a0032398

Trippas, D., Handley, S. J., & Verde, M. F. (2014). Fluency and belief bias in deductive reasoning: New indices for old effects. *Frontiers in Psychology, 5,* 1–7. doi:10.3389/fpsyg.2014.00631

Trippas, D., Handley, S. J., Verde, M. F., & Morsanyi, K. (2016). Logic brightens my day: Evidence for implicit sensitivity to logical validity. *Journal of Experimental Psychology: Learning, Memory, and Cognition, 42,* 1448–1457. doi:10.1037/xlm0000248

Trippas, D., Pennycook, G., Verde, M. F., & Handley, S. J. (2015). Better but still biased: Analytic cognitive style and belief bias. *Thinking & Reasoning, 21,* 431–445. doi:10.1080/13546783.2015.1016450

Trippas, D., Thompson, V. A., & Handley, S. J. (2017). When fast logic meets slow belief: Evidence for a parallel-processing model of belief bias. *Memory & Cognition, 45,* 539–552. doi:10.3758/s13421-016-0680-1

Trippas, D., Verde, M. F., & Handley, S. J. (2014). Using forced choice to test belief bias in syllogistic reasoning. *Cognition, 133,* 586–600. doi:10.1016/j.cognition.2014.08.009

Verschueren, N., Schaeken, W., & d'Ydewalle, G. (2005). Everyday conditional reasoning: A working memory – dependent tradeoff between counterexample and likelihood use. *Memory & Cognition, 33,* 107–119. doi:10.3758/BF03195301

Wilkins, M. C. (1929). The effect of changed material on ability to do formal syllogistic reasoning. *Archives of Psychology, 102,* 83.

Woodworth, R. S., & Sells, S. B. (1935). An atmosphere effect in formal syllogistic reasoning. *Journal of Experimental Psychology, 18,* 451–460. doi:10.1037/h0060520

4
BIAS, CONFLICT, AND FAST LOGIC

Towards a hybrid dual process future?

Wim De Neys

Introduction

Daily life experiences and scientific research on human thinking indicate that people's intuitions can often lead them astray. An intriguing illustration is the impact of "low-fat" food labels. Somewhat ironically, these labels can cause people to overeat and gain weight (Wansink & Chandon, 2006). Clearly, if you eat a low-fat alternative instead of the original version of your, say, favorite potato chips, you will have consumed fewer calories (e.g., 60% of the regular x calories). However, the problem is that we seem to intuitively equate "low fat" with "healthy". Because people see no danger in eating healthy food, the simple intuitive association will make it more likely that they consume more of it – and finish a second bag of potato chips, for example.

What is striking is that one would expect that upon some minimal reflection and deliberation, people would spot their error. Indeed, one doesn't need to be a rocket scientist to realize that when doubling your intake, the low-fat alternative becomes the least healthy option (e.g., 60% of regular x calories + 60% of regular x calories = 120% of regular x calories). Nevertheless, it seems hard for people to avoid this type of fallacious thinking.

Since the 1960s seminal work in the reasoning and decision-making field has shown how similar intuitive thinking can bias our inferences and make people violate the most basic logical and probabilistic rules. The dual process view of thinking was originally adopted to account for this bias phenomenon (Evans, 2016; Kahneman, 2011; Wason & Evans, 1975). At the heart of any dual process model lies the idea that human reasoning relies on two different types of systems or processes, which one can simply label System 1 and System 2 (Stanovich, 1999). System 1 (often also called the intuitive or heuristic system) is assumed to operate fast and effortlessly. It is this system that is supposed to mediate intuitive thinking and make us associate "low fat" with "healthy", for example. System 2 (often also called the deliberate or analytic system) is assumed to be slower and more effortful in the sense that it burdens our limited executive cognitive resources. It is this second system that is supposed to mediate the type of deliberate thinking that is typically required for sound logical inferencing, for example.[1]

Although different types of dual process models have been proposed through the years (Evans, 2008), the most influential one is the so-called serial or default-interventionist (DI) model that has been advocated and popularized through the groundbreaking work of prominent scholars such as Jonathan Evans (2006; Evans & Stanovich, 2013), Daniel Kahneman (2011), or Keith Stanovich (2010). At the core of this model lies a serial view on the interaction between System 1 and System 2. The key idea is that when people are faced with a reasoning problem, they will typically rely on System 1 to generate an answer. This is the default system. If needed, people can activate System 2 in a later phase to intervene and correct System 1 output. But this System 2 engagement only occurs after System 1 has been engaged, and it is also optional. That is, activation of System 2 is not guaranteed. More generally, in the serial DI model reasoners are conceived as cognitive misers who try to minimize cognitive effort (Kahneman, 2011). Because System 2 thinking is hard, people will tend to refrain from it and stick to the default System 1 response. Consequently, in cases in which System 1 cues a response that conflicts with more logical considerations – as in the typical classic reasoning task – most people will not detect this conflict. Hence, reasoners end up being biased because they simply don't notice that their intuitive response is unwarranted. And the few people who do notice it will need to correct the initially cued System 1 response after demanding System 2 intervention.

There is little doubt that the serial DI model offers an appealing explanation for the massive bias that has been observed in the reasoning and decision-making literature. It is also clear that the model has been highly instrumental in organizing and generating new research questions. However, in recent years evidence is amassing that its underlying assumptions might be problematic. As I noted in the opening chapter, this was one of the reasons for putting this volume together. In the present chapter I will specifically focus on work from my own team that has led me to re-think the way we need to conceive of the interaction between the two systems. I have organized the chapter in four sections. I start with a short theoretical discussion of alternative dual process models. In the second and third sections I give an overview of my empirical work. Finally, in the fourth section I discuss emerging themes, outstanding questions, and future directions.

Three theoretical models: serial, parallel, and hybrid

Before digging into the empirical data I want to introduce two alternatives to the dominant serial DI model: the parallel and hybrid models. Figure 4.1 presents a schematic illustration. I will return to a more detailed discussion in the remainder

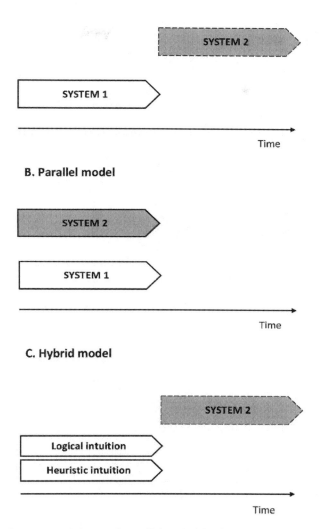

FIGURE 4.1 Illustration of the serial, parallel, and hybrid view on the relation between System 1 and System 2 processing. System 1 is represented by white bars and System 2 by grey bars. The horizontal axis represents the time flow. The dashed lines represent the optional nature of the System 2 engagement in the serial and hybrid model.

of the chapter, but I believe that briefly sketching the basic model features might be helpful to position the empirical work.

It is important to bear in mind that although the serial DI dual process model has been highly influential, rival models have always been around. The most well-known traditional competitor is the parallel processing model such as it has been presented in the work of Sloman (1996) or Epstein (1994), for example. Whereas the serial DI model assumes that System 2 is activated after System 1, the parallel model assumes that both systems are activated simultaneously from the start of the reasoning process. The fact that System 2 is engaged does not imply that its operations will always be successfully completed, but it at least suffices to detect possible conflict between the two systems. One implication is that, in contrast to the serial model, the parallel model does not postulate that biased reasoners are blind to the logically questionable nature of their response.

The hybrid model is a more recent competitor to the serial (and parallel) model. It is this model that is, in my opinion, best supported by recent empirical data. Although the serial and parallel models make different assumptions about biased reasoners' conflict detection efficiency, they both assume that detection of the erroneous nature of a System 1 response results from System 2 activation (the difference is that the serial model postulates that this System 2 activation only occurs for correct responders). Here lies the key difference with the hybrid model. At the most general level, the hybrid model postulates that the response that is traditionally considered to be computed by System 2 can also be cued by System 1. Hence, System 1 is assumed to generate (at least) two different types of intuitive responses. One of these is the traditional "heuristic" intuitive response based on semantic and visuospatial associations that is also assumed to be cued intuitively by the serial and parallel model. The other one is what I refer to as a "logical" intuitive response based on elementary knowledge of basic logical and probabilistic principles. The underlying idea here is that even biased reasoners implicitly grasp elementary logical and probabilistic principles and activate this knowledge automatically when faced with a reasoning task. This intuitive logical knowledge allows one to detect that the heuristic intuition is questionable in the case of conflict without a need to engage in demanding System 2 computations.

It should be clear that the hybrid model shares some key features with both the serial and parallel models (hence, its name). Just like the serial model, it assumes that System 1 and System 2 are activated in a serial fashion. So just like the serial model, it postulates that System 2 activation is optional and only occurs after initial System 1 activation. But just like the parallel model, the hybrid model also entails that there is parallel activation. However, the parallel activation concerns activation of different types of System 1 intuitions rather than parallel activation of System 1 and System 2.

In the next section I will review the empirical findings that have led me to favor the hybrid model. But before doing so, I want to clarify some common misconceptions that may confuse readers. First, in the dual process literature authors sometimes tend to equate System 2 processing and normative correctness. That is, the System 1 response is often referred to as the incorrect response, whereas the System 2 response is referred to as the correct response. This is a handy simplification because in most classic reasoning tasks that are studied in the field, it is typically the case that the intuitively cued response is incorrect from a normative point of view (i.e., within traditional standard logic, probability theory, or mathematics), whereas arriving at the correct response is assumed to require the type of deliberative thinking that is typical of System 2. However, it should be clear that there is obviously nothing "magical" about System 2 computation that makes its output universally normatively correct. It is simply the case that the two features (i.e., whether a response has been generated by System 1 or System 2 and whether it is normatively correct or not) are often correlated in the type of problems we typically study (Evans, 2012). Obviously, there are cases in which the System 1 response will be correct as well. For example, there is no doubt whatsoever that adults can give the correct answer to a problem such as "How much is 5 + 5?" intuitively without any deliberation. Likewise, there can be situations in which too much deliberation will lead you astray (e.g., Reyna, 2004). Hence, one needs to bear in mind that the normative correctness of a response is not a defining feature of System 1 and System 2 processing. It's a convenient overgeneralization that facilitates writing.

Second, the labels "serial", "parallel", and "hybrid" are functional labels to describe the postulated processing architecture during the core reasoning process. Literally speaking, a response to a reasoning problem can never be purely intuitive. That is, before System 1 can cue an intuitive response, one will need to read or listen to the problem premises, for example. It is well established that such reading and comprehension processes can require deliberation and draw on the very same executive resources that System 2 requires. Consequently, one can argue that every reasoning process starts with initial System 2 activation. Likewise, one might argue that every reasoning process also ends with System 2 activation. That is, once I have computed a response to a problem, I will need to verbalize, write down, or type my answer. This answer production may also require System 2. In this sense, it can be said that even the serial DI model assumes that System 2 is always "on". But the idea here is that System 2 is in a "low-effort" mode in which it simply accepts the suggestions made by System 1 without checking them (Kahneman, 2011). Hence, it does not engage in any proper deliberation, so its core function is not activated. In sum, it is useful to keep in mind that the debate between the different models concerns the processing during the actual "reasoning" stage and not the initial encoding of the preambles or the ultimate overt response production.

Empirical findings: conflict blind spot?

The processing architecture that is put forward by the serial dual process model leads to at least two testable core predictions. First, biased responding in classic reasoning tasks results from a failure to activate System 2 and detect that an intuitively cued System 1 response conflicts with deliberate System 2 computations. Second, correct responding in these cases requires a correction of the intuitively cued System 1 response by System 2. Put differently, biased reasoners should not notice that they are biased, and correct reasoners will correct their initial answer after deliberation. For convenience, I will refer to these core predictions as the "conflict blind spot" and "System 2 correction" assumption. Most of my work in the last ten years has focused on an empirical testing of these hypotheses. I review the work on the conflict blind spot in this section and move to the System 2 correction studies in the next one.

Evidence for successful conflict detection

The conflict blind spot entails that biased reasoners who violate elementary logical and probabilistic principles in classic reasoning and decision-making tasks will not detect that their intuitive answer conflicts with them. This is based on the assumption that taking these principles into account depends on System 2 processing and this optional System 2 processing is not engaged for biased reasoners who stick to the default System 1 response. In other words, biased reasoners will be blind to their bias and will not detect that their intuitively cued System 1 response is incorrect. One can see how this can easily lead to a somewhat grim characterization of the biased reasoner as a blind fool who errs without having any clue she's doing so (De Neys, Rossi, & Houdé, 2013; Hoffrage & Marewski, 2015). In my work on conflict detection during thinking, I have directly tested this assumption.

The methodological rationale is simple. Classic reasoning tasks that have been used to study intuitive bias in the field are typically constructed such that System 1 generates an appealing but incorrect intuitive response which conflicts with some normative logical, probabilistic, or mathematical principle. Take, for example, the infamous bat-and-ball problem (Frederick, 2005):

> "A bat and a ball together cost $1.10. The bat costs $1 more than the ball. How much does the ball cost?"

Intuitively, the answer "10 cents" immediately springs to mind because people naturally parse the $1.10 in $1 and 10 cents (Kahneman, 2011). However, although it is intuitively appealing, the answer is obviously wrong. Clearly, if the ball costs 10 cents and the bat costs $1 more, then the bat would cost $1.10. In this case, the bat and ball together would cost $1.20 and not $1.10 as stated in the problem. After some reflection, it is clear that the ball must cost 5 cents and the bat costs – at a dollar more – $1.05 which gives us a total of $1.10.

Now, in addition to the traditional "conflict" problems, participants in the conflict detection studies are also presented with control "no-conflict" problems. By introducing small content transformations, the intuitively cued System 1 response is made coherent with the appropriate System 2 response in these versions. In other words, in the control problems, the intuitively cued response is also correct. For example, a no-conflict control problem of the bat-and-ball problem might read:

> "A bat and a ball together cost $1.10. The bat costs $1. How much does the ball cost?"

Obviously, in this control version the intuitive splitting of $1.10 and selection of the "10 cents" answer is also mathematically correct.

To test reasoners' conflict or bias detection sensitivity, we can simply contrast their processing of the conflict and control versions. Basic studies on conflict or error monitoring in the cognitive control field (e.g., Botvinick, 2007) have long shown that error and conflict detection results, for example, in longer response latencies and decreased response confidence. The key difference between the conflict and control problems is the fact that the intuitively cued System 1 response happens to be incorrect in the conflict problem. If biased reasoners are sensitive to the erroneous nature of their answer, one can expect that this detection will affect their processing. And this is precisely what has been observed (e.g., De Neys & Glumicic, 2008; De Neys et al., 2013; De Neys, Cromheeke, & Osman, 2011). Biased reasoners who solve the conflict problems typically need more time to solve them and are less confident about the correctness of their response compared to the control problem (on which their intuitively cued response is also correct). This directly implies that biased reasoners are not blind to the questionable nature of their biased response.

Critically, these findings have been validated with a range of methods and tasks. For example, gaze tracking and memory studies indicate that biased reasoners also fixate on the logically crucial problem parts longer and show better recall of this information on the conflict problems (De Neys & Glumicic, 2008; Franssens & De Neys, 2009). Neuroimaging work further indicates that the anterior cingulate cortex – the brain region that is often assumed to mediate conflict and error detection (e.g., Botvinick, 2007) – shows increased activation when biased reasoners solve conflict vs. control problems (e.g., De Neys, Vartanian, & Goel, 2008; Simon, Lubin, Houdé, & De Neys, 2015). Hence, in line with the behavioral findings this suggests that even biased incorrect responders to traditional (i.e., conflict) reasoning problems are detecting that the intuitively cued System 1 answer is questionable.

As I noted, in addition to multiple methods, the conflict sensitivity effects have been observed on a range of classic tasks (e.g., conjunction fallacy, bat-and-ball problem, ratio bias, belief bias syllogisms, base-rate neglect problems, number conservation task; see De Neys, 2015). Clearly, any finding that is based on a single method or single problem is open to confounds (Aczel, Szollosi, & Bago, 2016; Mata, Schubert, & Ferreira, 2014; Pennycook, Fugelsang, & Koehler, 2012; Singmann, Klauer, & Kellen, 2014). Hence, the generalization across methods and tasks lends credence to the findings. In this sense it is also important to highlight that similar findings have been reported by different teams (e.g., Bonner & Newell, 2010; Gangemi, Bourgeois-Gironde, & Mancini, 2015; Morsanyi & Handley, 2012 Pennycook, Trippas, Handley, & Thompson, 2014; Thompson & Johnson, 2014; Villejoubert, 2009; Stupple, Ball, Evans, & Kamal-Smith, 2011). In sum, taken together, there seems to be reliable evidence against the conflict blind spot hypothesis (De Neys, 2014, 2015).

Evidence for intuitive conflict detection

The finding that biased reasoners show successful conflict detection is not predicted by the serial DI model. However, it fits with both the parallel and hybrid models. Indeed, proponents of the parallel model have long predicted that biased reasoners will show conflict sensitivity. The key difference with the hybrid model is that this conflict sensitivity is believed to result from effortful parallel System 2 engagement. The hybrid model entails that it results from automatically activated competing System 1 intuitions. Hence, after having established that there is evidence for biased reasoners' conflict sensitivity, the critical next step is to determine where this sensitivity is coming from: Is it driven by System 1 or System 2?

Addressing this issue is also relatively straightforward. The defining feature of System 2 processing is that it is slow and cognitive resource demanding. By depriving people of the time or resources to engage in System 2, we can experimentally "knock out" System 2. For example, we can limit the time people get to give an answer (i.e., time pressure manipulation) or force them to allocate their cognitive resources to another task during reasoning (i.e., concurrent load manipulation). In my studies I often show people a complex spatial dot pattern (e.g., four dots placed in a 3 × 3 grid) before the reasoning task which they have to memorize during reasoning. Because this memorization task requires executive resources needed for System 2 deliberation, System 2 processing will be hampered. If the conflict sensitivity effects (e.g., longer decisions times and lower confidence on conflict vs. control problems) result from System 2 processing, they should be attenuated under load or time pressure. Because System 1 operations do not require executive resources, they should, by definition, not be hampered by the executive load.

By now a range of studies have shown that conflict detection is typically preserved under load and time pressure (Bago & De Neys, 2017a; Franssens & De Neys, 2009; Johnson, Tubau, & De Neys, 2016; see also Pennycook et al., 2014; Thompson & Johnson, 2014). Hence, knocking out System 2 does not affect the efficiency of conflict detection, which suggests it is an intuitive System 1 process.

It is this evidence for the intuitive nature of successful conflict detection that has led me to propose a hybrid model and postulate that people have logical intuitions. If biased reasoners show sensitivity to violations of basic logico-mathematical principles in the absence of System 2 deliberation, we have to assume that they have some knowledge of these principles and activate these automatically when faced with the reasoning problem.

Empirical findings: corrective nature of System 2?

After having initially focused on the conflict blind spot assumption, my more recent empirical work shifted to an empirical test of the alleged corrective nature of System 2 processing. Bluntly put, one might say that whereas the conflict detection work primarily focused on incorrect responders, the focus here lies specifically on those few participants who do respond correctly. To recap, the "corrective System 2" assumption entails that on classic reasoning tasks in which System 1 cues an incorrect heuristic response, correct responding requires System 2 operations to override the initially cued System 1 response. So the idea is that people who respond correctly in the end initially also generate the incorrect "heuristic" System 1 response. In other words, in the time course of the reasoning process, the correct response is always preceded by the incorrect response: everyone is intuitively biased at first, but System 2 helps some people to correct this initial incorrect answer. Note that this assumption is made by both the traditional serial DI and parallel model. Although the parallel model entails that both systems are activated simultaneously, the fact that System 1 is faster implies that its output will be available first and will need to be overridden by the slower System 2 to respond correctly in case of conflict.

In recent work with Bence Bago we have begun to test this corrective time-course assumption directly (Bago & De Neys, 2017a, 2017b). Initially we were somewhat surprised to see that given how central the corrective assumption is for traditional dual process models, there is, in fact, little hard empirical evidence that supports it. I suspect that one reason is that the assumption seems so self-evident. Introspectively, it certainly feels that on traditional conflict tasks such as the bat-and-ball problem the intuitive response pops up immediately ("it's 10 cents!") and we have to think harder to correct it. However, we know that introspective impressions can be misleading (e.g., Mega & Volz, 2014). One might also argue that latency studies have clearly established that correct responses take longer than biased responses (e.g., De Neys, 2006; Pennycook, Fugelsang, & Koehler, 2015). Although this supports the dual process claim that System 1 is faster than System 2, it does not entail that people who gave the correct response initially considered the incorrect heuristic response. They might have needed more time for System 2 calculations without ever having considered the System 1 response.

To obtain more direct evidence, we adopted the two-response paradigm that has been introduced by Valerie Thompson and colleagues (e.g., Thompson, Prowse Turner, & Pennycook, 2011). In the paradigm participants are asked to give a first initial response as quickly as possible, and subsequently they are given all the time they want to reflect on the problem and select a final response. This simple procedure allows us to examine the time course of reasoners' (potential) answer change. The serial DI and parallel models predict two types of response patterns on traditional reasoning tasks. In line with classic findings in the literature, most people should be biased, so both their initial and final responses will be incorrect (we can label this a "00" pattern, i.e., two subsequent incorrect responses). In addition, some people will initially generate the incorrect response but will correct this in the end after they had the time to engage in System 2 deliberation (we can label this a "01" pattern).

Obviously, it is important to make absolutely sure that participants respect the instructions and indeed respond with the first response that comes to mind. If participants were to "cheat" and actually reflect before entering their initial response, it would not be surprising that they might give the correct answer as their first response. Therefore, in our version of the two-response paradigm we experimentally "knock out" System 2 by imposing both time pressure and a load task. Participants need to enter their initial response within a very strict deadline (e.g., 4 s for our studies with the bat-and-ball problem – the time needed in a pretest to simply read the problem). In addition, during the initial response phase they are burdened with a load task (e.g., the dot memorization task I introduced earlier) to further minimize the possibility that they deliberate during the first response phase. With this procedure we can be maximally sure that the initial response is truly intuitive in nature (Bago & De Neys, 2017a).

In one published (Bago & De Neys, 2017a) and one ongoing study (Bago & De Neys, 2017b) we have run this paradigm with three different reasoning tasks (i.e., base-rate task, syllogisms, and the bat-and-ball problem) in a total of 12 experiments in which we tested about 1000 participants. The results are highly consistent. Not surprisingly, the dominant response pattern (48% to 76% of trials) is the "00" case in which participants give the intuitively cued heuristic response both as their final and initial answer. Obviously, this is what all models would predict: in line with classic findings, people are typically biased when solving these infamous reasoning problems. In line with serial DI (and parallel) predictions, we also find a small subset of "01" trials (7% to 10% of trials) on which participants initially give the incorrect heuristic response and correct this after deliberation in the second response stage. They key finding is that we also frequently observe a "11" pattern (15% to 42% of trials) in which the correct response is already given in the initial response stage. Overall, this "11" pattern is about two times more frequent than the "01" pattern. In other words, of those participants who manage to give the correct answer as their final response, the vast majority (+66%) already selects this response as their initial answer. This implies that the corrective pattern that is envisaged by the traditional serial and parallel dual process models is the exception rather than the rule. People who respond correctly after deliberation do not necessarily need to override their initial response; they already give this correct answer intuitively.

For completeness, note that it is not the case that correct intuitive responses simply result from random guessing. We always present multiple conflict (and no-conflict) items. Participants' response patterns across items are almost perfectly stable. That is, if you give a correct intuitive response on one trial, you do so on all trials. If initial correct responses resulted from guessing, people should obviously show more variability in their responses. Likewise, we also control for problem familiarity (e.g., if participants have seen the problem before and know the solution, it would not be surprising that they do not need to deliberate about it).

As I noted, our empirical findings have been highly consistent across the different tasks and studies we have run. Moreover, independent work by Valerie Thompson and colleagues is pointing towards the same trends (Newman, Gibb, & Thompson, 2017). Hence, the empirical data seem to be robust. But how do we make theoretical sense of this? Clearly, the finding that correct deliberation is preceded by correct intuitive responding is hard to account for by the serial DI and parallel model. However, the logical intuition idea in the hybrid model suggests an explanation. A core feature of the model is that people have both a heuristic and logical intuition. However, this does not imply that both intuitions are necessarily equally strong. Indeed, for most people, the heuristic intuition will be stronger than the logical intuition (De Neys, 2012). This explains why heuristic responses still dominate and most people are biased on these tasks. Although the presence of a logical intuition allows them to detect the unwarranted nature of their heuristic response, it remains hard to override the dominant heuristic intuition. But in line with recent suggestions by Pennycook et al. (2015), it is reasonable to assume that there can be individual differences in the strength of both intuitions. That is, everyone has both intuitions but they vary in activation strength. For example, the dominant "00" case will be characterized by a very strong heuristic and weaker logical intuition. Intuitive correct "11" responders will show the opposite pattern with a very strong logical and weak heuristic intuition. For the "01" responders who correct their answer after deliberation, both intuitions would be more moderate and similar in strength.

Interestingly, conflict detection findings support the strength theorizing. In our two response experiments we always present participants with conflict and no-conflict control problems, as in the conflict detection studies discussed in the previous section. Although all reasoners show a conflict detection effect at the initial response stage (i.e., decreased response confidence for conflict vs. no-conflict problems), this effect is much more pronounced for the "01" responders whose intuitions are assumed to be most similar in strength (Bago & De Neys, 2017a). Hence, it is quite reasonable to conclude that the more similar the intuitions are, the more you are in doubt. This fits with a view in which our reasoning performance is determined by the absolute (which intuition dominates?) and relative (how big is the strength difference?) difference in the strength of the competing intuitions. Figure 4.2 presents an illustration of this idea.

Our work on the corrective System 2 assumption clearly indicates that people can answer some of the most infamous classic reasoning problems correctly without deliberation. This strengthens the case for the hybrid model's postulation of logical intuitions. Hence, in addition to logical responding on the basis of slow deliberate System 2 operations – as it is traditionally conceived – we need to postulate a type of fast, intuitive logical responding on the basis of System 1 operations. However, it

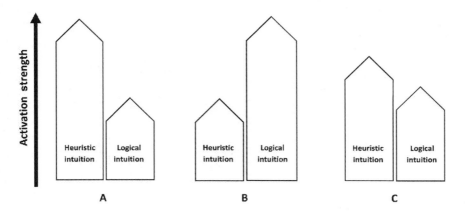

FIGURE 4.2 In the hybrid model different intuitions can differ in activation strength. The modal case (A) is the one in which the heuristic intuition will dominate. The more dominant the logical intuition becomes, the more likely that the reasoner will give an intuitive correct response (B). The smaller the relative strength difference between the competing intuitions, the more likely that deliberation will lead to correction (C).

is important to stress that although these "fast" and "slow" logical operations might result in the same output, they are assumed to originate from two different types of processes (System 1 and System 2, respectively) and will have different characteristics. In our studies with the bat-and-ball problem we also tried to pinpoint these different characteristics experimentally (Bago & De Neys, 2017b). For example, we simply asked participants to explain and justify why their answer was correct – both after the initial and final response. We observed that at the final response stage the vast majority of reasoners who gave the correct response managed to justify why their answer was correct (e.g., they typically referred to variants of the mathematical equation "$[x + (x + 100) = 110]$ so $[x = (110-100)/2]$"). However, these same participants did not manage to come up with such a justification after the initial response stage (i.e., they typically refer to an undefined "gut feeling" here). Hence, although they systematically gave the correct response based on mere intuitive processing, they could not explain why it was correct. It seems that deliberative System 2 thinking is indispensable in this respect (see further).

The point I want to clarify is that in talking about "fast" or "intuitive" logic, I do not entail that people are going through the exact same complex calculations as they would during System 2 processing. Bago and De Neys (2017a) have tried to illustrate this by drawing an analogy with the recall and recognition distinction in memory research (e.g., Haist, Shimamura, & Squire, 1992). Imagine you are presented with a list of ten names you need to memorize. Ten minutes later you might explicitly recall and jot down that "Tom", "Mary", "Chris", and "Peter" were on the list. But in addition your recognition memory might allow you to decide whether or not a certain item was on the list when it is presented to you (e.g., you might manage to say "yes" when asked whether "Tim" was among the presented names or not). Sometimes you might not be able to recall a name, but you could still recognize whether you saw it on the list or not. Recall and recognition can both allow us to retrieve a memory trace, but they differ in the processes involved in memory retrieval (among other things). This recall/recognition dichotomy is akin to what I am alluding to here. The idea is that the type of fast logical responding can be conceived of as a more superficial, recognition memory-like process that activates a stored logical principle and allows us to recognize that a competing heuristic intuition is questionable, without us being able to explicitly label or justify the principle (Bago & De Neys, 2017a). Hence, the key point is that the logical intuition theorizing does not entail that fast System 1 logical responses are similar – let alone superior – to System 2 logical responses.

Emerging themes, outstanding issues, and future directions

I hope to have illustrated in this chapter that there are good empirical reasons to revise key assumptions of the traditional dual process model and move to a hybrid view. However, it is also important to highlight that the development of this new hybrid model is a work in progress. I do not consider the theoretical model that I suggested as an endpoint. More work is needed to fine-tune the model, and this will lead to further revisions and developments. In this final section I will point to some key emerging issues that will require more attention in the coming years.

Individual differences

When I have argued that biased reasoners show conflict detection, I am talking about the average or modal biased reasoner (De Neys & Bonnefon, 2013). That is, the empirical conflict detection studies are always run at the group level. The analyses focus on the group of biased reasoners as a whole and test whether this group shows a significant conflict detection effect. As I outlined, we typically observe that this is the case. This suggests that the "average" biased reasoner does not have a conflict or bias blind spot. However, this does not imply that every single individual in the group shows this effect. This point has been rightly stressed by a number of colleagues and commentators (Mata et al., 2014; Mata, Ferreira, Voss, & Kollei, 2017; Mevel et al., 2015; Pennycook et al., 2015; Stupple et al., 2011).

In ongoing work I am actively focusing on this issue in collaboration with Darren Frey. One methodological problem is that conflict detection measures (e.g., confidence ratings, response latencies, etc.) are quite noisy. One of the reasons why psychologists have generally preferred to run studies at the group level is that by averaging over a large number of participants, we can reduce the intrinsic measurement noise. When we analyze the data of one single subject, the noise can easily lead to misclassifications. In our ongoing work we tackle this problem by co-registering different conflict detection measures. If an individual consistently shows detection effects across different measures (e.g., shows both more doubt *and* longer latencies on conflict problems), we are more certain that the effect does not result from chance or a measurement error. Our initial results show that the majority of biased reasoners indeed consistently show conflict detection effects across multiple measures (Frey, Johnson, & De Neys, 2017). However, we also find a smaller subgroup of reasoners (up to 15% of biased reasoners) who consistently fail to show any detection effects. Hence, there are definitely exceptions to the rule that biased reasoners show error or conflict sensitivity: some individuals do show a conflict detection blind spot. One of our future goals is to characterize and predict who these non-detecting individuals are (e.g., in terms of cognitive capacity and/or personality traits). In the same vein, we would obviously also like to characterize and predict which reasoners will show a dominant logical intuition and manage to solve problems correctly without deliberation. I envisage that this individual differences work will become ever more important in coming years.

Nature of the logical intuition signal

In my opinion there are good empirical reasons for the postulation of logical intuitions. People show sensitivity to violations of logical principles, and some reasoners even manage to give intuitive correct responses. However, more work is needed to pinpoint the exact nature of these logical intuitions. It is clear that one can conceive of logical intuitions at different levels of specificity (e.g., Travers, Rolison, & Feeney, 2016). If we take the bat-and-ball problem, for example, I believe we can distinguish at least three levels (e.g., high, moderate, or low specificity). A high level of specificity would imply that people intuitively figure out and know that the correct response is "5 cents". A moderate level of specificity might entail that people detect that the heuristic "10 cents" response is questionable because they realize it is too high. That is, people intuitively realize that "10 + (100 + 10) > 110", for example, but without actually knowing that the correct response is "5 cents". A low level of specificity might entail that people doubt the heuristic "10 cents" response that is cued by System 1 because they detect that they did not properly process the preambles. That is, people intuitively realize they neglected the "more than" statement (e.g., people detect that "100 ≠ (100 + 10)"), but without knowing that the correct response is "5 cents" or even whether the "10 cents" are too high or too low.

At present the available data do not really allow us to clearly differentiate between these different levels. This is crucial because it is evident that the different specificity levels might be based on quite different underlying computations. Furthermore, there might also be individual differences here. Although all (or most) reasoners might have a logical intuition, these intuitions might differ in specificity for different individuals. For example, it might be that intuitive correct responders in our two-response paradigm (e.g., the "11" group) have a highly specify intuition, whereas incorrect responders (e.g., the "00" group) have only a low or moderately specific intuition. Obviously, such fine-grained characterization will be an important challenge for future work.

Nature of System 2: why do we need System 2?

In the traditional serial DI and parallel dual process models the role of System 2 is well defined: it will help to correct the initial heuristic System 1 response. In the hybrid model, such correction is not necessarily needed. But if we do not need System 2 deliberation to correct System 1, what do we need it for? Why do we need System 2 if we can generate the correct response intuitively?

I believe that the key role of System 2 lies in a justification and validation process. Although reasoners might have an intuitive hunch about the correct response, they do not seem to be able to explicitly justify it in the absence of deliberate thinking. Such justification or validation is important for at least two reasons. First, it can function as a safeguard. It allows you to reduce possible erroneous conclusions. People might not have correct intuitions about each and every problem they will be faced with in daily life. Hence, deliberatively double-checking your intuitive hunches in those cases where you have the time to do so can help minimize errors. Second, deliberation will allow you to come up with a valid justification. This allows you to produce a good explanation or argument for why your response is correct. Such arguments are critical for communicative purposes (e.g., Mercier & Sperber, 2011). Imagine that we're having a discussion and I try to convince you that my answer to a problem is the correct one. If I just tell you that X is correct "because I felt it", I will not be very successful in convincing you. If I come up with a good explanation, however, you will be much more likely to change your mind (Trouche, Sander, & Mercier, 2014). Such argumentative persuasion has been argued to be the evolutionary driving force behind the development of the human capacity to reason (Mercier & Sperber, 2011). It is here, in the production of good, communicable arguments, that I see a key role for System 2.

In a sense one could claim that in my work I have been arguing that we need to upgrade the role of System 1. Indeed, I strongly believe that System 1 is capable of more than we have traditionally assumed in the field. However, this should not be conceived of as an argument against the role or importance of System 2. Upgrading the role of System 1 does not imply we have to downplay the role of System 2. Although we shouldn't underestimate the capacity of System 1, there are also things it cannot do and for which System 2 will be indispensable. The point here is not whether one system is "better" than the other. More generally, I believe that the reason the *two* systems evolved – and we still have them – is precisely because they are both valuable and needed.

Generalization

In the introduction I stated that it is hard to overestimate the impact of the serial DI dual process view. One illustration is that the ideas of prominent advocates such as Evans and Kahneman have inspired the construction of dual process models in other fields as well. Two examples are the dual process model of cooperation in economic interactions (Rand, Greene, & Nowak, 2012) and the dual process model of moral cognition (Greene, 2014). In a nutshell, the dual process model of human cooperation focuses on cases in which self-interest can conflict with group interest (e.g., get more money yourself or share more with others). The dual process model of moral cognition focuses on situations in which utilitarian and deontological considerations can lead to conflicting moral decisions (e.g., is it acceptable to torture a terrorist if it can save the lives of innocent civilians?). These models have been highly influential in their respective fields and generated an impressive amount of empirical work. Although I find these applications fascinating and I am impressed by the breadth of the studies, I also feel that the critical question about the precise interaction between the two postulated systems has been largely neglected. The research reviewed here indicates that there are good reasons to question core assumptions of the traditional (serial *and* parallel) dual process models during logical and probabilistic reasoning. I believe it is paramount to examine the implications of these findings for the applications of the dual process framework in other fields too (e.g., see Bialek & De Neys, 2016, 2017; Gürçay & Baron, 2017, for some initial explorations in the moral cognition case). Is there better support for the serial (parallel) assumptions in the case of moral reasoning and cooperation decisions, or should we favor a hybrid processing architecture in these cases too?

The general point I want to make is that I believe we need a much closer interaction between the type of "generic" dual process theorizing in the reasoning and decision-making field that is discussed in this chapter (and book) and applications of the dual process model in other fields. On one hand, other fields can use the alternative models (and methods) as a starting point. The exploration of the interaction issue does not need to start from scratch, but can build on existing models and methodological paradigms. On the other hand, it allows "generic" dual process theorists to test the generality of their models. That is, the end goal of our research should not be to build a model of logical or probabilistic reasoning per se, but a model of human thinking in all its different facets. I realize this might be an (overly) ambitious or even naive goal, but I nevertheless feel it is important to keep this general cross-field applicability of our models in mind. Here, too, I see an important challenge for future work.

Conclusion

In this chapter I have tried to review my empirical work and sketch the rationale behind the hybrid dual process model that I favor. Although the traditional dual process models have been instrumental for the field, I believe the emerging evidence is pointing to a clear need to revise core assumptions. For me personally, these revisions feel like a quite natural development and illustration of the way science proceeds. Just like dual process theorists have not been afraid to revise their initial theorizing in light of new evidence in the past (e.g., Evans, 2006), we're at the point where we need to reconsider the way we conceive of the interplay between System 1 and System 2. Obviously, not all scholars will agree with the specific model and ideas I proposed here, but I believe that we should at least acknowledge that it is time to move to a new conceptualization.

Note

1 I use "logical" loosely in this chapter as a general header and handy shortcut to refer to reasoning in line with classic norms in standard logic, probability theory, or mathematics.

References

Aczel, B., Szollosi, A., & Bago, B. (2016). Lax monitoring versus logical intuition: The determinants of confidence in conjunction fallacy. *Thinking & Reasoning, 22*, 99–117.

Bago, B., & De Neys, W. (2017a). Fast logic? Examining the time course assumption of dual process theory. *Cognition, 158*, 90–109.

Bago, B., & De Neys, W. (2017b). The smart system 1: Evidence for the intuitive nature of correct responding in the Bat-and-Ball problem. Manuscript submitted for publication.

Bialek, M., & De Neys, W. (2016). Conflict detection during moral decision making: Evidence for deontic reasoners' utilitarian sensitivity. *Journal of Cognitive Psychology, 28*, 631–639.

Bialek, M., & De Neys, W. (2017). Dual processes and moral conflict: Evidence for deontological reasoners' intuitive utilitarian sensitivity. *Judgment and Decision Making, 12,* 148–167.
Bonner, C., & Newell, B. R. (2010). In conflict with ourselves? An investigation of heuristic and analytic processes in decision making. *Memory & Cognition, 38,* 186–196.
Botvinick, M. M. (2007). Conflict monitoring and decision making: Reconciling two perspectives on anterior cingulate function. *Cognitive, Affective, & Behavioral Neuroscience, 7,* 356–366.
De Neys, W. (2006). Automatic – heuristic and executive – analytic processing during reasoning: Chronometric and dual-task considerations. *The Quarterly Journal of Experimental Psychology, 59,* 1070–1100.
De Neys, W. (2012). Bias and conflict: A case for logical intuitions. *Perspectives on Psychological Science, 7,* 28–38.
De Neys, W. (2014). Conflict detection, dual processes, and logical intuitions: Some clarifications. *Thinking & Reasoning, 20,* 169–187.
De Neys, W. (2015). Heuristic bias and conflict detection during thinking. In B. Ross (Ed.), *The psychology of learning and motivation* (pp. 1–32). Burlington: Academic Press.
De Neys, W., & Bonnefon, J. F. (2013). The whys and whens of individual differences in thinking biases. *Trends in Cognitive Sciences, 17,* 172–178.
De Neys, W., Cromheeke, S., & Osman, M. (2011). Biased but in doubt: Conflict and decision confidence. *PloS One, 6,* e15954.
De Neys, W., & Glumicic, T. (2008). Conflict monitoring in dual process theories of thinking. *Cognition, 106,* 1248–1299.
De Neys, W., Rossi, S., & Houdé, O. (2013). Bats, balls, and substitution sensitivity: Cognitive misers are no happy fools. *Psychonomic Bulletin & Review, 20,* 269–273.
De Neys, W., Vartanian, O., & Goel, V. (2008). Smarter than we think: When our brains detect that we are biased. *Psychological Science, 19,* 483–489.
Epstein, S. (1994). Integration of the cognitive and the psychodynamic unconscious. *American Psychologist, 49,* 709–724.
Evans, J. St. B. (2006). The heuristic-analytic theory of reasoning: Extension and evaluation. *Psychonomic Bulletin & Review, 13,* 378–395.
Evans, J. St. B. (2008). Dual-processing accounts of reasoning, judgment, and social cognition. *Annual Review of Psychology, 59,* 255–278.
Evans, J. St. B. (2012). Spot the difference: Distinguishing between two kinds of processing. *Mind & Society, 11,* 121–131.
Evans, J. St. B. (2016). Reasoning, biases and dual processes: The lasting impact of Wason (1960). *The Quarterly Journal of Experimental Psychology, 69,* 1–17.
Evans, J. St. B., & Stanovich, K. E. (2013). Dual process theories of higher cognition advancing the debate. *Perspectives on Psychological Science, 8,* 223–241.
Franssens, S., & De Neys, W. (2009). The effortless nature of conflict detection during thinking. *Thinking & Reasoning, 15,* 105–128.
Frederick, S. (2005). Cognitive reflection and decision making. *The Journal of Economic Perspectives, 19,* 25–42.
Frey, D., Johnson, E., & De Neys, W. (2017). Individual differences in conflict detection during reasoning. *Quarterly Journal of Experimental Psychology.* Advance online preprint.
Gangemi, A., Bourgeois-Gironde, S., & Mancini, F. (2015). Feelings of error in reasoning – in search of a phenomenon. *Thinking & Reasoning, 21,* 383–396.
Greene, J. D. (2014). *Moral tribes: Emotion, reason and the gap between us and them.* Bloomsbury: Atlantic Books.

Gürçay, B., & Baron, J. (2017). Challenges for the sequential two-system model of moral judgement. *Thinking & Reasoning, 23*, 49–80.

Haist, F., Shimamura, A. P., & Squire, L. R. (1992). On the relationship between recall and recognition memory. *Journal of Experimental Psychology: Learning, Memory, and Cognition, 18*, 691–702.

Hoffrage, U., & Marewski, J. N. (2015). Unveiling the lady in black: Modeling and aiding intuition. *Journal of Applied Research in Memory and Cognition, 4*, 145–163.

Johnson, E. D., Tubau, E., & De Neys, W. (2016). The doubting system 1: Evidence for automatic substitution sensitivity. *Acta Psychologica, 164*, 56–64.

Kahneman, D. (2011). *Thinking, fast and slow*. New York, NY: Farrar, Straus and Giroux.

Mata, A., Ferreira, M. B., Voss, A., & Kollei, T. (2017). Seeing the conflict: An attentional account of reasoning errors. *Psychonomic Bulletin & Review*. Advance online preprint.

Mata, A., Schubert, A.-L., & Ferreira, M. B. (2014). The role of language comprehension in reasoning: How "good-enough" representations induce biases. *Cognition, 133*, 457–463.

Mega, L. F., & Volz, K. G. (2014). Thinking about thinking: Implications of the introspective error for default-interventionist type models of dual processes. *Frontiers in Psychology, 5*, 864.

Mevel, K., Poirel, N., Rossi, S., Cassotti, M., Simon, G., Houdé, O., & De Neys, W. (2015). Bias detection: Response confidence evidence for conflict sensitivity in the ratio bias task. *Journal of Cognitive Psychology, 27*, 227–237.

Mercier, H., & Sperber, D. (2011). Why do humans reason? Arguments for an argumentative theory. *Behavioral and Brain Sciences, 34*, 57–74.

Morsanyi, K., & Handley, S. (2012). Does thinking make you biased? The case of the engineers and lawyer problem. *Proceedings of the Annual Meeting of the Cognitive Science Society, 34*, 2049–2054.

Newman, I., Gibb, M., & Thompson, V. A. (2017). Rule-based reasoning is fast and belief based reasoning can be slow: Challenging current explanations of belief-bias and base-rate neglect. *Journal of Experimental Psychology: Learning, Memory, & Cognition, 43*,1154–1170.

Pennycook, G., Fugelsang, J. A., & Koehler, D. J. (2012). Are we good at detecting conflict during reasoning? *Cognition, 124*, 101–106.

Pennycook, G., Fugelsang, J. A., & Koehler, D. J. (2015). What makes us think? A three-stage dual-process model of analytic engagement. *Cognitive Psychology, 80*, 34–72.

Pennycook, G., Trippas, D., Handley, S. J., & Thompson, V. A. (2014). Base rates: Both neglected and intuitive. *Journal of Experimental Psychology: Learning, Memory, and Cognition, 40*, 544–554.

Rand, D. G., Greene, J. D., & Nowak, M. A. (2012). Spontaneous giving and calculated greed. *Nature, 489*, 427–430.

Reyna, V. F. (2004). How people make decisions that involve risk: A dual-processes approach. *Current Directions in Psychological Science, 13*, 60–66.

Simon, G., Lubin, A., Houdé, O., & De Neys, W. (2015). Anterior cingulate cortex and intuitive bias detection during number conservation. *Cognitive Neuroscience, 6*, 158–168.

Singmann, H., Klauer, K. C., & Kellen, D. (2014). Intuitive logic revisited: New data and a Bayesian mixed model meta-analysis. *PloS One, 9*, e94223.

Sloman, S. A. (1996). The empirical case for two systems of reasoning. *Psychological Bulletin, 119*, 3–22.

Stanovich, K. E. (1999). *Who is rational? Studies of individual differences in reasoning*. Hove, UK: Psychology Press.

Stanovich, K. E. (2010). *Rationality and the reflective mind*. New York: Oxford University Press.

Stupple, E. J. N., Ball, L. J., Evans, J. St. B., & Kamal-Smith, E. (2011). When logic and belief collide: Individual differences in reasoning times support a selective processing model. *Journal of Cognitive Psychology, 23*, 931–941.

Thompson, V., & Johnson, S. C. (2014). Conflict, metacognition, and analytic thinking. *Thinking & Reasoning, 20*, 215–244.

Thompson, V., Prowse Turner, J. A., & Pennycook, G. (2011). Intuition, reason, and metacognition. *Cognitive Psychology, 63*, 107–140.

Travers, E., Rolison, J. J., & Feeney, A. (2016). The time course of conflict on the cognitive reflection test. *Cognition, 150*, 109–118.

Trouche, E., Sander, E., & Mercier, H. (2014). Arguments, more than confidence, explain the good performance of reasoning groups. *Journal of Experimental Psychology: General, 143*, 1958–1971.

Villejoubert, G. (2009). Are representativeness judgments automatic and rapid? The effect of time pressure on the conjunction fallacy. *Proceedings of the Annual Meeting of the Cognitive Science Society, 30*, 2980–2985.

Wansink, B., & Chandon, P. (2006). Can "low-fat" nutrition labels lead to obesity? *Journal of Marketing Research, 43*, 605–617.

Wason, P. C., & Evans, J. St. B. T. (1975). Dual processes in reasoning? *Cognition, 3*, 141–154.

5
COMPARING DUAL PROCESS THEORIES

Evidence from event-related potentials

Adrian P. Banks

Overview

Research on the electrophysiology of reasoning is comparatively rare, but it has the potential to offer considerable insights into the time course of cognitive processes and contribute to a wide range of theoretical questions such as the role of dual processes in reasoning. Although a behavioural response to a reasoning problem can indicate a single time point at which a complex series of cognitive events ends, event-related potentials (ERPs) can be used to examine the timing of different events as they unfold during the reasoning process. That is, it is possible to measure cognitive events in the window between presentation of the problem and the behavioural response. Theories differ crucially about what occurs in this window, and ERPs offer the potential to observe this activity. A small number of studies have been conducted with the aim of identifying the electrophysiological correlates of reasoning on tasks that have been used more widely to examine dual process theory. In this chapter I will review the ERP research that has aimed to test dual process theories of reasoning, discuss the findings, and explore both the potential and the limitations of this technique. Finally, I will discuss how the theoretical implications of these findings support the idea that Type 1 processes are fast and automatic, occur in parallel, and when acquired over time, can reproduce any thinking process that can be automated, including both normatively correct logical responses and belief-based responses within a belief bias task.

Belief bias and dual process theories

So far, ERP studies of dual process theory have examined the widely studied belief bias paradigm. Belief bias is the tendency to judge conclusions to reasoning problems based on prior beliefs rather than logical validity (Evans, Barston, & Pollard, 1983;

Klauer, Musch, & Naumer, 2000). Although belief bias has been studied in a number of different reasoning tasks, the seminal experimental paradigm was developed by Evans et al. (1983). In this, participants are asked to evaluate the logical validity of a conclusion to a syllogism. The problems are constructed to independently manipulate both logical validity and belief of the conclusion. For example:

> No cigarettes are inexpensive
> Some addictive things are inexpensive
> Therefore, some addictive things are not cigarettes

This syllogism has a conclusion that is both valid and believable. Whereas:

> No addictive things are inexpensive
> Some cigarettes are inexpensive
> Therefore, some cigarettes are not addictive

This syllogism has a conclusion that is valid but unbelievable. Evans et al. found that participants were more likely to accept valid conclusions, as instructed, but were also more likely to accept believable conclusions, and interestingly there was a greater effect of belief on invalid than valid conclusions. These key findings have been replicated many times and have been an important line of evidence in developing and testing dual process theories (e.g. De Neys, 2006; Evans & Curtis-Holmes, 2005; Stupple, Ball, Evans, & Kamal-Smith, 2011).

Dual process theories propose two types of thinking, one referred to as heuristic, Type 1, or System 1 thinking and the other referred to as analytic, Type 2, or System 2 thinking. In this chapter I will mostly use the terms Type 1 and 2 thinking, but this largely refers to the same concept as System 1 and 2. De Neys (this volume) has characterised three types of dual process models, and explaining the phenomenon of belief bias has played a notable part in developing and contrasting these models. Many studies of belief bias have explained the effect using the default-interventionist model (Evans, 2006; Evans & Stanovich, 2013). This is a serial process in which a fast, heuristic, belief-based judgement is made initially, but analytic processes may override this response with the logical solution under certain circumstances. Parallel models, in contrast, propose that both of these types of thinking are engaged simultaneously from the beginning of the reasoning process (e.g. Sloman, 1996). This allows for a conflict to be detected if the two types of thinking lead to different responses, but raises other questions such as whether it is maladaptive to always engage both processes when in most cases the simpler process will provide the best response. Finally, hybrid models such as the logical intuition model (this volume; De Neys, 2012), the three-stage dual process model of analytic engagement (Pennycook, Fugelsang, & Koehler, 2015), or the parallel model of Trippas and Handley (this volume; Handley & Trippas, 2015) draw on elements of both serial and parallel models. They propose an initial response made using Type 1 processes followed by the subsequent engagement of analytic Type 2 processes under certain circumstances. However, they propose that the initial Type 1 processes can occur in parallel. Furthermore, amongst the parallel Type 1 processes are those that are logical and cue the normatively correct response. This contrasts with the assumption in other dual process models that Type 1 processes tend to cue heuristic responses that may not be normatively correct.

These three types of dual process models differ in fundamental ways in their description of how reasoning occurs. There are two areas in which ERP research is beginning to contribute to resolving the debate between these models. First, the temporal resolution of ERPs means that they can be used to assess if and when reasoning occurs serially or in parallel. Second, the fact that ERPs can be measured prior to a behavioural response means that they can be used to examine the initial fast reasoning processes to assess if these cue biased or normatively correct responses.

Event-related potentials and reasoning

An electroencephalogram, or EEG, is a recording of the electrical activity of the brain. Embedded within it is the electrical activity generated as a result of many different cognitive processes. In order to extract from this the response to a specific event, the same event is repeated across many trials, the same time window is extracted from each of these trials, and then the time windows are averaged together. This process means that random noise in the signal is averaged out across trials, leaving a clearer signal that is the ERP. The ERP is a series of positive and negative voltage deflections, or components, that are labelled P or N to indicate a positive- or negative-going component and numbered to indicate the relative position in the waveform (P1 is the first positive component, P2 is the second positive component, etc.). Each of these components relates to different cognitive processes, so finding differences in either the amplitude or latency of components provides information about differences in the cognition between experimental conditions. It provides a continuous measure of cognitive processing between the presentation of the task and the behavioural response, and this is done with high temporal resolution.

Initial work on reasoning has begun to identify the components associated with several standard tasks. The most common component that is influenced by reasoning complexity is the P3. This is a positive deflection that typically occurs 300 ms to 500 ms after an event and indicates updating of working memory (Polich, 2007). It is found in conditional reasoning (Bonnefond & Van der Henst, 2013; Bonnefond, Kaliuzhna, Van der Henst, & De Neys, 2014), relational reasoning (Bonnefond, Castelain, Cheylus, & Van der Henst, 2014), and syllogistic reasoning (Qiu, Li, Luo, Zhang & Tu, 2009). However, these experiments vary in their procedure and so the full interpretation of the P3 in reasoning has not yet been settled. The N2 has also been found in conditional reasoning (Bonnefond et al., 2014) and the Wason selection task (Cai, et al., 2011). The N2 is a negative deflection that is typically found 200 ms to 350 ms after the event and indicates the resolution of conflict (Folstein & Van Petten, 2008). Late positivity or positive slow waves have also been found in conditional reasoning (Bonnefond & Van der Henst, 2009) and syllogistic reasoning (Luo et al., 2013). Despite the name, this component is still found before the behavioural response to a reasoning task (e.g. 1000 ms to 2000 ms after the stimulus). The cognitive processes associated with this component are less well defined, but include sustained attention (Gevins, et al., 1996) or the retrieval of information from working memory (García-Larrea & Cézanne-Bert, 1998). Finally, a P2 component has been found, although rarely (Bonnefond & Van der Henst, 2009). The P2 component indicates the detection of expected features (e.g. Luck & Hillyard, 1994) and in language comprehension tasks is greater for expected than unexpected words (Federmeier, Mai, & Kutas, 2005).

Event-related potentials and dual process theories of reasoning

The first ERP study that relates to dual process theory investigated the effect of belief bias on syllogistic reasoning (Luo, Yuan, Qiu, Zhang, Zhong, & Huai, 2008). Syllogisms were constructed with beliefs that were either consistent with or conflicted with the logically correct answer, referred to by the authors as facilitatory and inhibitory beliefs. There was also a baseline condition in which there was no connection between the two premises. Premises were presented serially – the major premise was presented, followed by the minor premise, followed by the conclusion. Participants responded after the presentation of the conclusion. The ERPs were time locked to the onset of the minor premise. No difference in accuracy was found between the facilitating and inhibiting beliefs, but response times were shorter for facilitating beliefs. The main ERP finding was an increased positivity between 300 ms and 500 ms and 1000 ms and 1600 ms for both facilitatory and inhibitory beliefs compared to baseline and an increased positivity between 300 ms and 600 ms for inhibitory compared to facilitatory beliefs. The authors suggest that this positive component indicates that more attentional resources were required to activate and apply rules of inference.

However, this study has some limitations that restrict the interpretation of these findings. First, the task differed from the typical paradigm used for studying belief bias. Whereas a typical task requires the evaluation of a conclusion that may or may not be believable, this study used a production task in which premise believability is manipulated to influence reasoning. As the ERPs were time locked to the minor premise rather than the conclusion, it is the role of beliefs in facilitating the integration of minor premise with major premise that is the focus of this study rather than the conflict of belief and logic in the evaluation of a conclusion. Also, by time locking to the onset of the minor premise, the recording conflates the reading process with the reasoning process. Second, all of the problems were invalid, and the same syllogistic format was used in all of the 160 reasoning trials (all A are B; all C are B; therefore, the relation between A and C is indefinite). Given the high level of accuracy (96% and 87% for facilitatory and inhibitory conditions), it is possible that the response became well practiced and responses made through recognition rather than reasoning. Furthermore, as no valid syllogisms were used, it is not possible to test the characteristic interaction of logic and belief that is assessed in typical belief bias studies.

Luo, Yang, Du, and Zhang (2011) applied the same approach to studying belief bias in conditional reasoning. Modus tollens and denial of the antecedent arguments were presented with facilitatory or inhibitory beliefs. ERPs were time locked to the onset of the minor premise, and greater negativity was observed in the 400ms to 600ms and 800ms to 1600ms windows for inhibitory compared to facilitatory modus tollens, but no differences were found for denial of the antecedent arguments. The authors suggest that the earlier negativity could be a delayed N2, which is a component associated with detecting conflict and could indicate that a conflict between logic and belief responses has been detected (Folstein & Van Petten, 2008). But the timing of the negativity is much later than is typically found for an N2, which questions this interpretation. No component is proposed to account for the later negativity. The differences between modus tollens and denial of the antecedent arguments was explained in terms of different strategies that may have been adopted based on the training received, but there is no direct evidence that this is what occurred.

As in Luo, Yuan, Qiu, Zhang, Zhong, and Huai (2008), time locking to the minor premise moves the focus of this study to integration of the premises. The same logical argument is again repeated many times – each one is presented sixty times – raising the possibility that the responses are learnt rather than reasoned. Neither Luo et al. (2008) nor Luo et al. (2011) report ratings of the strength of belief in the problems, and weak beliefs undermine the belief bias phenomena (Banks, 2013). The items in the paper do not seem compelling, for example, an inhibitory belief item is 'If a person is rich, then the person will be happy. Somebody is not happy. The person is not rich.' and it may be that there was not a sufficiently strong belief to elicit the effect, although accuracy was significantly greater with facilitatory problems. The main concern though is that the pattern of ERPs cannot be readily explained in terms of the components that are evoked and the theoretical mechanisms that they might indicate.

Luo et al. (2013) shift the focus to the evaluation of conclusions in syllogisms in which the logically validity of the conclusion either conflicted or did not with the believability of the conclusion. This study is more comparable with the majority of behavioural studies of belief bias and therefore provides more direct evidence to differentiate between competing theoretical accounts of belief bias and dual process theories. Luo et al. presented the major and minor premises together, followed by the conclusion, at which point a response was made. The ERPs were time locked to the response. This provides an indication of the reasoning process when the response is decided upon rather than the reasoning process as the premises are integrated and the conclusion is presented. Conflict problems were found to evoke more positivity −400ms to −200ms prior to the response than no conflict problems. The authors suggest that this late positive component (so called because it is one of the later ERP components, but it still precedes the behavioural response) reflects cognitive control as the heuristic response is inhibited and the analytic response made. If so, this finding provides initial support for dual process theories of belief bias, as it demonstrates that a conflict between belief and logic must be resolved prior to responding.

Although this study enables a stronger conclusion to be made about responses to belief bias problems than the previous studies, there are still some methodological limitations. Only one valid and one invalid syllogism were used in all the conditions, each repeated eighty times and potentially leading to a learnt rather than a reasoned response. There was also no assessment of the strength of belief of the conclusions, with some conclusions not seeming to evoke a compelling belief, for example, 'Therefore, the relation between small dogs and black dogs is uncertain'. These two factors may partly account for the comparatively small difference in accuracy between conflict and no conflict problems: 53% and 58%, respectively.

Overall, these studies demonstrate the potential to record ERPs during reasoning and evoke differences between conflict and no-conflict problems (or inhibition and facilitation). But no clear pattern emerges across the studies. With syllogisms, both Luo et al. (2008) and Luo et al. (2013) find that inhibition or conflict is associated with early positivity – although one is time locked to the minor premise and the other to the response – whereas with conditionals Luo et al. (2011) find that inhibition is associated with early negativity, but only for modus tollens inferences. It is hard to draw a persuasive theoretical interpretation from these contrasting findings. This could be for a number of methodological reasons that were already highlighted earlier. In our studies we sought to overcome these methodological issues and provide a clearer test of the electrophysiology of reasoning.

Methodologically, we (Banks & Hope, 2014) sought to develop a task that enabled ERPs to be assessed whilst ensuring as far as possible comparability with standard tasks in this domain in order that the findings could be used to test current theories of dual process theory. Theoretically, our aim was to exploit the precise temporal resolution of ERPs to compare serial and parallel dual process theories. To do this, we measured the ERPs evoked by the conclusion rather than the premises or time locked to the response as has been the case in previous research. The problems were designed so that it was not possible to evaluate the conclusion until the final word was presented. ERPs were time locked to the onset of this word. We manipulated both logic and belief in a full factorial design and used a wider range of different problem types than in previous studies. Relational reasoning problems were used, as there are a wide range of possible problems, they are relatively pure strategically, and they are not prone to variations in premise interpretations (Roberts, 2000). A nonsense term was used to ensure that no premise conflicted with prior knowledge, as this can be difficult to integrate into a coherent representation (Klauer et al., 2000). Here's an example of a typical problem:

Premise 1	Giraffes are bigger than elephants
Premise 2	Zoots are bigger than elephants

Premise 3	Mice are bigger than zoots
Initial conclusion	Mice are bigger than
Final conclusion word	Elephants

The main prediction of this experiment contrasts serial and parallel dual process models. If the initial evaluation of the conclusion is based only on belief or only on logic, as predicted by serial models, the ERP elicited by the conclusion will only be influenced by one factor (e.g. the believability but not the logical validity of the conclusion). If the initial evaluation of the conclusion is based on both belief and logic, as predicted by parallel models, the ERP elicited by the conclusion will be influenced by the interaction of both factors (e.g. problems where logic and belief conflict will differ from problems where there is no conflict). The main finding of this study was a larger P3 component for both conditions in which logic and belief conflict (logically valid but unbelievable and logically invalid but believable conclusions) than for both conditions in which logic and belief do not conflict (logically valid and believable and logically invalid and unbelievable conclusions). This supports the parallel dual process models, as it indicates that both belief and logic are processed at the same time, and very rapidly after the presentation of the conclusion – within the 300ms to 500ms time window. Furthermore, there was no difference in the latency of the peak of the P3 component between the four conditions. This also indicates that the initial evaluation of the conclusion is influenced by both belief and logic in parallel rather than serially.

Our interpretation of these findings is that participants are constructing a representation, a mental model, of the relations between the items in the problem as they read the premises. This is a dynamic process in which the mental model is updated to incorporate new information as each word of the problem is read. Participants typically seek to construct a single, coherent, isomeric representation of relational reasoning problems in which new items and relations are incorporated and represented efficiently (Schaeken, Van der Henst, & Schroyens, 2007). As the conclusion is read, it, too, is represented in some form. In the no-conflict condition this conclusion is coherent with the current representation, but in the conflict condition the conclusion is inconsistent and requires the representation of the problem in working memory to be updated. As the P3 is a component that is associated with updating of working memory, the P3 amplitude is greater in the conflict condition. Although further research is required to explore exactly how dual processes influence working memory updating during reasoning, the empirical findings as they stand provide support for models in which the initial evaluation of the conclusion is influenced by both belief and logic rapidly and in parallel rather than serially.

Our second study sought to examine the time course of belief and logic-based processes further (Banks & Dunne, in prep.). A typical belief bias task is based on a paradigm in which the logical task is rather difficult, often a syllogism with low levels of accuracy, and a belief that is compelling. From this paradigm it is concluded that the belief judgement is fast and occurs by default and the logic judgement is slow and may not occur at all. There is a wide range of evidence supporting this serial or default-interventionist model (Evans & Stanovich, 2013). More recently, evidence has been presented for a parallel processes interpretation of this phenomenon. These theories suggest that both belief- and logic-based processing occur in parallel but that they vary in time course according to factors such as the complexity of the judgement. That is, different, less complex, logical problems might be faster to evaluate than the belief judgement. This research implies the apparently default nature of belief judgements and that slower intervention of logical analysis is a consequence of the type of problems that have been studied historically rather than an inherent property of logic and belief.

Handley, Newstead, and Trippas (2011) provided the first evidence for this. They introduced a manipulation in which participants evaluated the believability of logical problems as well as the more common logical validity of belief-based problems. They found that logic influenced the evaluations of belief more than belief influenced the evaluation of logic. This is not consistent with the application of a belief heuristic by default. In this case logic-based processing appears to have been applied by default, in effect a 'logic bias'. Second, they studied different logical problems to those typically employed in belief bias research. They chose problems with simpler logical forms than is typical: conditionals and disjunctions. They suggest that these simpler forms may lead to inferences that are made automatically because of the familiarity to participants. As a result, the inferences are made without intentional control and conflict with the belief-based judgement. Trippas, Thompson, and Handley (2016) provide further evidence for parallel logic and belief-based processes that vary in their time course. They manipulated the complexity of the logical problems and were able to show that when the processing of complex logical problems was greater than the processing of belief judgements, belief interfered with logic. But with simpler logical problems the processing was less than the processing of belief judgements, and then logic interfered with belief. It is the relative complexity of the logic and belief judgement task that determines the interaction, rather than an inherent property of logic or belief.

These behavioural studies introduce new ways of examining the dual process theories by manipulating instructions and the logical complexity. Our second study again exploited the temporal resolution of ERPs to provide direct evidence for the time course of logic and belief-based processing. We used the instructional manipulation of Handley et al. (2011) in which participants judged either the believability or the logical validity of the problems in order to examine belief as well as logical processing. We used a simpler logical form in order to examine familiar inferences that may occur more automatically than the complex task used in our previous study. However, we did introduce some methodological changes in order to assess ERPs adequately. As before, we studied relational reasoning (three term series) and time locked to the onset of the final word of the conclusion. It was not possible to evaluate the conclusion until this word was presented. A typical problem is:

>   Premise 1   Sheep are bigger than toads
>   Premise 2   Toads are bigger than hippos
>   Conclusion   Sheep are bigger than hippos

We also adapted the belief judgement task in order to more closely parallel the logical task. In each case there were either two believable statements and one unbelievable statement or one believable statement and two unbelievable statements. The belief judgement task was to assess if the statements were mostly believable or mostly unbelievable. This could only be resolved when the final statement was read. Therefore, much like the logical task, each statement had to be read in turn, a representation of them held in working memory, and a belief-based evaluation of all three made after they have been presented. This is similar to a process of logical reasoning in which the premises are read and held in working memory and a logical evaluation is made when the third statement, the conclusion, is presented.

As in our earlier study, we aimed to compare serial and parallel dual process models by examining the timing of the influence of logic and belief on conclusion evaluation. Serial models predict an initial influence on ERPs of just one factor (e.g. belief) whereas parallel models predict that both factors influence the initial evaluation of the conclusion, causing a difference between no conflict problems (where the two factors lead to the same evaluation) and conflict problems (where they lead to different evaluations).

Under logic instructions we found that the judgements accurately reflected the logical validity of the problems but were not influenced by their believability. However, under belief instructions we found that the judgements accurately reflected the believability of the problems and that responses were influenced by their logical validity. That is, logic influenced belief-based judgements, but that belief did not influence logic-based judgements. This replicates the behavioural findings of Handley et al.'s task instructions using a different task.

The key question though is the influence that the task instructions have on the ERPs. The main finding was an interaction between task instructions and conflict such that the difference in P2 amplitude between no-conflict and conflict conditions was greater under belief task instructions than logic task instructions. This difference was found in the 125ms to 200ms time window – an earlier stage of the process than our first experiment that used a more complex reasoning task. P2 is a component that in sentence comprehension tasks is larger for expected words than unexpected words (Federmeier et al., 2005). Our interpretation of these findings is that the expectation of the final concluding word can be influenced by both belief and logic. Where expectations from each of these factors are the same (i.e. in no-conflict problems), the final word is more expected than in conflict problems where different expectations are generated by belief and logic. Therefore under belief instructions, both belief and logic are influencing the conclusion evaluation in parallel because in this condition the P2 was greater for no-conflict than conflict problems. However, interestingly, no difference between no-conflict and conflict problems was found under logic instructions. In this condition the believability of the conclusion did not influence the judgements of logical validity.

These findings provide further support for parallel models, as logic and belief can influence conclusion evaluation at the same time on presentation of the conclusion. Also, as there was an influence of logic under belief instructions, they provide further evidence that with simpler logic problems, automatic logical inferences are made that can influence judgements by default and without intentional control.

Parallel processing and automatic inferences: evidence from ERPs

The ERP studies described earlier provide a new line of evidence for investigating dual process theory. Empirically, there are several new findings. The main finding that was present in some form in all of the studies was that conflict (or inhibitory belief) problems differed from no-conflict (or facilitatory belief) problems. Although conflict detection has repeatedly been found in behavioural studies, these ERP data add to the findings by providing more precise information about when the cognitive processing of conflict and no-conflict problems begins to differ. This occurred early in the evaluation (typically within the first 1000 ms), and Banks and Hope (2014) directly assessed the latencies and showed no difference between belief and logic conditions. The findings show that there is not an initial difference between conditions based on belief followed by a later conflict with logic. Instead, the initial difference contrasts conflict with no-conflict problems that both logical and belief-based evaluations have been made in parallel.

The second set of empirical findings relates to the ERP components elicited by reasoning, and this pattern of findings is less clear. The two studies that time-lock to the minor premise (Luo et al., 2008; Luo et al., 2011) find opposite effects – increased positivity and increased negativity, respectively, for conflict problems. There are also some concerns about the methods used in these studies, and resolving these will lead to clearer findings about the integration of the minor premise in reasoning. Examining conclusion processing, Luo et al. (2013) and Banks and Hope (2014) both used a typical belief bias task and found increased positivity in conflict problems – late positivity for Luo et al. and a P3 for Banks and Hope. These components indicate that the application of attentional resources is elicited by the conflict, either exerting cognitive control in inhibiting a response or updating a representation required by the task. These studies used complex logical problems, and increased attentional resources are required to resolve the conflicting responses from difficult logic and simple belief. In contrast, the simpler logical problems tested by Banks and Dunne (in prep.) evoked differences in an earlier component, the P2, which indicates an expectation for a final concluding word. There was no difference in the P3. This indicates that differences in the cognitive processing of conflict and no-conflict problems emerge prior to the updating of working memory representations. This suggests more automatic, less working memory–dependent processes for the simpler three-term series problem. Interestingly, this effect was greater under belief instructions than logic instructions, indicating that the automatic expectations generated by the logical structure of the problem had a greater effect on belief judgements than automatic beliefs had on logical judgements. Under belief instructions the simple three-term series apparently generated an automatic logical inference that conflicted with the belief judgements, despite no instructions to reason logically. That is, the normatively correct logical response was generated by an automatic process.

These conclusions are still tentative as the small number of studies and range of methodological approaches used mean that there is not yet a solid body of replicated empirical evidence that firmly establishes the ERP components that are found when reasoning. Nonetheless, it is possible to consider the theoretical implications of the findings to date.

It is difficult to reconcile these findings with a serial, default-interventionist model in which an initial judgement is made based solely on heuristic processes followed under certain circumstances by a later logical judgement based on analytic processes. None of the studies found a time window prior to the behavioural response in which conditions differed only by belief-based heuristic, with an interaction with logic intervening later. They all indicate an evaluation of logic and belief in parallel. Several different parallel models have been proposed, and the ERP studies further discriminate between them. One traditional theory is that analytic and heuristic processes are engaged from the onset of the problem (Sloman, 1996). Although this is a possibility, it is notable that the components influenced by conflict are comparatively early (i.e. 200 to 300 ms after conclusion presentation), whereas this model has typically not emphasised fast logical processing; that is, in particular, logical responding for a typical belief bias task is generally expected to be analytic and slow. If the conflict arises because of the simultaneous engagement of slow analytic processing and fast heuristic ones, it should be expected to arise much later (i.e. when the slow logical process has completed its response generation) than the 300ms to 500ms time window that was found by Banks and Hope (2014). The findings are easier to reconcile with more recent parallel models (or so-called "hybrid" models, De Neys, this volume), in particular the logical intuition model (De Neys, 2012) and the three-stage dual process model of analytic engagement (Pennycook et al., 2015), or the parallel model of Trippas and Handley (Handley & Trippas, 2015). These models predict an initial stage involving only fast, Type 1 processes that operate in parallel followed by a later stage in which analytic processes generate a response if the Type 1 processes conflict. These models account for the ERP data well, explaining the differences between conflict and no-conflict problems that are found soon after the presentation of the conclusion.

Different ERP components are associated with different cognitive processes, so the ERP studies not only provide data about the timing of dual processes, but also the components elicited provide information about the type of cognitive process evoked by the different problems. The most interesting distinction is between the complex logical problems tested by Luo et al. (2013) and Banks and Hope (2014) and the simpler logical problems tested by Banks and Dunne (in prep.). The former tasks were more typical of tasks used to study belief bias and conflict evoked components associated with working memory updating and cognitive control. The simpler logical problems, however, evoked differences in an earlier component associated with expectations generated automatically as the problem is read. Future research on the different components evoked by different reasoning tasks will generate further insight into the different elements and stages of the reasoning process as it unfolds.

The ERP evidence presented here demonstrates that the technique is best suited to examining fast, Type 1 processes that are not directly measurable with behavioural paradigms. It is well suited to further test the theoretical accounts of Type 1 processes. One possibility is that automaticity is the basis for Type 1 logical intuitions (e.g. De Neys, 2012), and the complementary theory has also been proposed, namely that working memory involvement is the basis of Type 2 analytic processes (Evans & Stanovich, 2013). Extensive research on automaticity on the acquisition and qualities of automatic cognition has identified different mechanisms for automatic cognition, including a shift towards direct memory retrieval (Logan, 1988), the proceduralisation of an algorithm after repeated practice (Anderson, 1982), or the consistent mapping between stimulus and response (Schneider & Shiffrin, 1977). If these mechanisms apply to reasoning, what forms of reasoning could be automated? A three-term series problem could be readily automated, either because it is more frequently encountered or because the simple form means that there is a more consistent mapping of the response to the stimulus, or both. But it may be that only some reasoning can be automated because the mapping between the stimulus and response is highly variable, providing a limit on what can and cannot become a Type 1 process. For example, this is likely to be the case when reasoning about moral dilemmas, as the utilitarian, Type 2 process will generate different responses to different dilemmas depending on what the alternative is. If, indeed, some Type 1 processes are automated inferences, the further implication is that a dual process theory requires more than an accurate account of the underlying cognitive architecture, but also an account of the interaction of the architecture with different properties of the reasoning task such as the consistency of mapping between premises and conclusion. Answering these questions requires further research on the speed of processing and level of attentional control for different problems. The studies described earlier show how ERPs can be used to measure the latency of cognitive processes, and the amplitude of different components can be used to index different cognitive processes, such as the allocation of attention. ERP research can contribute to answering these theoretical questions.

ERP methodology

Although ERP studies offer new lines of evidence, they also bring new methodological challenges. All of the experiments described earlier have introduced some changes to the typical presentation of reasoning problems, and this is true of all EEG studies of reasoning. It is a necessary response to the constraints of ERP methodology and worth evaluating to what extent these changes limit the interpretation of the findings (Roser et al., 2015). The studies described earlier differ from the typical behavioural paradigms in two ways. First, there is a very large number of trials. The large number of trials is a potential limitation, as it is possible that responses are learnt rather than reasoned. If so, then the ERPs would reflect the recognition of a problem within a given experimental paradigm rather than the intended cognitive process. We mitigated this issue by using a wider range of problems which were constructed so that it was not possible to predict the conclusion before it was presented. Our second study also used a number of filler problems to reduce the predictability of the trials. We also found the expected behavioural effects in the responses of participants, indicating that the study elicited the phenomena of interest. Future ERP studies should continue to minimise this methodological constraint. Second, information is presented serially (one sentence or word at a time) rather than in parallel (the entire problem presented at once). This has been found to influence reasoning performance, thereby reducing belief bias (Morley, Evans, & Handley, 2004). It is a necessary constraint in order to minimise eye movement artefacts that render the EEG too noisy to analyse and to identify an exact point of interest to time-lock the ERPs to.

Whereas the former issue is a methodological problem, the latter raises interesting theoretical questions. When a dual process theory describes two processes occurring in parallel, at what point does this begin? Even when using a parallel presentation format, when reading a problem, the information is not actually absorbed in parallel but sequentially as each word is read. For example, a typical base-rate neglect problem presents base-rate information about the population followed by information about a specific individual. One set of information is used to reason normatively and the other heuristically. Differences in time at which both of these reasoning processes end (measured by a behavioural response) may reflect not just how fast each process is, but also the point in time at which the reasoning began. If one process begins before the other, then it may finish first and trigger a behavioural response, but it is not necessarily a faster process overall. More precise timing of reasoning can help distinguish if the cognitive processes truly are occurring in parallel or if strategic online processing as the problem is read or interleaving of cognitive processes is giving rise to that impression.

Conclusion

The main contribution of ERP research at present lies in the investigation of fast, Type 1 processes that are difficult to tap using behavioural paradigms. The studies described here illustrate different ERP components that are evoked by different logical problems, indicating the timing and the type of cognition involved prior to the behavioural response. The early interaction of belief and logic in all of the problems suggests that these factors are evaluated in parallel at the onset of the conclusion rather than serially. The simpler logical problems differed from the more complex logical problems and evoked an automatic logical inference that interfered with belief judgements, suggesting that within a belief bias task, the Type 1 processes could be logic based as well as belief based.

Together, these findings provide evidence about the initial cognitive response to reasoning, an area where dual process theories disagree. These findings are most consistent with parallel Type 1 processes that may generate belief- or logic-based responses. The data support the idea that these responses are automatic and will be acquired when a person has repeated exposure to consistent patterns, be they logical forms or other patters of inference. Examining this idea requires further work on the conditions under which automatic inferences can be acquired and the timing and cognitive processes that index their formation. Developing reasoning tasks for ERP studies will help in answering these questions.

References

Anderson, J. R. (1982). Acquisition of cognitive skill. *Psychological Review*, 89, 369–406.
Banks, A. P. (2013). The influence of activation level on belief bias in relational reasoning. *Cognitive Science*, 37, 544–577.
Banks, A. P., & Dunne, L. (in prep.). Logic and belief instruction in belief bias: Evidence from event-related potentials. Manuscript in preparation.
Banks, A. P., & Hope, C. (2014). Heuristic and analytic processes in reasoning: An event-related potential study of belief bias. *Psychophysiology*, 51, 290–297.
Bonnefond, M., Castelain, T., Cheylus, A., & Van der Henst, J. B. (2014). Reasoning from transitive premises: An EEG study. *Brain and Cognition*, 90, 100–108.
Bonnefond, M., Kaliuzhna, M., Van der Henst, J. B., & De Neys, W. (2014). Disabling conditional inferences: An EEG study. *Neuropsychologia*, 56, 255–262.
Bonnefond, M., & Van der Henst, J. B. (2009). What's behind an inference? An EEG study with conditional arguments. *Neuropsychologia*, 47, 3125–3133.
Bonnefond, M., & Van der Henst, J. B. (2013). Deduction electrified: ERPs elicited by the processing of words in conditional arguments. *Brain and Language*, 124, 244–256.
Cai, X., Li, F., Wang, Y., Jackson, T., Chen, J., Zhang, L., & Li, H. (2011). Electrophysiological correlates of hypothesis evaluation: Revealed with a modified Wason's selection task. *Brain Research*, 1408, 17–26.
De Neys, W. (2006). Dual processing in reasoning: Two systems but one reasoner. *Psychological Science*, 17, 428–433.
De Neys, W. (2012). Bias and conflict: A case for logical intuitions. *Perspectives on Psychological Science*, 7, 28–38.
Evans, J. St. B. (2006). The heuristic-analytic theory of reasoning: Extension and evaluation. *Psychonomic Bulletin & Review*, 13, 378–395.
Evans, J. S. B., Barston, J. L., & Pollard, P. (1983). On the conflict between logic and belief in syllogistic reasoning. *Memory & Cognition*, 11, 295–306.
Evans, J. S. B., & Curtis-Holmes, J. (2005). Rapid responding increases belief bias: Evidence for the dual-process theory of reasoning. *Thinking & Reasoning*, 11, 382–389.
Evans, J. S. B., & Stanovich, K. E. (2013). Dual-process theories of higher cognition: Advancing the debate. *Perspectives on Psychological Science*, 8, 223–241.
Federmeier, K. D., Mai, H., & Kutas, M. (2005). Both sides get the point: Hemispheric sensitivities to sentential constraint. *Memory & Cognition*, 33, 871–886.

Folstein, J. R., & Van Petten, C. (2008). Influence of cognitive control and mismatch on the N2 component of the ERP: A review. *Psychophysiology, 45,* 152–170.

García-Larrea, L., & Cézanne-Bert, G. (1998). P3, positive slow wave and working memory load: A study on the functional correlates of slow wave activity. *Electroencephalography and Clinical Neurophysiology/Evoked Potentials Section, 108,* 260–273.

Gevins, A., Smith, M. E., Le, J., Leong, H., Bennett, J., Martin, N., McEvoy, L., Du, R., & Whitfield, S. (1996). High resolution evoked potential imaging of the cortical dynamics of human working memory. *Electroencephalography and Clinical Neurophysiology, 98,* 327–348.

Handley, S. J., Newstead, S. E., & Trippas, D. (2011). Logic, beliefs, and instruction: A test of the default interventionist account of belief bias. *Journal of Experimental Psychology: Learning, Memory, and Cognition, 37,* 28–43.

Handley, S. J., & Trippas, D. (2015). Chapter two-dual processes and the interplay between knowledge and structure: A new parallel processing model. *Psychology of Learning and Motivation, 62,* 33–58.

Klauer, K. C., Musch, J., & Naumer, B. (2000). On belief bias in syllogistic reasoning. *Psychological Review, 107,* 852–884.

Logan, G. D. (1988). Toward an instance theory of automatization. *Psychological Review, 95,* 492–527.

Luck, S. J., & Hillyard, S. A. (1994). Electrophysiological correlates of feature analysis during visual search. *Psychophysiology, 31,* 291–308.

Luo, J. L., Liu, X., Stupple, E. J., Zhang, E., Xiao, X., Jia, L., Yang, Q., Li, H., & Zhang, Q. (2013). Cognitive control in belief-laden reasoning during conclusion processing: An ERP study. *International Journal of Psychology, 48,* 224–231.

Luo, J. L., Yang, Q., Du, X. M., & Zhang, Q. L. (2011). Neural correlates of belief-laden reasoning during premise processing: An ERP study. *Neuropsychobiology, 63,* 112–118.

Luo, J. L., Yuan, J. J., Qiu, J., Zhang, Q. L., Zhong, J., & Huai, Z. C. (2008). Neural correlates of the belief-bias effect in syllogistic reasoning: An event-related potential study. *Neuroreport, 19,* 1075–1079.

Morley, N. J., Evans, J. S. B., & Handley, S. J. (2004). Belief bias and figural bias in syllogistic reasoning. *Quarterly Journal of Experimental Psychology Section A, 57,* 666–692.

Pennycook, G., Fugelsang, J. A., & Koehler, D. J. (2015). What makes us think? A three-stage dual-process model of analytic engagement. *Cognitive Psychology, 80,* 34–72.

Polich, J. (2007). Updating P300: An integrative theory of P3a and P3b. *Clinical Neurophysiology, 118,* 2128–2148.

Qiu, J., Li, H., Luo, Y., Zhang, Q., & Tu, S. (2009). The neural basis of syllogistic reasoning: An event-related potential study. *Brain Research, 1273,* 106–113.

Roberts, M. J. (2000). Strategies in relational inference. *Thinking and Reasoning, 6,* 1–26.

Roser, M. E., Evans, J. S. B., McNair, N. A., Fuggetta, G., Handley, S. J., Carroll, L. S., & Trippas, D. (2015). Investigating reasoning with multiple integrated neuroscientific methods. *Frontiers in Human Neuroscience, 9,* 41.

Schaeken, W., Van der Henst, J., & Schroyens, W. (2007). The mental models theory of relational reasoning: Conclusions' phrasing, and cognitive economy. In W. Schaeken, A. Vandierendonck, W. Schroyens, & G. d'Ydewalle (Eds.), *The mental model theory of reasoning: Refinements and extensions* (pp. 129–150). Mahwah, NJ: LEA.

Schneider, W., & Shiffrin, R. M. (1977). Controlled and automatic human information processing: I. detection, search, and attention. *Psychological Review, 84,* 1–66.

Sloman, S. A. (1996). The empirical case for two systems of reasoning. *Psychological Bulletin, 119,* 3–22.

Stupple, E. J., Ball, L. J., Evans, J. S. B., & Kamal-Smith, E. (2011). When logic and belief collide: Individual differences in reasoning times support a selective processing model. *Journal of Cognitive Psychology, 23*, 931–941.

Trippas, D., Thompson, V. A., & Handley, S. J. (2016). When fast logic meets slow belief: Evidence for a parallel-processing model of belief bias. *Memory & Cognition, 45*, 539–552.

6
THE FUZZY-TRACE DUAL PROCESS MODEL

Valerie F. Reyna, Shahin Rahimi-Golkhandan, David M. N. Garavito, and Rebecca K. Helm

Overview

In this chapter, we provide an overview of the basic tenets and empirical findings that are relevant to fuzzy-trace theory (FTT). FTT is part of a movement that involves rethinking the traditional dual process model that distinguishes intuition from deliberation, conserving its strengths but moving beyond it. Our framework allows reasoning, judgment, and decision-making to be understood in a new way that makes meaning central to cognition and places intuition – defined as meaningful gist-based thinking – at the apex of advanced cognition. However, the theory is not just a framework for new thinking. Rather, FTT encompasses findings generated from multiple perspectives, with the aim of bringing them together in a parsimonious and predictive theory. First, we discuss the assumptions of the theory, followed by critical tests of predictions and key differences from alternative approaches.

Tenets of fuzzy trace theory

FTT distinguishes *verbatim* representations of information that are literally similar to information as presented from gist representations of information – the essential meaning of that same information (Abadie, Waroquier, & Terrier, 2013; Reyna, 2012). FTT's verbatim–gist distinction was inspired by classic psycholinguistic findings, including those of Bransford and Franks (1971) and Clark and Clark (1977). However, FTT's assumptions about verbatim and gist representations and core predictions differ from those in classic psycholinguistics (Reyna, 2012). Bransford and Franks (and others) claimed that verbatim representations of the surface form of presented sentences (e.g., The ants ate the sweet jelly; the jelly was on the table.) are processed to extract gist representations of meaning (e.g., The ants ate the jelly on the table.) and then the verbatim surface form is discarded, such that actually presented sentences and gist-consistent inferences cannot be discriminated.

However, both the psycholinguistic assumptions about semantic abstraction and the findings of no discrimination were called into question (e.g., Alba & Hasher, 1983; Reyna, Corbin, Weldon, & Brainerd, 2016; Reyna & Kiernan, 1994). Sensitive tests showed that verbatim and gist representations were not related to one another; for example, forgetting of verbatim memories was not related to misrecognition of gist-based inferences as having been presented. Instead, verbatim and gist memories were stochastically independent, which means that recognizing the presented sentences had no relationship with misrecognizing the inferences. In addition, when recognition instructions were clarified by giving examples of gist-consistent inferences that should be *rejected*, people discriminated presented sentences from inferences – in contrast to Bransford and Franks' (1971) key result of no discrimination (e.g., Reyna & Kiernan, 1994).[1] Many other effects and re-analyses of data from multiple (skeptical) laboratories have confirmed FTT's assumptions about verbatim versus gist representations (e.g., Brainerd & Reyna, 1992). Thus, the use of the terms "verbatim" and "gist" does not involve merely recycling the same ideas used in earlier theories. Although there is some overlap in definitions, the assumptions and predictions of FTT differ substantially from those of earlier verbatim–gist conceptualizations (Reyna & Brainerd, 1995).

In FTT, each kind of mental representation generally supports a different kind of processing: gist representations tend to support "fuzzy" (imprecise) impressionistic, generally unconscious processing, whereas verbatim representations tend to support more precise processing (Kühberger & Tanner, 2010). The outputs of processing include recognition judgments, logical inferences, probability judgments, and risky choices, which are produced by applying verbatim and gist processing in parallel (Reyna & Brainerd, 1992). Other dual process theories do not make this verbatim–gist distinction the cornerstone of their approaches.

Mental representations of information are needed, regardless of whether reasoners use working memory to represent information that is written down (and currently visible) to solve a problem or whether they retrieve information from long-term memory to solve a problem. The inputs or stimulus – the premises of a logical argument, the numbers in a mathematical problem, or the options in a decision task – must be mentally represented in order to be operated on by the mind. FTT proposes that these mental representations are encoded from the stimulus in two roughly parallel streams: verbatim (precise words, numbers, pictures, etc.) and gist (imprecise meanings). Multiple gist representations of the same stimulus are routinely encoded that vary in precision, but only one may be used to answer the question at hand (Reyna, Lloyd, & Brainerd, 2003). Gist representations are not just imprecise in the sense that they are vague – they also distill the meaning of experience into its *essence*. Gist representations also reflect limitations in people's understanding, for example, representing stereotypes (De Neys & Vanderputte, 2011[2]).

Once encoded, representations of stimuli cue memorized operations or general principles that are applied to the encoded representations. An example of a general reasoning principle is "more frequent is more probable" (i.e., if two classes of events vary in their frequency of occurrence, whichever class is more frequent is more probable, all else being equal). Because of the encoding specificity property of retrieval (i.e., like cues like), precise verbatim representations tend to cue precise rote operations, and general gist representations tend to cue general principles (Reyna & Brainerd, 1995). By encoding specificity, we mean that recall is enhanced if the circumstances surrounding recall match that of encoding. That is, the form of the cue determines the form of the recalled memory: verbatim cues elicit verbatim memories, and gist cues elicit gist memories. Encoding, retrieval, and processing also proceed roughly in parallel and can cycle multiple times to produce a response.

For example, if asked what 2 multiplied by 8 equals, many adults retrieve a memorized rote response (the answer of 16) from long-term memory. This kind of "reasoning" corresponds to stimulus–response learning. At the same time, adults encode the approximate magnitude of the numbers, the gist: these are all pretty small numbers, compared to numbers like 100,000 (Reyna, Nelson, Han, & Dieckmann, 2009). If the task were choice, the gist of numbers such as 16 and 100,000 (small vs. large) might be sufficient to accomplish the task of choosing. For instance, a general principle, such as more money is better than less money, could be applied to a choice between $16 and $100,000, and $100,000 would be preferred without regard to the exact numerical difference. An exact response is required to the multiplication question, but a vague ordinal number sense is all that is needed for the choice task (Thompson & Siegler, 2010).

After a buffer task or delay after presentation of numbers, people might not remember verbatim numbers, but they usually remember the gist that the numbers were pretty small or that a presented fraction such as one-third was "less than half." When researchers contrive tasks that require exact numbers or precise wording to perform, the ability to use gist is constrained or eliminated, and such tasks do not necessarily reflect how people make judgments or decisions in the real world.

Even when adults have access to verbatim representations (i.e., they *remember* them) and perform numerical calculations, they nevertheless rely more on gist representations to *reason* in familiar domains. This is referred to as the "fuzzy-processing preference." For example, if 2 out of 7 patients are saved with Treatment A and 3 out of 5 patients are saved with Treatment B, the latter is preferred whether or not people calculate exact proportions (Furlan, Agnoli, & Reyna, 2016; Reyna & Brainerd, 1994). Similarly, many people prefer winning (a) $1 million for sure over (b) an 89% chance to win $1 million plus a 10% chance to win $5 million and 1% chance to win nothing (the "Allais" problem, so named because it was invented by Maurice Allais; Reyna & Brainerd, 2011). People prefer option (a) because they can rely on the simplest gist, even simpler than an ordinal distinction between small and large, to accomplish the task of choosing, which turns on the categorical possibility of receiving nothing in option (b). That is, the gist of the options boils down to winning (a lot of) money versus maybe winning nothing. This preference for the sure option frequently holds even for those who realize that option (b) is numerically superior to option (a); the gist trumps the verbatim representation (Reyna, 2012).

People are more likely to prefer the sure option when decision options are equivalent numerically compared with when they are not equivalent (i.e., one option is numerically superior), showing that both gist and verbatim representations of the options are processed (Reyna & Brainerd, 1995). Verbatim analysis (e.g., multiplying each probability by its outcome) reduces preferences for the sure option when options are not equivalent numerically (when the risky gamble is superior mathematically). However, as adults think more deeply and consider the *meaningful* distinctions between options, some are more likely to prefer the sure $1 million in the Allais problem noted earlier. One of the key aspects of the Allais problem is that it pits simple, meaningful gist distinctions against quantitative verbatim details, and many adults depend on the gist to make decisions.

We should point out that when we say "rely" on verbatim or gist representations, we do not imply that only those representations are encoded or processed. Research on FTT has shown that verbatim and multiple gist representations are encoded, but the default preference is typically the simplest gist that can accomplish the task (Reyna & Brainerd, 1995). The ability to accomplish the task is driven by the specificity of the required response, among other factors. Although most adults prefer gist, individual differences also have been shown to influence processing preferences (e.g., in aging or in autism; Reyna & Brainerd, 2011).

Important advantages of gist representations in reasoning are that they are imprecise, and thus fit many specific situations, and are meaningful and thus capture non-superficial conceptual relations (Reyna & Brainerd, 1995). For example, if 2 and 8 were the length in feet of the sides of a rectangle and a reasoner were asked to calculate the area of that rectangle, retrieving and applying the rote operation of length multiplied by width would yield the correct answer of 16 square feet (Wertheimer, 1982). However, if the figure were a parallelogram, the same rote formula would yield the wrong answer. Understanding why the formula for a rectangle generates the right answer facilitates successful transfer to the parallelogram problem.

Prior to FTT, Gestalt theorists studied reasoning and distinguished between thinking that was (a) non-productive, such as memorized operations that are rigid and do not transfer to new problems that differ superficially from previous learning (i.e., stimulus–response learning of the behaviorists), and (b) productive thinking that does transfer to novel problems because of deep conceptual understanding (Sternberg & Davidson, 1995). This distinction is echoed in FTT's verbatim–gist difference, although FTT contains assumptions not found in Gestalt theory, and many other aspects of Gestalt theory are not adopted in FTT. Thus, gist-based intuition in FTT is not associative processing (i.e., stimulus–stimulus or stimulus–response association) (cf. Sloman, 2002).

Surprisingly, many contemporary theories do not have mechanisms to account for near and far transfer (when superficial features of a "new" problem differ a little or a lot from old learning and yet reasoners apply the old learning). Critical empirical tests show that theories must include mechanisms for far transfer to explain such replicated effects as learning sets (e.g., specific features of a maze change, but maze-experienced subjects learn new mazes in a few trials), cognitive maps (e.g., subjects execute dissimilar responses to get to the same goal in a maze, such as swimming left rather than running right by using cognitive maps), transposition effects (e.g., subjects learn abstract relations among magnitudes and transfer this abstraction to new problems, rejecting options that match prior reinforced responses literally), comprehension of novel metaphors (e.g., subjects interpret expressions such as "Juliet is the sun" not as Juliet is literally hot and gaseous), and many other phenomena (Reyna & Brainerd, 1992, 1995). For these phenomena, the literal stimulus–response mappings of old learning do not apply to the new transfer situation, but successful reasoners rely on having meaningful insight into the gist of the concepts to solve new problems.

Meaningful insight into concepts does not necessarily imply insight into cognition itself, called "metacognition," which is a distinct construct in FTT (Liberali, Reyna, Furlan, Stein, & Pardo, 2012). Metacognition is, by definition, cognition about cognition and encompasses reflection about the processes or outputs of thinking (Evans & Stanovich, 2013). However, as demonstrated in research, a reasoner can understand the gist of concepts, such as probability or the area of a rectangle, without being able to articulate or be reflective about his or her understanding, which is recognized in FTT (Reyna & Mills, 2007). Moreover, detecting and inhibiting impulsive or inconsistent responses need not be conscious or effortful (Franssens & De Neys, 2009; Reyna & Mills, 2007) and may be linked to personality traits, such as behavioral inhibition and the need for cognition (Evans & Stanovich, 2013; Reyna et al., 2011).

People can exhibit biases in their reasoning under circumstances that do not prompt self-examination, but then engage in heightened monitoring, detection, and inhibition when their biases are more obvious (Reyna & Brainerd, 1994; Stanovich & West, 2008). For example, when the same information is framed in terms of gains and losses, but the framing difference is manipulated between subjects (i.e., each group receives a different frame), people show framing effects (e.g., greater risk seeking for losses than gains; see later). That framing effect is diminished when the gain and loss versions of the same information are presented to the same subjects. More generally, research on FTT has shown that monitoring and associated inhibition of compelling responses requires a parameter that is separate from parameters that capture verbatim and gist representations to adequately model memory, judgment, and decision-making (e.g., Brainerd, Reyna, & Howe, 2009; Reyna & Brainerd, 1998, 2011; Reyna & Mills, 2007).

In addition to representational distinctions and processes that inhibit impulsive or inconsistent responses, FTT integrates other building blocks of motivation (e.g., reward-seeking motivation), emotion (e.g., valence and arousal), and social/moral values (e.g., human lives should be saved) (Bookbinder & Brainerd, in press; Broniatowski, Hilyard, & Dredze, 2016; Reyna, Wilhelms, McCormick, & Weldon, 2015). Thus, although FTT began as a cognitive theory that focused on mental representations, it has grown to include concepts that translate mental representations into behavior that serves motivational, emotional, and social goals. The theory accomplishes this translation by assuming that cognitive representations combine with socioemotional and motivational factors to jointly determine behavior.

For example, how people mentally represent options interacts with their attraction to rewards (Reyna et al., 2011). The Allais problem mentioned earlier presents options that vary in both risk and reward. A verbatim analysis of the precise numbers highlights the tradeoff between risk and reward, the classical analysis of choice in economics: from this perspective, the certainty of a lower reward ($1 million) may be more than offset by a risky but potentially higher reward ($5 million). In addition, there are individual and developmental differences in sensitivity to reward (Casey, Galvan, & Somerville, 2016; Steinberg, 2008). Therefore, adolescents, who are more likely to emphasize verbatim representations and are more sensitive to rewards compared with adults, are more attracted to risky options with higher rewards (Reyna & Farley, 2006). Cognitive representations (verbatim and gist) and reward sensitivity have unique but synergistic effects (Reyna et al., 2011).

Both adolescents and adults encode verbatim and gist representations of decision options, but adults' fuzzy-processing preference for gist means that their preferences hinge on the simple contrast between some and none: receiving some money for sure as opposed to either receiving some money or no money. Because some money is valued over no money, adults tend to prefer the sure option. As the emphasis on gist processing increases with development, risky preferences for choices such as these decline, a developmental trend that supports FTT (for a meta-analysis, see Defoe, Dubas, Figner, & van Aken, 2014). As we discuss later, developmental differences in verbatim and gist processing contribute to critical tests of FTT's fundamental assumptions.

Findings and empirical tests

Early studies on FTT showed that children and adults encoded verbatim and gist representations of problem information in many paradigms (e.g., probability judgment, conservation, mental arithmetic, transitive inference, class-inclusion reasoning, etc.; Reyna & Brainerd, 1995). People used verbatim memory to answer immediate questions about exact details of the problem information and used gist memory to reason or make inferences even when the exact details were accessible. Reliance on simple gist occurred as long as problems could be solved that way, and many problems could be solved better with gist than with verbatim memory for myriad reasons (e.g., gist was more meaningful, flexible, and memorable).

For example, if presented with photos of 7 women and 3 men and asked whether there were more women or more people, comparing 7 to 3 turns out to be a bad idea; it is a source of the typical class-inclusion error of answering "more women." The better that reasoners remember 7 women and 3 men, the more they commit the error; taking away a display with this information improves reasoning because the exact number of women and men becomes hazy in memory. Then, rather than focus on the verbatim information that is salient in the display, reasoners think about the gist. The simple qualitative gist that women *are* people comes into focus, and the details about how many more women than men there are recedes. Adults do not commit this error very often, but their response time is long, and they will err systematically under speeded conditions, implying an inhibitory process.

This systematic class-inclusion error is not due mainly to linguistic ambiguity or misinterpretation, although some responses occur because "people" in the question is interpreted as "men." There are multiple arguments against linguistic ambiguity, but one is that reasoners commit the error after they are asked to count the women, men, and people out loud and they correctly count 7, 3, and 10, respectively. Thus, the problem is confusing not because of ambiguity – although reasoners are thinking of the relative number of women and men when they answer the question incorrectly. All problems that involve overlapping "vertical" (e.g., the hierarchical relationship between women and people) and "horizontal" (e.g., the relative magnitude relationship between women and men) class-inclusion relationships are confusing. Piaget's explanation for this reasoning error was a deficit in logical reasoning, and others have argued that working-memory limitations play a role; both explanations have been ruled out with careful experiments. For example, problems with a higher memory load – with more classes – were easier to solve than the standard class-inclusion problems when the classes did not overlap, although memory performance was lower under specific conditions (see Table 6.1). Similarly, increasing the number of premises in a transitive inference task (e.g., the green rod is longer than the orange rod, the orange rod is longer than the purple rod, and so on) decreases memory, but improves reasoning (the ability to infer that the purple rod is shorter

TABLE 6.1 Illustrative arrays for class inclusion problems

Type of problem					
One superordinate set	C C	S S	G G	D D	H H
	C C	S S	G G	D D	
	C C	S S	G G		
	C C	S S			
	C C				
Two superordinate sets	C C	H H		V V	P P
	C C			V V	P
	C C			V V	
	C C			V V	
				V	

Note. The problem at the top includes one superordinate set (C = cow, S = sheep, G = goat, D = dog, H = horse), and the one at the bottom includes two (C = cow, H = horse, V = violin, P = piano). The problems with a higher memory load – with more classes – were easier than the standard class-inclusion problems, but memory performance was worse under specific conditions (see Brainerd & Reyna, 1995).

than the green rod) because the pattern of decreasing length becomes more obvious (see Reyna & Brainerd, 1995). Moreover, in another empirical test of FTT, verbatim memory for the number of objects in each class was found to be stochastically independent of reasoning performance grounded in gist (e.g., the gist that women and men are people, so people are more; Reyna & Brainerd, 1995, 2008).

Applying FTT, similar explanations were advanced to explain conjunction fallacies (e.g., ranking Linda as more likely to be a feminist bank teller than to be a bank teller because of a compelling verbal description that evokes a stereotype of feminism; Tversky & Kahneman, 1983) as well as other logical reasoning errors that again involve overlapping classes, including disjunction fallacies, base-rate neglect, conversion errors in conditional probability judgments, and other class-inclusion confusions (Reyna, 2004). The argument that using frequencies (or counts) rather than probabilities reduces these fallacies turns out not to be true. Instead, the key to these fallacies are overlapping classes that confuse the reasoner along with a compelling gist that competes with the gist required by the question, thereby usurping reasoning. Therefore, a critical test of FTT's explanation is to eliminate overlapping classes to determine whether the fallacies are reduced or eliminated.

As a critical test, that segregation of classes can be accomplished by using Venn diagrams, placing distinctive tags (e.g., on all of the photos so that the number of tags may be compared to the number of women), or with 2×2 tables (e.g., so that estimates can be made separately for the classes of feminists who are bank tellers, bank tellers who are not feminists, those who are both, and those who are neither). The marginal totals can be easily computed, and base rates (e.g., the probability of being a bank teller) can be distinguished from conditional probabilities that have different marginal totals as denominators (e.g., the probability of being a feminist given that one is a bank teller vs. the probability of being a bank teller given that one is a feminist; Reyna & Brainerd, 1994, 2008). As shown in a series of experiments, these simple manipulations are effective in reducing or eliminating class-inclusion fallacies (e.g., Wolfe & Reyna, 2010). For example, it is readily apparent from a 2×2 table (which reasoners fill in with their own probability estimates about Linda) that the probability of being a bank teller who is a feminist and the probability of being a bank teller who is not a feminist add up to the total (marginal) probability of being a bank teller. Reasoners are not told the answers; they have the competence to reason logically and coherently once the classes are discrete (Reyna & Brainerd, 1994; Reyna et al., 2003).

Competence to reason logically has also been assessed by asking children and adults to make transitive inferences, also called linear syllogisms (e.g., Reyna et al., 2016). Children as young as 6 years old are able to make transitive inferences (e.g., Carmen is older than Ida) from presented premises, such as Carmen is older than Ben and Ben is older than Ida. Reyna and Kiernan (1994) presented such sentences (plus filler sentences) for many stories, administering gist-based reasoning tests to one group and verbatim-based recognition tests to another group both immediately and after a week's delay. On the gist-based test, people were asked to judge whether sentences were true or false, regardless of whether they were explicitly presented, *based on* what was presented. Judgments for presented sentences were positively related to judgments for true paraphrases and true inferences because all of these were based on the gist of presented sentences (statistical tests were likelihood ratios of conditional and unconditional probabilities that determine whether there is any dependency at all between pairs of presented and unpresented sentences within each story; Reyna & Kiernan, 1994). As also expected by FTT, there was little effect of delay on dependencies because judgments consistently drew on stable gist representations.

For the verbatim group, people made old-new recognition judgments, again to presented sentences, paraphrases of presented sentences (e.g., Ben is younger than Carmen), true and false inferences with presented wording (e.g., Carmen is older than Ida), and true and false inferences with novel wording (e.g., Ida is younger than Carmen). Consistent with FTT's predictions, on the immediate test, recognition of presented sentences (based on verbatim memory) was stochastically independent of misrecognition of true inferences (based on gist memory). Verbatim memory was not only not perfectly correlated with gist memory for any of the true sentences, it was also completely unrelated, just as verbatim and gist memory had been unrelated in earlier research on cognitive development. However, after a delay, when verbatim memory became inaccessible and gist memory dominated judgments of both presented and unpresented true sentences, previously independent sentences and inferences became positively dependent, just as in the gist (meaning) condition.

Other experiments showed that boosting verbatim memory for sentences in stories (through repetition, etc.) created negative dependency on immediate tests, as expected by FTT, because people said "yes" more often to presented sentences but "no" more often to true paraphrases and inferences; they used verbatim memory to reject true sentences (Reyna & Brainerd, 1995). Similar effects are found with words and other meaningful stimuli. Another counterintuitive but predicted result was that people rejected gist-consistent distractors more often than unrelated distractors, called "false-recognition reversal." To illustrate, when people study a word list with "cat" on it, they tend to "falsely" recognize the related word "animal" on a later recognition test more often than the unrelated word "book" – called *false recognition*. However, if verbatim memory for "cat" is strengthened by repeating it on the study list, the test word "animal" elicits verbatim memory for "cat," so that "animal" is rejected more often (false-recognition *reversal*) than the unrelated word "book" (Reyna & Brainerd, 1995).

Each of these findings with the old-new recognition test and with the true-false meaning test were predicted by FTT (Reyna et al., 2016; Reyna & Kiernan, 1994). Along with other FTT findings of predicted dissociations, they are strong evidence for distinct representational and processing systems of this specific sort – verbatim and gist systems. These theoretical conclusions about sentences require testing verbatim-consistent and gist-consistent sentences (and also controlling for wording that matches presented wording) and varying instructions to different groups to affirm either verbatim-consistent or gist-consistent sentences. Subsequent work used these carefully designed types of test stimuli and instructions, including related distractors such as true inferences, to construct mathematical models that separated such processes as verbatim-based acceptance of presented sentences, verbatim-based rejection of true inferences (and paraphrases), gist-based acceptance of true inferences (and paraphrases), and the degree to which people inhibit responses (Reyna et al., 2016). These FTT models were tested for goodness of fit against real data, meaning that they could be rejected by the data if the theoretical assumptions of the model were wrong; they fit the data. Parameters also "jumped" in response to experimental manipulations in ways that validated their theoretical interpretations. FTT's approach to measurement and manipulation addresses criticisms of dual process theories, providing evidence against single-system accounts (cf. Keren & Schul, 2009; Osman, 2004). FTT also accounts for the sometimes vivid *phenomenology* of gist-based "false" memories (Reyna et al., 2016). These memories are called "false" because the item tested, such as a true inference, is not literally identical to what was experienced, and yet people can remember the gist as vivid under conditions predicted by FTT. FTT was the first (and only) theory to predict that such memories would increase from childhood to adulthood (Brainerd, Reyna, & Forrest, 2002; Reyna & Kiernan, 1994), a result later replicated over 50 times (Brainerd & Reyna, 2012). The developmental *increase* in technically *inaccurate* but substantive memories tells us something important about the human mind and functionality, underlining the likely advantages of gist for advanced cognition (Reyna, Chick, Corbin, & Hsia, 2014; Reyna & Lloyd, 2006). We called this pattern a "developmental reversal" because it violates the usual expectations about developmental increases in precision and accuracy.

Developmental reversals are also observed for gain–loss framing effects (Reyna & Ellis, 1994; Reyna et al., 2011). In framing, as in the Allais problem, decision makers typically choose between a sure versus a risky option. In the gain frame, they might choose between $40 for sure or a two-thirds chance of winning $60 and a one-third chance of winning $0. In the corresponding "loss" frame, decision makers could be given an endowment of $60 but must choose between losing $20 for sure versus a two-thirds chance of losing $0 and a one-third chance of losing $60. Despite the net equivalence of the gain and loss versions of the decision (e.g., $60 − $40 = $20), adults prefer the sure option in the gain frame and the risky option in the loss frame (Tversky & Kahneman, 1986). However, children treat these frames as equivalent, modulating their risk preference based on probabilities and outcomes; framing differences emerge with age (Reyna & Ellis, 1994; Reyna et al., 2011; Weller, Levin, & Denburg, 2011). The ability to perform numerical computations improves during the same period that preference for relying on these details declines, consistent with FTT (Reyna & Brainerd, 1994; Weller et al., 2011).

There are numerous tests of FTT's explanation of decision-making phenomena such as the Allais problem and gain–loss framing effects (Reyna, 2012; Reyna & Brainerd, 2011). One of the straightforward tests involves truncating or deleting the zero part of the risky option in framing problems, the part that is responsible for the simplest qualitative distinction between options of receiving something or nothing. All of the elements needed to perform a quantitative analysis of the pros and cons of each option remain (e.g., $40 for sure vs. a two-thirds chance of winning $60). Moreover, the deleted zero part of the risky option (e.g., one-third chance of $0) is provided prior to choice to eliminate ambiguity. Nevertheless, deleting the zero part of the risky option for gains and losses eliminates framing effects, contrary to theories of risky decision-making other than FTT (Reyna & Brainerd, 1991). This and other types of truncation effects that test theoretical predictions have been replicated (Kühberger & Tanner, 2010; Reyna et al., 2014).

The advantages of FTT for advanced cognition, including decision-making, also have been examined experimentally by inducing gist-based thinking (Abadie et al., 2013; Fukukura, Ferguson, & Fujita, 2013; Reyna & Mills, 2014; Wolfe et al., 2015). Better decisions often reflect gist-based thinking (e.g., simple categorical thinking such as "it only takes once to get HIV-AIDS), rather than verbatim-based thinking (e.g., focusing on details and weighing the probabilities and potential outcomes of an array of options by trading off[3]). Thus, FTT predicts that adolescents who take risks are more likely to think in terms of risk–reward tradeoffs than adults, confirmed by Kwak, Payne, Cohen, and Huettel (2015). Using eye tracking, they showed that adolescents used a more detailed exhaustive approach to explore probabilities and outcomes than adults before making decisions in a risky-choice framing task. In contrast, decisions by young adults were influenced by task-relevant heuristics that simplified the decision problem.

FTT assumes that both gist and verbatim processing occur – those who rely on gist are often aware of the details and the tradeoffs, but they reject that way of thinking as the final arbiter of their decisions when the stakes are high. Instead of thinking that a low probability of a seriously bad outcome is okay because rewards are high, possibility (of the seriously bad outcome) rules over probability in decision-making. This is not because people do not understand probability, as evidenced by the fact that people who show this effect pass probability tests, but because possibility captures the essence of the risky option, as reflected in the adage that the probability is 100% if it happens to you (Reyna & Brainerd, 1994).

It is also not the case that gist thinkers necessarily have higher perceptions of risk; they are often aware that the objective probabilities of bad outcomes are, in fact, low. Critical tests of these hypotheses include randomizing adolescents to a gist-thinking versus verbatim-thinking curriculum about sexual risk taking, but maintaining all the same information about objective risks (Reyna & Mills, 2014). The gist curriculum facilitated health-promoting knowledge, attitudes, and thinking and was associated with better self-reported behavioral outcomes (e.g., delayed initiation of sex).

As an advanced type of cognition, in each of the domains of reasoning, judgment, and decision-making that we have discussed, FTT has predicted developmental increases in reliance on gist. Although gist-based intuition supports globally less error-prone reasoning and healthier decisions, it also produces systematic biases that paradoxically increase from childhood to adulthood. As discussed earlier, FTT motivated the first study on gain–loss framing effects in children (Reyna & Ellis, 1994), and it has subsequently been applied to a host of other reasoning, judgment, and decision-making biases. Conjunction fallacies, being determined by both compelling gist and class-inclusion confusion, also increase during this period when gist is pitted against verbatim details (e.g., as they are in the Linda and Allais problems). For example, Morsanyi, Chiesi, Primi, and Szűcs (2016) showed that children were more sensitive to numerical details about the frequencies of different classes and, hence, less likely to exhibit the conjunction fallacy. They also found that children's tendency to be less biased than adults was not due to their lack of knowledge about social stereotypes (e.g., as in the example of Linda), but rather their heavy reliance on explicit, literal information in the task description. False memory increases during this same period (shown to be due to gist by multiple empirical tests) and cannot be explained away by references to knowledge differences between children and adults: when materials were normed to equate knowledge requirements for children and adults, the predicted growth of gist-based memory and judgment biases was retained (Brainerd & Reyna, 2012). Although we have discussed effects separately, recent research has related them empirically to one another; for example, individuals who show framing biases have more gist-based false memories (Corbin, Reyna, Weldon, & Brainerd, 2015; Helm & Reyna, in press).

Conclusions, implications, and how theories differ

We have presaged many of the differences between FTT and alternative theories in the prior sections because tests of FTT have also been tests of alternatives. These effects include independence of verbatim and gist representations in logical inference; variations of this independence effect with delay and with instructions; better reasoning once problem information is forgotten; better reasoning with higher cognitive load; developmental reversals in memory, judgment, and decision-making; framing in risky choice and a variety of truncation effects; reduction of conjunction and other class-inclusion fallacies, including base-rate neglect with 2×2 tables (using probabilities not frequencies); and effects of inducing gist thinking on real-world judgments and decision-making. Note that methods reported in the original studies matter. For example, we are not saying that reasoning is always better when problem information is forgotten; instead, that effect holds when verbatim details support judgments that contradict the gist of problem information (Reyna et al., 2003). The bottom line is that FTT predicts these effects, and traditional dual process theories do not explain them easily. Indeed, many results clearly refute predictions of those theories (e.g., of prospect theory; Kahneman, 2011).

Findings such as independence between verbatim-based memory performance and gist-based reasoning performance may seem to contradict many findings that memory and reasoning correlate. However, that contradiction is more apparent than real. In FTT research, contingencies were computed within each story or problem; for instance, presented premises were related only to the true inferences that followed from those premises, as opposed to relating memory in general to reasoning in general. Using this approach, it is possible to assess whether accurate reasoning performance depends – even to a small degree – on working memory for problem information, a defining feature of current dual process models (Evans & Stanovich,

2013). The answer in many instances appears to be "no" because advanced reasoning bypasses the constraints of verbatim memory by relying on gist.

Traditional dual process models capture fundamental aspects of human thinking that should be conserved in newer approaches that expand our notions of intuition beyond a lazy default, which requires intervention to engage advanced processing and reduce biases, to parallel processes that incorporate intuitive insight (De Neys, 2012; Reyna, 2012). To be sure, there are reasoning and decision-making errors attributable to fast cognitive tempo (Kahneman, 2011), inadequate reflection (Evans & Stanovich, 2013), and immature executive processes (Casey et al., 2016; Steinberg, 2008), as recognized in FTT. However, literal thinking and failures to "get the gist" – failures of meaningful insight – cannot be remedied simply by slowing down processing and adding more "RAM" to augment human computation. Although some errors are reduced when individuals process more details more slowly and precisely, life skills can be impaired; gist-based thinking, rather than verbatim-based thinking, is often associated with healthier outcomes (Blalock & Reyna, 2016; Reyna & Brainerd, 2011). Relevant to real-world outcomes, FTT underlines the difference between processing *more* versus processing *more meaningfully*. As is well known in psycholinguistics, context, knowledge, and experience shape the meaning (or interpretation) of information, and thus FTT incorporates these factors by emphasizing essential meaning as central to cognition and its development.

Development offers an important perspective on adult competence. Unless development is devolution, which is unlikely, the increase in many systematic biases and fallacies cannot be ignored by theories of adult reasoning and decision-making (for a list of such developmental reversals, see Weldon, Corbin, & Reyna, 2013). Traditional dual process approaches assume an evolutionarily and developmentally advanced role for Type 2 (reflective) processing in reducing biases produced by Type 1 (intuitive) processing. More recent approaches (e.g., Stanovich, West, & Toplak, 2011) have acknowledged that development of intuitive biases might conform to an inverted U-shaped function, rather than decreasing from childhood to adulthood, as traditional theories assume. However, the observed developmental relationships from multiple laboratories tend to be monotonic, not an inverted U-shape.

Two types of biases or fallacies have been conflated from the perspective of FTT: those that involve failures of executive processes (e.g., of computation or inhibition) that decrease from childhood to adulthood and those that involve gist-based intuition that increase during this period (or, equivalently, increase with greater experience and expertise; Reyna et al., 2014). This conclusion is buttressed not just by the increase in such systematic biases with development, but by the detailed process models of those biases that we have only touched on briefly. The critique that counterintuitive developmental patterns were a side effect of using materials that were inappropriate for young children (e.g., that biases drew on knowledge they had yet to acquire) has been ruled out in studies on gist-based false memory, framing effects, the conjunction fallacy, and other phenomena (cf. De Neys & Vanderputte, 2011; Stanovich et al., 2011; Toplak, West, & Stanovich, 2014; see

Morsanyi et al., 2016; Weldon et al., 2013). Therefore, the evidence supports the theoretical ideas that motivated predictions of developmental reversals, and it is not necessary to turn to post hoc speculations to explain these effects.

Our analysis leaves many open questions, such as whether reasoning is the implementation of concrete beliefs, abstract structures, or something else entirely (Evans, Thompson, & Over, 2015). Verbatim and gist are both symbolic representations, but verbatim is more concrete and literal than is gist. However, gist is not an abstract (i.e., contentless) representation. Gist consists of schematic representations that incorporate semantic and pragmatic knowledge. Reasoning is, then, a process of applying general but not universal principles to meaningful representations of information. However, formalisms that capture meaningful content, not mindless associations that simulate effects of meaning, are needed. Additional work is also needed to characterize levels of gist and the processes through which representations are simplified to distill the nub of information to arrive at the gist. In the era of big data and overwhelming access to detailed information, appreciating the essence of information is more important than ever to improve human reasoning, judgment, and decision-making.

Acknowledgements

Valerie F. Reyna, Shahin Rahimi-Golkhandan, David M. N. Garavito, and Rebecca K. Helm are affiliated with the Human Neuroscience Institute and Department of Human Development, Cornell University. Preparation of this manuscript was supported in part by grants from the National Institutes of Health grant (award R01NR014368–01), National Science Foundation (award 1536238), and National Institute of Food and Agriculture (awards NYC-321423 and NYC-321436) to V. F. Reyna. Correspondence should be directed to Valerie F. Reyna, Human Neuroscience Institute, Cornell University, MVR G331, Ithaca, NY 14853 USA. E-mail: vr53@cornell.edu.

Notes

1 Note that people still erroneously accept gist-consistent inferences as presented more often than they accept gist-*in*consistent sentences as presented.
2 Stereotypes may also reflect memorized superficial features that are applied verbatim (i.e., without thinking).
3 The definition of a "better" decision has been written about in FTT (Adam & Reyna, 2005; Reyna & Brainerd, 1994; Reyna et al., 2003; Reyna & Farley, 2006).

References

Abadie, M., Waroquier, L., & Terrier, P. (2013). Gist memory in the unconscious-thought effect. *Psychological Science*, 24, 1253–1259. doi:10.1177/0956797612470958

Adam, M. B., & Reyna, V. F. (2005). Coherence and correspondence criteria for rationality: Experts' estimation of risks of sexually transmitted infections. *Journal of Behavioral Decision Making*, 18(3), 169–186. doi:10.1002/bdm.493

Alba, J. W., & Hasher, L. (1983). Is memory schematic? *Psychological Bulletin, 93*(2), 203–231.
Blalock, S. J., & Reyna, V. F. (2016). Using fuzzy-trace theory to understand and improve health judgments, decisions, and behaviors: A literature review. *Health Psychology, 35*(8), 781–792. doi:10.1037/hea0000384
Brainerd, C. J., & Reyna, V. F. (1992). Explaining "memory-free" reasoning. *Psychological Science, 3*(6), 332–339. doi:10.1111/j.1467–9280.1992.tb00042.x
Brainerd, C. J., & Reyna, V. F. (1995). Autosuggestibility in memory development. *Cognitive Psychology, 28*(1), 65–101. doi:10.1006/cogp.1995.1003
Brainerd, C. J., & Reyna, V. F. (2012). Reliability of children's testimony in the era of developmental reversals. *Developmental Review, 32*, 224–267. doi:10.1016/j.dr.2012.06.008
Brainerd, C. J., Reyna, V. F., & Forrest, T. J. (2002). Are young children susceptible to the false-memory illusion? *Child Development, 73*(5), 1363–1377. doi:10.1111/1467–8624.00477
Brainerd, C. J., Reyna, V. F., & Howe, M. L. (2009). Trichotomous processes in early memory development, aging, and neurocognitive impairment: A unified theory. *Psychological Review, 116*(4), 783–832. doi:10.1037/a0016963
Bransford, J. D., & Franks, J. J. (1971). The abstraction of linguistic ideas. *Cognitive Psychology, 2*(4), 331–350.
Bookbinder, S. H., & Brainerd, C. J. (2017). Emotionally negative pictures enhance gist memory. *Emotion, 17*(1), 102–119. doi: 10.1037/emo0000171.
Broniatowski, D. A., Hilyard, K. M., & Dredze, M. (2016). Effective vaccine communication during the Disneyland measles outbreak. *Vaccine, 34*(28), 3225–3228. doi:10.1016/j.vaccine.2016.04.044
Casey, B. J., Galvan, A., & Somerville, L. H. (2016). Beyond simple models of adolescence to an integrated circuit-based account: A commentary. *Developmental Cognitive Neuroscience, 17*, 128–130.
Clark, H. H., & Clark, E. V. (1977). *Psychology and language: An introduction to psycholinguistics.* New York, NY: Harcourt College Publishing.
Corbin, J. C., Reyna, V. F., Weldon, R. B., & Brainerd, C. J. (2015). How reasoning, judgment, and decision making are colored by gist-based intuition: A fuzzy-trace theory approach. *Journal of Applied Research in Memory and Cognition, 4*, 344–355. doi:10.1016/j.jarmac.2015.09.001
Defoe, I. N., Dubas, J. S., Figner, B., & Van Aken, M. A. (2014). A meta-analysis on age differences in risky decision-making: Adolescents versus children and adults. *Psychological Bulletin, 141*(1), 48–84. doi:10.1037/a0038088
De Neys, W. (2012). Bias and conflict: A case for logical intuitions. *Perspectives on Psychological Science, 7*(1), 28–38. doi:10.1177/1745691611429354
De Neys, W., & Vanderputte, K. (2011). When less is not always more: Stereotype knowledge and reasoning development. *Developmental Psychology, 47*(2), 432–441.
Evans, J. St B. T., & Stanovich, K. E. (2013). Dual-process theories of higher cognition: Advancing the debate. *Perspectives on Psychological Science, 8*(3), 223–241. doi:10.1177/1745691612460685
Evans, J. St B. T., Thompson, V. A., & Over, D. E. (2015). Uncertain deduction and conditional reasoning. *Frontiers in Psychology, 6*, 398, 1–12.
Franssens, S., & De Neys, W. (2009). The effortless nature of conflict detection during thinking. *Thinking & Reasoning, 15*(2), 105–128. doi: 10.1080/13546780802711185.
Fukukura, J., Ferguson, M. J., & Fujita, K. (2013). Psychological distance can improve decision making via reduction of information overload via gist memory. *Journal of Experimental Psychology: General, 142*(3), 658–665. doi:10.1037/a0030730
Furlan, S., Agnoli, F., & Reyna, V. F. (2016). Intuition and analytic processes in probabilistic reasoning: The role of time pressure. *Learning and Individual Differences, 45*, 1–10. doi:10.1016/j.lindif.2015.11.006

Helm, R. K., & Reyna, V. F. (2017). Logical but incompetent plea decisions: A new approach to plea bargaining grounded in cognitive theory. *Psychology, Public Policy, and Law, 23*(3), 367–380. doi: 10.1037/law0000125.

Kahneman, D. (2011). *Thinking fast and slow*. London, UK: Penguin.

Keren, G., & Schul, Y. (2009). Two is not always better than one: A critical evaluation of two-system theories. *Perspectives on Psychological Science, 4*, 533–550.

Kühberger, A., & Tanner, C. (2010). Risky choice framing: Task versions and a comparison of prospect theory and fuzzy-trace theory. *Journal of Behavioral Decision Making, 23*(3), 314–329. doi:10.1002/bdm.656

Kwak, Y., Payne, J. W., Cohen, A. L., & Huettel, S. A. (2015). The rational adolescent: Strategic information processing during decision making revealed by eye tracking. *Cognitive Development, 36*, 20–30. doi:10.1016/j.cogdev.2015.08.001

Liberali, J. M., Reyna, V. F., Furlan, S., Stein, L. M., & Pardo, S. T. (2012). Individual differences in numeracy and cognitive reflection, with implications for biases and fallacies in probability judgment. *Journal of Behavioral Decision Making, 25*, 361–381. doi:10.1002/bdm.752

Morsanyi, K., Chiesi, F., Primi, C., & Szűcs, D. (2017). The illusion of replacement in research into the development of thinking biases: The case of the conjunction fallacy. *Journal of Cognitive Psychology, 29*(2), 240–257. doi:10.1080/20445911.2016.1256294.

Osman, M. (2004). An evaluation of dual-process theories of reasoning. *Psychonomic Bulletin & Review, 11*, 988–1010.

Reyna, V. F. (2004). How people make decisions that involve risk: A dual-process approach. *Current Directions in Psychological Science, 13*(2), 60–66. doi:10.1111/j.09637214.2004.00275.x

Reyna, V. F. (2012) A new intuitionism: Meaning, memory, and development in Fuzzy-Trace Theory. *Judgment and Decision-Making, 7*(3), 332–359.

Reyna, V. F. & Brainerd, C. J. (1991). Fuzzy-trace theory and framing effects in choice: Gist extraction, truncation, and conversion. *Journal of Behavioral Decision Making, 4*, 249–262. doi:10.1002/bdm.3960040403

Reyna, V. F., & Brainerd, C. J. (1992). A fuzzy-trace theory of reasoning and remembering: Paradoxes, patterns, and parallelism. In A. Healy, S. Kosslyn, & R. Shiffrin (Eds.), *From learning processes to cognitive processes: Essays in honor of William K. Estes* (Vol. 2, pp. 235–259). Hillsdale, NJ: Erlbaum.

Reyna, V. F., & Brainerd, C. J. (1994). The origins of probability judgment: A review of data and theories. In G. Wright & P. Ayton (Eds.), *Subjective probability* (pp. 239–272). New York, NY: Wiley.

Reyna, V. F., & Brainerd, C. J. (1995). Fuzzy-trace theory: An interim synthesis. *Learning and Individual Differences, 7*(1), 1–75. doi:10.1016/1041–6080(95)90031-4

Reyna, V. F., & Brainerd, C. J. (1998). Fuzzy-trace theory and false memory: New frontiers. *Journal of Experimental Child Psychology, 71*(2), 194–209.

Reyna, V. F., & Brainerd, C. J. (2008). Numeracy, ratio bias, and denominator neglect in judgments of risk and probability. *Learning and Individual Differences, 18*(1), 89–107. doi:10.1016/j.lindif.2007.03.011

Reyna, V. F., & Brainerd, C. J. (2011). Dual processes in decision making and developmental neuroscience: A fuzzy-trace model. *Developmental Review, 31*, 180–206. doi:10.1016/j.dr.2011.07.004

Reyna, V. F., Chick, C. F., Corbin, J. C., & Hsia, A. N. (2014). Developmental reversals in risky decision-making: Intelligence agents show larger decision biases than college students. *Psychological Science, 25*(1), 76–84. doi:10.1177/0956797613497022

Reyna, V. F., Corbin, J. C., Weldon, R. B., & Brainerd, C. J. (2016). How fuzzy-trace theory predicts true and false memories for words and sentences. *Journal of Applied Research in Memory and Cognition, 5*(1), 1–9. doi:10.1016/j.jarmac.2015.12.003

Reyna, V. F., & Ellis, S. C. (1994). Fuzzy-trace theory and framing effects in children's risky decision making. *Psychological Science*, 5, 275–279. doi:10.1111/j.1467-9280.1994.tb00625.x

Reyna, V. F., Estrada, S. M., DeMarinis, J. A., Myers, R. M., Stanisz, J. M., & Mills, B. A. (2011). Neurobiological and memory models of risky decision making in adolescents versus young adults. *Journal of Experimental Psychology: Learning, Memory, and Cognition*, 37(5), 1125–1142. doi:10.1037/a0023943

Reyna, V. F., & Farley, F. (2006). Risk and rationality in adolescent decision making. *Psychological Science in the Public Interest*, 7(1), 1–44. doi:10.1111/j.1529-1006.2006.00026.x

Reyna, V. F., & Kiernan, B. (1994). Development of gist versus verbatim memory in sentence recognition: Effects of lexical familiarity, semantic content, encoding instructions, and retention interval. *Developmental Psychology*, 30(2), 178–191. doi:10.1037/0012-1649.30.2.178

Reyna, V. F., & Lloyd, F. J. (2006). Physician decision making and cardiac risk: Effects of knowledge, risk perception, risk tolerance, and fuzzy processing. *Journal of Experimental Psychology: Applied*, 12(3), 179–195. doi:10.1037/1076-898X.12.3.179

Reyna, V. F., Lloyd, F. J., & Brainerd, C. J. (2003). Memory, development, and rationality: An integrative theory of judgment and decision-making. In S. Schneider & J. Shanteau (Eds.), *Emerging perspectives on judgment and decision research* (pp. 201–245). New York: Cambridge University Press.

Reyna, V. F., & Mills, B. A. (2007). Interference processes in fuzzy-trace theory: Aging, Alzheimer's disease, and development. In D. Gorfein & C. MacLeod (Eds.), *Inhibition in cognition* (pp. 185–210). Washington: APA Press.

Reyna, V. F., & Mills, B.A. (2014). Theoretically motivated interventions for reducing sexual risk taking in adolescence: A randomized controlled experiment applying fuzzy-trace theory. *Journal of experimental psychology: general*, 143(4), 1627. doi:10.1037/a0036717.

Reyna, V. F., Nelson, W., Han, P., & Dieckmann, N. F. (2009). How numeracy influences risk comprehension and medical decision making. *Psychological Bulletin*, 135, 943–973. doi:10.1037/a0017327

Reyna, V. F., Wilhelms, E. A., McCormick, M. J., & Weldon, R. B. (2015). Development of risky decision making: Fuzzy-trace theory and neurobiological perspectives. *Child Development Perspectives*, 9(2), 122–127. doi:10.1111/cdep.12117

Sloman, S. A. (2002). Two systems of reasoning. In T. Gilovich, D. Griffin, & D. Kahneman (Eds.), *Heuristics and biases: The psychology of intuitive judgment* (pp. 379–396). New York: Cambridge University Press.

Stanovich, K. E., & West, R. F. (2008). On the relative independence of thinking biases and cognitive ability. *Journal of Personality and Social Psychology*, 94(4), 672–695. doi:10.1037/0022-3514.94.4.672

Stanovich, K. E., West, R. F., & Toplak, M. E. (2011). The complexity of developmental predictions from dual process models. *Developmental Review*, 31(2), 103–118. doi: 10.1016/j.dr.2011.07.003.

Steinberg, L. (2008). A social neuroscience perspective on adolescent risk taking. *Developmental Review*, 28(1), 78–106. doi:10.1111/j.1467-8721.2007.00475.x.

Sternberg, R. J., & Davidson, J. E. (Eds.). (1995). *The nature of insight*. Cambridge, MA: Bradford/MIT Press.

Thompson, C. A., & Siegler, R. S. (2010). Linear numerical-magnitude representations aid children's memory for numbers. *Psychological Science*, 21(9), 1274–1281. doi:10.1177/0956797610378309

Toplak, M. E., West, R. F., & Stanovich, K. E. (2014). Rational thinking and cognitive sophistication: Development, cognitive abilities, and thinking dispositions. *Developmental Psychology*, 50(4), 1037–1048. doi:10.1037/a0034910

Tversky, A., & Kahneman, D. (1983). Extensional versus intuitive reasoning: The conjunction fallacy in probability judgment. *Psychological Review, 90*, 293–315.

Tversky, A., & Kahneman, D. (1986). Rational choice and the framing of decisions. *Journal of business, 4*(2), S251–S278.

Weldon, R. B., Corbin, J. C., & Reyna, V. F. (2013). Gist processing in judgment and decision making: Developmental reversals predicted by fuzzy-trace theory. In H. Markovits (Ed.), *The developmental psychology of reasoning and decision-making* (pp. 36–62). New York: Psychology Press.

Weller, J. A., Levin, I. P., & Denburg, N. L. (2011). Trajectory of risky decision making for potential gains and losses from ages 5 to 85. *Journal of Behavioral Decision Making, 24*, 331–344. doi:10.1002/bdm.690

Wertheimer, M. (1982). *Productive thinking* (Enlarged ed., Phoenix ed.). Chicago: University of Chicago Press.

Wolfe, C. R., & Reyna, V. F. (2010). Semantic coherence and fallacies in estimating joint probabilities. *Journal of Behavioral Decision Making, 23*(2), 203–223. doi:10.1002/bdm.650

Wolfe, C. R., Reyna, V. F., Widmer, C. L., Cedillos, E. M., Fisher, C. R., Brust-Renck, P. G., & Weil, A. M. (2015). Efficacy of a web-based intelligent tutoring system for communicating genetic risk of breast cancer: A fuzzy-trace theory approach. *Medical Decision Making, 35*, 46–59. doi:10.1177/0272989X14535983

7
CONFLICT AND DUAL PROCESS THEORY
The case of belief bias

Linden J. Ball, Valerie A. Thompson and Edward J. N. Stupple

Introduction

Our prior beliefs influence our reasoning in profound ways, as confirmed by nearly a century's worth of scientific research on the phenomenon of *belief bias* (see Wilkins, 1929, for pioneering work). Belief bias refers to the reliable finding that people judge believable conclusions to presented arguments as more acceptable than unbelievable conclusions, regardless of their logical validity (Evans, Barston, & Pollard, 1983). This belief-bias effect occurs irrespective of the strength of presented arguments (Stanovich & West, 1997) and regardless of whether tasks involve formal or informal reasoning (Thompson & Evans, 2012).

Despite extensive research, there is still no consensus as to how best to explain belief bias. Indeed, recent research has, if anything, complicated the explanatory puzzle, with new methodologies (e.g., rapid-response paradigms) giving rise to unexpected results that often fail to align readily with long-standing theories (cf. Ball & Thompson, in press). These established theories of belief bias almost universally advance *dual process* explanations (Evans, in press; Evans & Stanovich, 2013a, 2013b), which hinge on the interplay between two qualitatively different types of reasoning processes, whose precise nature is the central concern of the present volume. The fact that recent findings provide important challenges to traditional dual process conceptualisation of belief bias means that it is timely to reflect on the current status of such accounts whilst also considering the potential directions for theoretical developments in this important area of reasoning research.

To provide a backdrop for our discussion of dual process theories of belief bias, we begin this chapter with a *task analysis* of the standard paradigm employed in most reported research. As this task analysis will show, a central feature of this paradigm is the use of reasoning problems whose conclusions involve either the presence or absence of a *conflict* between the conclusion's logical status and its belief status. Of course, the logic/belief conflict built into particular problems is intentional and key to the researcher's construction of effective materials in which conclusion validity and conclusion believability are systematically permuted across items. However, whether this logic/belief conflict has psychological consequences is an empirical matter lying at the heart of nearly all belief-bias studies.

In this chapter, we discuss what empirical evidence has revealed about belief-bias effects and the implications of this evidence for a dual process view of belief bias. Throughout our review it will become readily apparent that there are a range of seemingly contradictory findings, especially when considering foundational studies of belief bias in the light of contemporary data. A recent attempt to reconcile such contradictory findings has been proposed by Ball and Thompson (in press), and in the penultimate section of this chapter we will rehearse the core tenets of their attempted rapprochement, which retains a key role for the interaction between dual-reasoning processes in the explanation of a wide variety of belief-bias effects.

Task analysis of the standard belief-bias paradigm

Belief bias has most commonly been studied using *categorical syllogisms* (see Table 7.1 for examples). These are deductive arguments involving two premises and a conclusion, each of which contains a standard logical quantifier (*all, no, some* or *some . . . are not*). From a logical standpoint, a *valid* conclusion describes the relationship between the premise terms in a way that is necessarily true. A conclusion that is consistent with the premises but that is not necessitated by them is *invalid*.

TABLE 7.1 Examples of the four permutations of belief-oriented syllogisms that arise from the systematic crossing of a conclusion's logical status with its believability status (items adapted from De Neys & Franssens, 2009). Logic/belief conflict problems are depicted in italic font, whereas no-conflict items are in standard font.

	Logical Status	
Believability Status	**Valid**	**Invalid**
Believable	Valid – Believable	Invalid – Believable
	All birds have wings	*All flowers need water*
	All crows are birds	*All roses need water*
	Therefore, all crows have wings	*Therefore, all roses are flowers*
Unbelievable	*Valid – Unbelievable*	Invalid – Unbelievable
	All mammals can walk	All meat products can be eaten
	All whales are mammals	All apples can be eaten
	Therefore, all whales can walk	Therefore, all apples are meat products

In belief-bias studies involving categorical syllogisms participants are typically asked to evaluate the validity of given conclusions whose validity and believability have been systematically manipulated across items. As Table 7.1 shows, the crossing of conclusion validity and conclusion believability produces two kinds of problems. First, there are *conflict* items (italic font) where conclusion validity and believability are in opposition (i.e., problems with valid–unbelievable conclusions and invalid–believable conclusions). Second, there are *no-conflict* items (standard font), where conclusion validity and believability are congruent (i.e., valid–believable conclusions and invalid–unbelievable conclusions).

The systematic way in which items are constructed in the belief-bias paradigm can tell us much about the factors that influence people's reasoning. If, for example, people's responses are primarily driven by prior beliefs, then believable conclusions will generally be accepted and unbelievable conclusions will generally be rejected, irrespective of their logical status. On the other hand, if people's responses are primarily determined by logical considerations, then valid conclusions will generally be accepted and invalid conclusions will generally be rejected, irrespective of their belief status. Such a pattern of findings, however, would need to be interpreted cautiously because it could be that people are responding to structural features of problems that are merely *correlated* with their logical properties, but without engaging in any formal reasoning process of determining whether conclusions are necessary given the premises (Klauer & Singmann, 2013).

Both of these aforementioned response patterns (i.e., logic-based responding versus belief-based responding) would indicate either that people lack any sensitivity to logic/belief conflict or, alternatively, that their sensitivity does not influence their ability to implement a belief-based or logic-based reasoning strategy. Any other systematic and reliable pattern of responding centred on conflict items would, we contend, suggest that participants are sensitive to the conflict. Again, a task analysis can reveal why this is so. Take, for example, the conflict items with valid–unbelievable conclusions. If people respond to items with valid–unbelievable conclusions purely on the basis of beliefs, then these conclusions should have similarly high rejection rates to items with invalid–unbelievable conclusions because both problem types have conclusions that run counter to beliefs. If, however, conflict items with valid–unbelievable conclusions show a consistently reduced rejection rate compared to items with invalid–unbelievable conclusions, then people are presumably being swayed by the validity of these former conclusions despite the fact that they run counter to beliefs. In other words, people would be demonstrating sensitivity to the logic/belief conflict inherent in these items. A similar analysis can be applied to invalid–believable conclusions relative to valid–believable ones, with similar consequences.

In sum, the way in which reasoners respond to conflict items relative to no-conflict items in a belief-bias paradigm can tell us much about people's sensitivity to the conflict between the logic and belief status of the conclusions to these items. Of course, if such sensitivity is apparent, then the challenge is to explain its psychological basis (cf. Evans, 2007).

Are people sensitive to logic/belief conflict?

What does the empirical evidence reveal in relation to the pattern of endorsement rates for belief-oriented syllogisms? From Evans et al.'s (1983) classic study of belief bias onward, evidence has consistently indicated that people show a high degree of sensitivity to logic/belief conflict when responding to both types of conflict syllogisms (i.e., items with valid–unbelievable conclusions and with invalid–believable conclusions). Table 7.2 shows representative data from Evans et al. (1983). Looking at the no-conflict items first, we can see that people are strongly inclined to endorse valid–believable conclusions (89% acceptance rate) and are strongly inclined to reject invalid–unbelievable conclusions (10% acceptance rate). This endorsement/rejection rate also appears to be *symmetrical* for these two types of no-conflict items (i.e., similarly high endorsement and rejection, respectively). For conflict items, however, it is evident that people are influenced by both logic and belief, because endorsement rates to the presented conclusions are close to neither ceiling nor floor levels. People endorse valid–unbelievable conclusions at a rate of 56% despite these conclusions being unbelievable, which is much higher than the rate with which their invalid counterparts are endorsed. This indicates a marked influence of logic. Likewise, people endorse invalid–believable conclusions at a rate of 71%, which is lower than their valid counterparts, again showing some influence of logic despite these conclusions being believable. Interestingly, the effect of logic on the two types of conflict problems seems *asymmetrical* in that the influence of logic is stronger on valid–unbelievable items compared to invalid–believable items.

This description is consistent with the modal statistical pattern of main and interactive effects of the manipulated variables (logic and belief), with analyses typically revealing three statistically significant findings. First, believable conclusions are more readily endorsed than unbelievable ones, which is the standard belief-bias effect indicating that people have a susceptibility to being unduly influenced by beliefs. Second, valid conclusions are more readily endorsed than invalid ones, indicating that as well as being biased by beliefs participants simultaneously show some logical ability. Third, there is an interaction between logic and belief such that the effect of logic is stronger for unbelievable conclusions than for believable

TABLE 7.2 Percentage of conclusions accepted as a function of their logical status and their believability status, aggregated across three experiments reported by Evans et al. (1983).

	Logical Status		
Believability Status	Valid	Invalid	Mean
Believable	89	71	80
Unbelievable	56	10	33
Mean	72	40	

These data are taken from Evans, Newstead, and Byrne (1993).

conclusions. This interaction effect again points to the asymmetrical sensitivity that people have to logic/belief conflict dependent on whether they are responding to unbelievable conclusions (associated with a stronger logic effect) or believable conclusions (associated with a weaker logic effect).

Numerous studies since Evans et al.'s (1983) pioneering research have corroborated the reliability of these three effects, and in an effort to explain them a variety of theories have been mooted and investigated. As noted earlier, these theories are typically couched in dual process terms, where the operation of two qualitatively different types of processing is central. According to Evans and Stanovich (2013a, 2013b), *Type 1* processes have two defining features: they are undemanding of working memory resources and they are autonomous, running to completion whenever a relevant cue triggers them. They also tend to be fast, high capacity, non-conscious and capable of running in parallel, but these are merely examples of correlated features rather than defining features. In contrast, Type 2 processes are defined in terms of requiring working resources and being focused on cognitive decoupling and mental simulation, which are critical for hypothetical thinking. Type 2 processes also tend to be slow, capacity limited, conscious and serial, but again, these are correlated features rather than defining features.

Since the 1980s these dual process notions have been drawn upon in a variety of ways to provide theoretical accounts of belief-bias effects. One especially dominant theoretical approach in this area has been to emphasise the *sequential* progression from relatively fast, autonomous Type 1 processes to relatively slow, working memory–demanding Type 2 processes. In the next section we review a key model of belief bias that has adopted these sequential-processing assumptions. We then overview the key strengths of this theory before progressing to a consideration of some of the possible limitations of this account in terms of its capacity to accommodate both historical and more recent challenges.

Logic/belief conflict and sequential dual processes: the selective processing model

Arguably the most well-formulated and compelling sequential, dual process theory of belief-bias effects is the *selective processing model*, which was originally proposed by Evans (2000; see also Evans, Handley, & Harper, 2001; Morley, Evans, & Handley, 2004), with similar ideas being mooted independently by Klauer, Musch, and Naumer (2000). According to this model, when people are asked to evaluate belief-laden conclusions to presented syllogisms, they tend to default to a Type 1 response bias and accept believable conclusions and reject unbelievable conclusions. This default predisposition explains why belief bias arises with both valid and invalid inferences, thereby accounting for the main effect of belief evident in conclusion-endorsement data. In addition, the model proposes that at least some of the time a Type 2 process occurs that involves motivated, analytic reasoning, with this process being driven by a conclusion's believability or unbelievability. Based on the following assumptions, this Type 2 intervention in the face of initial, default evaluations can explain the sensitivity that people demonstrate to logic/belief conflict:

> *First, if people engage in motivated Type 2 reasoning, then they attempt to construct a single integrated representation or "mental model" of the presented premise information.*
>
> *Second, this mental-model construction process is biased by the believability of the presented conclusion, such that: (i) for a believable conclusion an attempt is made to construct a single model that supports the conclusion; whereas (ii) for an unbelievable conclusion an attempt is made to construct a single model that refutes the conclusion.*

In addition to explaining the main effects of logic and belief, these assumptions provide a clear rationale for the emergence of the commonly observed logic-by-belief interaction, where logic has a greater impact when conclusions are unbelievable than when they are believable. This explanation rests on the asymmetry in the probability of finding confirming and disconfirming models. For unbelievable conclusions, a motivated search for a single counterexample model will reveal such a model when the conclusion is invalid, but will fail to reveal such a model when the conclusion is valid. Thus, there is the potential for a strong influence of logic on unbelievable conclusions in line with the belief-bias data in Table 7.2. When, however, conclusions are believable, then a motivated search for a single supporting model will typically reveal such a model *both when the conclusion is valid and when it is invalid*, leading to a high rate of acceptance for invalid–believable conclusions. This would thereby weaken any effect of logic for believable conclusions – again entirely in line with the data depicted in Table 7.2.

Key strengths of the selective processing model of belief bias

There is much to recommend Evans et al.'s (2001) selective processing model of belief bias and its underpinning *default–interventionist* concepts. As we have explained, the assumption that belief biases arise from two distinct processes can account for the logic-by-belief interaction in conclusion endorsement rates, which results from a differential sensitivity to logic/belief conflict with valid–unbelievable items relative to invalid–believable ones. Moreover, the selective processing model has gained support when its assumptions have been tested experimentally. For example, because the Type 1 response bias is assumed to precede Type 2 motivated-reasoning, the overarching belief-bias effect should increase if people have to make rapid conclusion evaluations. Using a speeded-response paradigm, Evans and Curtis-Holmes (2005) demonstrated this predicted increase in belief bias. Their study also revealed the disappearance of the logic-by-belief interaction, which is also explicable according to the model because participants would have had insufficient time to engage in motivated reasoning (see also Shynkaruk & Thompson, 2006; Thompson & Johnson, 2014).

The explanatory strength of the selective processing model is also borne out by its capacity to account for data deriving from studies using dual-task methodologies, which require people to evaluate belief-oriented syllogisms under a working memory (WM) load such as memorising information unrelated to the reasoning task that subsequently needs to be recalled. Because Type 2 processing is assumed to be WM dependent, any evidence of impaired reasoning under a WM load would suggest that Type 2 processing is involved in the reasoning task. De Neys (2006) reported a study using this paradigm in which participants who varied in their individual WM capacities tackled belief-oriented syllogisms under a secondary WM load. The results supported the selective processing model in that the WM load reduced reasoning success for logic/belief conflict items, but did not disrupt reasoning success for the no-conflict items where the conclusion's belief status was sufficient to engender a correct response. In addition, although participants with higher WM capacities performed better on logic/belief conflict items than participants with lower WM capacities, all reasoners were similarly susceptible to the disruptive effects of WM load on reasoning.

Other research examining individual differences in reasoning (Stanovich, 1999; Stanovich & West, 2008; Toplak, West, & Stanovich, 2011) has likewise supported the selective processing model. In particular, Stanovich and colleagues have amassed substantial evidence for two important individual-difference variables in the susceptibility to belief bias that are consistent with selective-processing assumptions. These two variables are general intelligence and the disposition to engage in analytic thinking. In relation to the first variable, individuals with higher general intelligence perform better on logic/belief conflict items than do individuals with lower general intelligence. This concurs with the selective-processing assumption that WM capacity is needed for Type 2 motivated reasoning to intervene to overturn Type 1 default responses, given that there is considerable evidence for the view that general intelligence is highly correlated with WM capacity (e.g., Conway, Kane, & Engle, 2003). In relation to the second variable, people who are more disposed to engage in Type 2 thinking also do better on logic/belief conflict problems than those who are less disposed to engage in Type 2 thinking, a finding that again aligns with the selective-processing perspective because it is only by having a disposition to deploy Type 2 processing that there is an opportunity to overturn default beliefs for logic/belief conflict items. This opportunity, of course, will depend on the availability of sufficient WM capacity and an effective reasoning process – or what Stanovich (2012; see also Stanovich, West, & Toplak, 2016) poignantly refers to as "mindware."

These latter considerations relating to the availability of sufficient working memory capacity and mindware to enable reasoners to profit from increased Type 2 engagement go a long way toward explaining why observed correlations between analytic thinking dispositions and reasoning success are rather modest. That is, there will be occasions when Type 2 thinking *is* engaged but where it still results in an incorrect answer (Evans, 2007; Evans & Stanovich, 2013a, 2013b; Stanovich, 2012). Indeed, the selective processing model predicts that this situation will arise for many reasoners when they are tackling invalid–believable conflict items, where the motivated search for a single model to support the believable conclusion will typically produce an affirmative result, leading to an erroneous conclusion endorsement. In effect, what we have here is an example of a *mindware gap* (Stanovich et al., 2016), inasmuch as reasoners are using conclusion believability as a directional steer to guide a biased reasoning strategy, with attendant negative consequences for reasoning accuracy.

It is important to mention a further important issue in relation to Type 2 processes, which is that although they may be engaged, reasoners may still apply them defectively with the aim of merely *justifying* or *rationalising* initial, default conclusions delivered by Type 1 processes (see Evans, in press). Thompson and colleagues (Shynkaruk & Thompson, 2006; Thompson, Turner, & Pennycook, 2011) have provided evidence for this view using a *two-response paradigm*, where reasoners are instructed to provide *two* responses: an initial, fast, intuitive response often under extreme time pressure, followed by a second, slower, considered response with no time constraint. In some reasoning tasks there is a slight increase in correct responding between the initial and the second response, but most of the time the second answer is the same as the first, despite an extensive re-thinking period. What this suggests is that this additional time is merely being used by reasoners to engage in Type 2 rationalisation of default, Type 1 evaluations.

We finally note that neuroimaging research has also provided evidence that is broadly consistent with the selective processing account, again affirming the model's strength. For example, brain-imaging studies have shown that logic/belief conflict is detected by the brain and is associated with increased activation within the anterior cingulate cortex. Other brain-imaging studies support the existence of a distinction between the underpinning brain regions associated with belief-based responses versus reasoning-based responses (De Neys, Vartanian, & Goel, 2008; Goel & Dolan, 2003; Houdé et al., 2000; Prado & Noveck, 2007; Tsujii & Watanabee, 2009). For example, the override of belief-based responding appears to be associated with activation within areas of the *right prefrontal cortex* that are typically associated with executive control, including the inhibition of salient but erroneous responses. Of interest, too, is evidence from De Neys and Franssens (2009) showing that belief bias appears to arise from participants' failure to *complete* the inhibition process rather than from a failure to recognise the need to inhibit inappropriate beliefs in the first place. This evidence is fascinating because it points to the conclusion that most people are sensitive to logic/belief conflict and strive to inhibit the influence of their beliefs, albeit often unsuccessfully (see also Banks & Hope, 2014; De Neys, 2012, 2014; Luo et al., 2013; Luo, Tang, Zhang, & Stupple, 2014).

In sum, there is a wealth of evidence deriving from a range of methodologies to support the key dual process concepts and default–interventionist assumptions of Evans et al.'s (2001) selective processing model of belief bias. In particular, there are good grounds for the view that belief-based responses reflect the operation of Type 1 processes that form default answers and that the likelihood of Type 2 reasoning being successfully engaged to overturn a belief-based answer varies according to a reasoner's cognitive capacity and cognitive motivation. However, despite the explanatory success of the selective processing model, evidence has arisen over the years that seems problematic for the account. In the next section, we examine key historical challenges to the model and the way in which it has accommodated or rebuffed these.

Historical challenges to the selective processing model of belief bias

When the selective processing model of belief bias first appeared in the literature, its primary focus was on providing a coherent explanation not only of typical conclusion-endorsement evidence but also of other important findings relating to people's processing of syllogistic arguments. Of particular relevance were data indicating that reasoners had a dominant tendency to base their conclusion-evaluation decisions on the construction of *single* mental models (Evans, Handley, Harper, & Johnson-Laird, 1999; Newstead, Handley, & Buck, 1999) as opposed to searching for potential counterexample models as assumed by the then-dominant mental models theory of deduction (e.g., Johnson-Laird & Byrne, 1991). Soon after being proposed, however, the selective processing model appeared to run into conceptual difficulties of its own, which arose from evidence garnered from time-based measures of reasoning. Such measures included people's latencies to register conclusion endorsement/rejection decisions as well as eye-tracking and mouse-tracking data obtained from monitoring reasoners' moment-by-moment direction of attention during their inspection of premises and conclusions.

In one key study, Thompson, Striemer, Reikoff, Gunter, and Campbell (2003) showed that response latencies are significantly longer when people respond to believable conclusions compared to unbelievable conclusions. This finding has since been replicated in studies using eye-tracking and mouse-tracking methodologies (Ball, Phillips, Wade, & Quayle, 2006; Stupple & Ball, 2008; see also Ball, 2013; Thompson, Morley, & Newstead, 2011a). The selective processing model, however, would seem to predict that both believable and unbelievable conclusions should be subjected to similar processing effort because participants should be equally likely to engage in the motivated search for a single model of the premises when confronted with either believable or unbelievable conclusions (albeit a confirming model for the former and a disconfirming model for the latter). Indeed, if anything, one might expect the search for a confirming model to be easier (and therefore quicker) than the search for a disconfirming model, meaning that believable conclusions should be processed more quickly than their unbelievable counterparts.

Chronometric studies have also produced evidence for a logic-by-belief interaction in participants' response-time data (Thompson et al., 2003) that is difficult to account for in the selective processing framework. For example, Ball et al. (2006) found that invalid–believable conflict items take significantly longer to process than no-conflict items, with there being a similar – albeit weaker – increase in processing times for valid–unbelievable conflict items relative to no-conflict items. To reconcile these findings with the selective processing model, Stupple, Ball, Evans, and

Kamal-Smith (2011) speculated that the long average processing times for invalid–believable items might arise because extended processing for a subset of reasoners swamps the data, markedly shifting the mean latency value upward. They further suggested that this subset of reasoners might be those of very high ability, who potentially possess the disposition, cognitive capacity and analytic mindware to evaluate these conclusions correctly, but whose reasoning necessitates time-consuming analytic processing.

Stupple et al. (2011) ran an inspection-time study that provided clear evidence to support these latter proposals, thereby successfully reconciling the selective processing model with apparently anomalous chronometric findings (see also Thompson et al., 2011a, for similar findings). In their study, Stupple et al. identified three distinct subsets of reasoners. First, they isolated a *low-logic* group, who showed high levels of belief bias and very rapid response times, seemingly indicative of the predominant operation of a Type 1 response bias. Second, they identified a *medium-logic* group, who showed moderate belief bias and slower response times, with the data being broadly consistent with an effort at motivated reasoning that was selectively biased by conclusion believability. Third, they determined that there was also a *high-logic* group, who showed low belief bias but increased processing times, especially for invalid–believable items. Stupple et al.'s (2011) results indicate that people of varying logical ability have different endorsement-rate and response-time profiles, with arguably the profile for the medium-ability group aligning most closely with the assumptions of the selective processing model. A further noteworthy aspect of Stupple et al.'s (2011) study was their finding that although the response-time difference for conflict versus no-conflict problems was particularly striking for high-ability reasoners, it was nevertheless still reliably present – albeit greatly diminished – for low-ability reasoners. This observation indicates that even for low-logic individuals who make their decisions primarily on the basis of a Type 1 response bias, there is evidence for them having some residual sensitivity to logic/belief conflict. We explore this important issue in the next section.

Moving on from chronometric data, another significant challenge to the credibility of the selective processing model arose from Dube, Rotello, and Heit's (2010) research that criticised the need to posit a Type 2 motivated-reasoning component to explain belief bias in addition to a more basic Type 1 response bias. Dube et al. argued that the characteristics of conclusion-endorsement data in the belief-bias paradigm necessitate conducting analyses using the methods of Signal Detection Theory (SDT; Macmillan & Creelman, 2005). Crucially, they claimed that when an SDT analysis is applied to the data, it reveals that *all* belief-bias effects, including the apparent logic-by-belief interaction, can be explained in terms of a *pure* response bias such that there is no need to postulate the existence of Type 2 motivated reasoning.

Although at first sight Dube et al.'s (2010) evidence seems devastating for the selective processing model, it turns out that their conclusion depends on debatable assumptions that can be disputed both empirically and conceptually (Klauer & Kellen, 2011; Trippas, Handley, & Verde, 2013; Trippas, Handley, &

Verde, 2014a). Moreover, recent studies that using SDT to analyse belief-bias data clearly reveal the existence of both a response-bias component *and* a motivated-reasoning component to belief bias, with logical accuracy being higher for unbelievable conclusions than for believable conclusions – as per selective-processing predictions. It does, seem, however, that certain conditions need to prevail for the motivated-reasoning component to emerge. In particular, it appears to arise for people of higher ability or who possess a more analytic cognitive style (Trippas et al., 2013). These observations also align with other findings (Stupple et al., 2011; Thompson et al., 2011a) that associate the motivated reasoning effect with reasoning ability.

Recent experiments reported by Trippas, Verde, and Handley (2014b) provide further evidence to support these conclusions. Trippas et al. used a two-alternative, forced-choice procedure in which participants were presented simultaneously with *two* syllogisms and were asked to choose which of the two associated conclusions was valid. Importantly, in some trials the believability of the two presented conclusions was equated (i.e., the two given conclusions were either both believable or were both unbelievable). This procedure ensured that the Type 1 response-bias component of belief bias could be entirely removed from a participant's decision-making process, thereby enabling any effects arising from Type 2 motivated reasoning to be isolated. More specifically, any Type 2 reasoning should reveal itself in the standard fashion as increased accuracy in the unbelievable-conclusion condition relative to the believable-conclusion condition.

In their first experiment Trippas et al. (2014b) found no effect of conclusion believability, which runs counter to the idea of a Type 2 motivated-reasoning component to belief bias. In subsequent experiments, however, they introduced procedural changes to create more standardised task formats, and they also took into account participants' cognitive ability and propensity to engage in motivated reasoning. Evidence from these follow-on experiments revealed that the more cognitively able and more analytic reasoners demonstrated the predicted motivated-reasoning effect, performing better with unbelievable than believable conclusions, whereas the less cognitively able and less analytic reasoners showed patterns consistent with a relatively pure response bias. We note that these findings also align with aspects of Stupple et al.'s (2011) data summarised earlier, which revealed that reasoners' endorsement-rate patterns and response-time profiles are mediated by individual differences in logical ability. Current research (Trippas, Pennycook, Verde, & Handley, 2015) suggests that analytic thinking dispositions may be the more critical predictor of Type 2 motivated reasoning than cognitive ability.

The data described thus far are consistent with the selective processing model. That said, we need to point out an apparent contradiction for the model that was identified by Ball and Thompson (in press). This concerns the discrepancy between the response-time findings reported by Stupple et al. (2011), which indicate that high-ability reasoners take longer on invalid–believable problems than on any other problem types, and the endorsement-rate findings of Trippas et al. (2014b), which indicate that such high-ability reasoners perform *more poorly* on believable than unbelievable problems. Ball and Thompson (in press) argued that these data suggest that achieving correct answers for invalid–believable conflict problems is both more difficult *and* more time consuming than getting the correct answers for valid–unbelievable conflict problems. Ball and Thompson (in press) also argued that these data may be reconciled within the selective processing framework. First, they note that to identify the correct answer to an invalid–believable conflict problem will require the reasoner to search for and discover an alternative model of the premises that is inconsistent with the given conclusion, which will presumably be both time consuming and error prone, even for high-ability reasoners. Second, they suggest that to find the correct answer for a valid–unbelievable conflict problem, the reasoner does not need to find an alternative representation of the premises, because any model of the premises (including the first one) will be consistent with the conclusion and thus be grounds to accept it. This process may be less time consuming and less error prone.

Ball and Thompson (in press) state that an important consequence of these speculative proposals is that "the signature that we have interpreted as motivated reasoning (better performance on unbelievable than believable problems) may be, instead, simply a difference in the type of reasoning required to achieve correct performance on the two types of problems." These issues certainly emphasise the need for further investigation using data analysis approaches that focus on individual differences in reasoning. In this respect Trippas (personal communication) may be correct to suggest that the likely way forward will require the *joint* modeling of response-time and choice data using sequential sampling approaches such as the diffusion model (e.g., Ratcliff, Smith, & McKoon, 2015).

To summarise, in this section we have reviewed some of the historical challenges that have been lodged against the dual process assumptions of the selective processing model, which claims that belief-bias effects arise from both Type 1 response bias and Type 2 motivated reasoning. We have shown that the model has generally accommodated what appeared to be problematic findings, although this has admittedly often been at the expense of having to add auxiliary assumptions to the model, especially in relation to the issue of individual differences in reasoning. To be fair, however, the model as initially proposed was geared toward accounting for aggregate data rather that the subtleties of individual variation in reasoning, and it appears to be a strength of the model that it has been able to be augmented in ways that make sense of individual variation in response-rate and response-time profiles. We have also shown how important methodological challenges – this time relating to the appropriate way to analyse belief-bias data – have largely given rise to findings that can be reconciled with the selective processing model and its prediction that belief-bias arises from both a response bias and from motivated reasoning. In the next section we examine more recent findings that appear to challenge the model in unexpected ways. We also assess whether it might be possible to retain the selective processing model, or at least some of its core dual process concepts, in light of these latest challenges.

Contemporary challenges to the selective processing model of belief bias

According to the selective processing model, when conclusion-endorsement rates reveal sensitivity to logic/belief conflict, this is a result of Type 2 motivated-reasoning overturning a Type 1 belief-based response. Such conflict sensitivity would be expected to emerge slowly because Type 2 processing is correlated with time-consuming sequential thinking (Evans & Stanovich, 2013a, 2013b). We have, however, already alluded to data from Stupple et al.'s (2011) study that run counter to the *slow* emergence of logic/belief conflict. Stupple et al. isolated a low-logic group showing marked belief bias and rapid response times indicative of Type 1 responding. This same low-logic group, however, still showed a reliable response-time difference for logic/belief conflict problems versus no-conflict problems, which is curious given the rapidity of these individuals' responses. In other words, these individuals were responding non-logically to conflict items, yet still seemed to show sensitivity to their validity or invalidity.

How might we account for this apparently *automatic* detection of logic/belief conflict at a Type 1 level? To address this question, De Neys (2012, 2014) has advanced a model in which sensitivity to logic/belief conflict is *entirely* Type 1 and intuitive in nature, being based on implicit and automatically activated knowledge rather than knowledge elicited and applied through motivated Type 2 reasoning. What De Neys proposes is that people are 'intuitive logicians', whose gut feelings to reasoning problems cue some awareness of their logical solutions (see also Morsanyi & Handley, 2012, for pioneering evidence of people's intuitive detection of logicality). One upshot of this logical intuitions model is that it provides a mechanism whereby conflict detection can trigger Type 2 reasoning in an attempt to resolve intuitively detected logic/belief conflict. This would readily explain how logic/belief sensitivity manifests in people's confidence ratings (De Neys, Cromheeke, & Osman, 2011; Thompson et al., 2011) and in electrodermal measures of autonomic activation (De Neys, Moyens, & Vansteenwegen, 2010; Morsanyi & Handley, 2012). In addition, the triggering of Type 2 processing based on intuitively detected logic/belief conflict would engender increased processing times for conflict items, as established in the literature reviewed earlier.

In essence, De Neys is proposing a dual process model of belief bias incorporating default-interventionist principles, albeit a model whereby much initial work is conducted by rapid, Type 1 processes that identify logic/belief conflict and trigger downstream Type 2 processing. The effectiveness of the latter will depend on individual variation in cognitive ability and reasoning dispositions, so the model can align with evidence for a motivated-reasoning component to belief-bias effects and evidence that high-ability reasoners can sometimes resolve logic/belief conflicts in favour of logical responses. There is, therefore, some potential for the logical intuitions model to be reconciled with the selective processing model, with the latter providing the Type 2 motivated-reasoning mechanism needed to explain what happens when logic/belief conflict is detected by Type 1 processes.

Key aspects of De Neys' logical intuitions model are also supported by recent research on *meta-reasoning* (e.g., Ackerman & Thompson, 2017, in press). Studies of meta-reasoning are concerned with the mechanisms that *regulate* reasoning by setting goals, determining how much effort to apply, deciding among strategies, monitoring ongoing progress and terminating activity (see Quayle & Ball, 2000, for early ideas regarding the role of such mechanisms in the emergence of belief-bias effects). Meta-reasoning research often assumes that people base their regulation decisions on their sense of ease or difficulty with a problem, including the *fluency* with which an initial solution comes to mind (Ackerman & Zalmanov, 2012). Indeed, answer fluency is a factor that Thompson and colleagues (e.g., Thompson et al., 2011; Thompson et al., 2013) have suggested is especially important in mediating a judgement that they term 'Feeling of Rightness' (FoR). This FoR seems to act as a *metacognitive trigger*, terminating processing when a Type 1 process has produced a rapid, intuitive answer that is attributed to be correct, or else switching processing to a Type 2 mode when the initial, intuitive answer is associated with a low FoR and is therefore felt likely to be incorrect. As such, there are important theoretical links between the Type 1 to Type 2 switching role played by FoR judgments in the Ackerman–Thompson meta-reasoning framework and De Neys' claims that there is a 'switch' mechanism that initiates Type 2 processing when logic/belief conflict is detected intuitively. Thompson and Morsanyi (2012) have also suggested that the switch decision might be affective in nature, which aligns with autonomic-arousal findings in belief-bias studies (e.g., De Neys et al., 2010).

To summarise the evidence discussed in this section so far, the role of selective processing in belief bias – at least as conventionally conceived – is challenged by findings suggesting that logic/belief conflict can be detected rapidly and intuitively purely on the basis of Type 1 processes. Such Type 1 conflict detection may cue a low FoR, with this metacognitive judgment triggering Type 2, motivated reasoning that might resolve the conflict in favour of logic or belief (e.g., through rationalisation). It is also possible that the Type 2 processing runs according to the motivated-reasoning process captured in the selective processing model, which would provide some degree of reconciliation between the selective processing model and the logical intuitions model.

The concept of Type 1 logical intuitions is clearly a radical departure from conventional notions of people's logical understanding, which is assumed to take time to achieve via analytic reasoning processes. Under this conventional view, a belief-based response should always be completed *before* a Type 2 response has even been initiated. One upshot of this default-interventionist view is that a Type 2 logic-based response should be unable to *interfere* with a Type 1 belief-based response (Newman, Gibb, & Thompson, 2017). This prediction has been tested in studies employing the novel methodology whereby reasoners are instructed to respond to problems on the basis of the *believability* of presented conclusions rather than their logical validity. When evaluating conclusions in this way, it has been found that participants are slower at making belief-based responses when a conclusion conflicts with a problem's logical validity than when it does not (Handley, Newstead, & Trippas, 2011; Handley & Trippas, 2015; Howarth, Handley, & Walsh, 2016). This finding again points directly to the existence of Type 1 logical intuitions.

Two important criticisms of this line of research have recently been articulated by Newman et al. (2017). First, they argued that the evidence for logical intuitions seems typically to arise in studies using very simple reasoning tasks such that any logical processing would be expected to be straightforward (cf. Evans, in press). Second, they point out that because people are not put under time pressure in studies demonstrating apparent logical intuitions, this allows for the possibility that the logic/belief conflict observed when using belief-based instructions arises slowly, with both the belief-based and logic-based processes being Type 2 in nature. Supporting this latter proposal is evidence that belief-based processing can indeed sometimes involve slow, Type 2 operations (e.g., De Neys, Schaeken, & d'Ydewalle, 2005; Markovits, Forgues, & Brunet, 2012; Verschueren, Schaeken, & d'Ydewalle, 2005).

Newman et al. (2017) report experiments addressing these issues by utilising complex reasoning problems and a two-response paradigm (Thompson et al., 2011b), whereby initial responses were elicited under logical-reasoning instructions with a short response-time deadline, with participants then having time to rethink their decisions. If Type 1 logical intuitions extend beyond simple inferences, then rapid, initial responses to complex problems should be sensitive to the manipulation of logical information. This prediction gained convincing support. Bago and De Neys (2017) report equivalent findings using the two-response paradigm and procedures to eradicate initial Type 2 processing, including challenging response deadlines and concurrent WM loads, although unlike in Newman et al.'s research, the reasoning problems used were relatively straightforward. Other recent research by Trippas, Thompson, and Handley (2017) lends further support to the view that fast, rule-based processes of a Type 1 variety can arise in a belief-bias paradigm even with complex reasoning problems. Trippas et al. (2017) report studies using low, moderate and high complexity problems under either belief-based or reasoning-based instructions. For the simplest problems they corroborated Handley et al.'s (2011) findings that conclusion validity interferes more with judgments of conclusion believability than the converse. For moderate-complexity problems they showed that the validity of conclusions interferes with evaluations of conclusion believability to the same extent that the believability of conclusions interfered with evaluations of conclusion validity. For complex reasoning problems, the interference pattern flipped, with conclusion believability interfering more with judgments of conclusion validity than vice versa. Trippas et al. (2017) view these findings as supporting a parallel-processing model in which multiple problem features – including belief content and logical structure – are processed *simultaneously*. In the case where both problem features can be assessed in a straightforward way, they can cause mutual interference, but in cases where either a belief-based or a logic-based response requires more complex processing, then an interference asymmetry can arise.

Conclusions

In this chapter we have examined the viability of Evans et al.'s (e.g., 2001) selective processing model of belief-bias effects in reasoning, where belief-oriented problems produce robust conclusion-endorsement findings, including main effects of belief and logic and a reliable logic-by-belief interaction. The latter finding indicates people's sensitivity to logic/belief conflict and is especially pronounced when they respond to unbelievable conclusions. The selective processing model emphasises the operation of dual processes within a default-interventionist framework, with relatively fast Type 1 processes delivering default belief-based responses and with slower Type 2 processes potentially intervening to deliver responses based on motivated reasoning. We have shown that until a few years ago the selective processing model seemed to accommodate a vast array of evidence, including sometimes challenging findings emerging from chronometric data and the application of signal detection theory analyses. In general terms the model captured the existence of both a response-bias component to belief bias (i.e., an overarching tendency to accept believable conclusions and reject unbelievable conclusions) and a secondary motivated-reasoning component to belief-bias, giving rise to stronger effects of logic for problems with unbelievable than believable conclusions.

More recently, however, methodological innovations have given rise to serious concerns regarding the sustainability of the selective processing model of belief bias. Indeed, our synoptic review of the evidence indicates a complex picture in which both logic-based and belief-based processes appear to operate *either* according to a fast Type 1 route *or* a slow Type 2 route. Ball and Thompson (in press) propose that such evidence can either be viewed as a deep challenge to the fundamental assumptions of traditional dual process accounts of belief bias, such as the selective processing model, or as the foundational components for constructing the next generation of dual process models. They adopt the latter approach and in this final, concluding section we summarise key suggestions forwarded by Ball and Thompson for how the findings outlined in the previous section might be integrated with basic dual process assumptions and default-interventionist concepts.

Ball and Thompson (in press) propose that although Type 1 and Type 2 processes may produce similar outputs, they may have different triggers and may differentially draw on WM resources. They propose that Type 1 processes produce answers autonomously in response to triggering conditions, which may relate to a problem's belief content or its structure, including features correlated with logical validity. These Type 1 processes tend to be fast, parallel and draw minimally upon WM capacity. In contrast, Type 2 processes require WM, rely on serial processing and tend to be slower. They can be triggered autonomously, as arises when a reasoner has a low FoR in their Type 1 response (Thompson et al., 2011b, 2013), or they can be initiated at the reasoner's behest (Thompson, 2013). Ball and Thomson also note that there is evidence that many, if not all, inferences rely, at least in part, on Type 1 processes. On this analysis, there will, therefore, typically be *two* Type 1 outputs generated in response to a belief-oriented problem: one based on beliefs and one based on structural features that may reflect logical validity. A corollary to this is the assumption that Type 1 processes are *default*, with Type 2 processes then being activated as needed, for example, to resolve a conflict between competing Type 1 outputs (e.g., De Neys, 2012, 2014) or in response to a low FoR regarding an initial solution (e.g., Thompson et al., 2011b, 2013). Type 2 processing may be further augmented because of a reasoner's inherent disposition to engage in actively open-minded thinking (e.g., Trippas et al., 2015).

The idea that Type 2 processing can overturn initial Type 1 output clearly concurs with the default-interventionist view that belief bias can arise from a combination of Type 1 response bias and Type 2 motivated reasoning. Also in line with default-interventionist assumptions are findings showing that initiating Type 2 processing is hampered by the absence of available time or the lack of WM resources. Data supporting the notion that Type 2 processing is WM dependent derives from Evans, Handley, Neilens and Over's (2010) study examining the role of cognitive capacity and Type 2 thinking in overcoming belief-based responding. Evans et al. asked participants to make inferences either under strict deductive instructions or under pragmatic instructions. They observed belief bias in both cases, but this disappeared for high-capacity reasoners in the strict-instructions group. In other words, the default response when reasoning pragmatically appears to be belief based, but when instructed to reason logically, this can be suppressed by those with high WM capacity. These findings strongly support the role of Type 2 thinking in overcoming beliefs.

We have also seen throughout our discussion of belief-bias findings that *problem complexity* is a factor that seems central to a full understanding of the interplay between Type 1 and Type 2 processes in generating responses, whether under belief or logic instructions (Handley et al., 2011; Howarth et al., 2016; Trippas et al., 2017). As Ball and Thompson (in press) argued, it may be that the selective processing model is best placed to capture belief-bias findings that arise with more complex reasoning problems of the type that were studied in many of the pioneering experiments up to a decade or so ago. In contrast, belief-bias effects seen with the easier problems featured in recent studies may rely more on Type 1 processes.

To conclude, we have come a long way in understanding belief bias in reasoning from the pioneering research of Wilkins nearly a century ago. Although important questions remain regarding the basis of belief-bias effects and people's inherent sensitivity to logic/belief conflict, it seems clear that dual process concepts continue to be central to understanding the complex interplay between people's basic understanding of logical principles and their inherent tendency to be influenced by the belief status of conclusions. We look forward to the emergence of new findings and theoretical insights that seem certain to extend our understanding of belief-bias effects in reasoning in the near future.

References

Ackerman, R., & Thompson, V. A. (2017). Meta-reasoning: Monitoring and control of thinking and reasoning. *Trends in Cognitive Sciences, 21,* 607–617.

Ackerman, R., & Thompson, V. A. (in press). Meta-reasoning: Shedding meta-cognitive light on reasoning research. In L. J. Ball & V. A. Thompson (Eds.), *The Routledge international handbook of thinking and reasoning.* Abingdon, UK: Routledge.

Ackerman, R., & Zalmanov, H. (2012). The persistence of the fluency – confidence association in problem solving. *Psychonomic Bulletin & Review, 19,* 1189–1192.

Bago, B., & De Neys, W. (2017). Fast logic? Examining the time course assumption of dual process theory. *Cognition, 158,* 90–109.

Ball, L. J. (2013). Eye-tracking and reasoning: What your eyes tell about your inferences. In W. De Neys & M. Osman (Eds.), *New approaches in reasoning research* (pp. 51–69). Hove, UK: Psychology Press.

Ball, L. J., & Thompson, V. A. (in press). Belief bias and reasoning. In L. J. Ball & V. A. Thompson (Eds.), *The Routledge international handbook of thinking and reasoning.* Abingdon, UK: Routledge.

Ball, L. J., Phillips, P., Wade, C. N., & Quayle, J. D. (2006). Effects of belief and logic on syllogistic reasoning: Eye-movement evidence for selective processing models. *Experimental Psychology, 53,* 77–86.

Banks, A. P., & Hope, C. (2014). Heuristic and analytic processes in reasoning: An event-related potential study of belief bias. *Psychophysiology, 51,* 290–297.

Conway, A. R., Kane, M. J., & Engle, R. W. (2003). Working memory capacity and its relation to general intelligence. *Trends in Cognitive Sciences, 7,* 547–552.

De Neys, W. (2006). Dual processing in reasoning: Two systems but one reasoner. *Psychological Science, 17,* 428–433.

De Neys, W. (2012). Bias and conflict: A case for logical intuitions. *Perspectives on Psychological Science, 7,* 28–38.

De Neys, W. (2014). Conflict detection, dual processes, and logical intuitions: Some clarifications. *Thinking & Reasoning, 20,* 169–187.

De Neys, W., Cromheeke, S., & Osman, M. (2011). Biased but in doubt: Conflict and decision confidence. *PLoS One, 6,* e15954.

De Neys, W., & Franssens, S. (2009). Belief inhibition during thinking: Not always winning but at least taking part. *Cognition, 113,* 45–61.

De Neys, W., Moyens, E., & Vansteenwegen, D. (2010). Feeling we're biased: Autonomic arousal and reasoning conflict. *Cognitive, Affective, & Behavioral Neuroscience, 10,* 208–216.

De Neys, W., Schaeken, W., & d'Ydewalle, G. (2005). Working memory and everyday conditional reasoning: Retrieval and inhibition of stored counterexamples. *Thinking & Reasoning, 11,* 349–381.

De Neys, W., Vartanian, O., & Goel, V. (2008). Smarter than we think: When our brains detect that we are biased. *Psychological Science, 19,* 483–489.

Dube, C., Rotello, C. M., & Heit, E. (2010). Assessing the belief bias effect with ROCs: It's a response bias effect. *Psychological Review, 117,* 831–863.

Evans, J. St. B. T. (2000). Thinking and believing. In J. Garcìa-Madruga, N. Carriedo, & M. J. González-Labra (Eds.), *Mental models in reasoning* (pp. 41–56). Madrid: UNED.

Evans, J. St. B. T. (2007). On the resolution of conflict in dual process theories of reasoning. *Thinking & Reasoning, 13,* 321–339.

Evans, J. St. B. T. (in press). Dual-process theories. In L. J. Ball & V. A. Thompson (Eds.), *The Routledge international handbook of thinking and reasoning.* Abingdon, UK: Routledge.

Evans, J. St. B. T., Barston, J. L., & Pollard, P. (1983). On the conflict between logic and belief in syllogistic reasoning. *Memory & Cognition, 11*, 295–306.

Evans, J. St. B. T., & Curtis-Holmes, J. (2005). Rapid responding increases belief bias: Evidence for the dual process theory of reasoning. *Thinking & Reasoning, 11*, 382–389.

Evans, J. St. B. T., Handley, S. J., & Harper, C. N. (2001). Necessity, possibility and belief: A study of syllogistic reasoning. *Quarterly Journal of Experimental Psychology, 54*, 935–958.

Evans, J. St. B. T., Handley, S. J., Harper, C. N., & Johnson-Laird, P. N. (1999). Reasoning about necessity and possibility: A test of the mental model theory of deduction. *Journal of Experimental Psychology: Learning, Memory, & Cognition, 25*, 1495–1513.

Evans, J. St. B. T., Handley, S. J., Neilens, H., & Over, D. (2010). The influence of cognitive ability and instructional set on causal conditional inference. *Quarterly Journal of Experimental Psychology, 63*, 892–909.

Evans, J. St. B. T., Newstead, S. E., & Byrne, R. M. J. (1993). *Human reasoning: The psychology of deduction*. Hove, UK: Erlbaum.

Evans, J. St. B. T., & Stanovich, K. E. (2013a). Dual-process theories of higher cognition: Advancing the debate. *Perspectives on Psychological Science, 8*, 223–241.

Evans, J. St. B. T., & Stanovich, K. E. (2013b). Theory and metatheory in the study of dual processing: Reply to comments. *Perspectives on Psychological Science, 8*, 263–271.

Goel, V., & Dolan, R. J. (2003). Explaining modulation of reasoning by belief. *Cognition, 87*, B11–B22.

Handley, S. J., Newstead, S. E., & Trippas, D. (2011). Logic, beliefs, and instruction: A test of the default interventionist account of belief bias. *Journal of Experimental Psychology: Learning, Memory, & Cognition, 37*, 28–43.

Handley, S. J., & Trippas, D. (2015). Dual processes and the interplay between knowledge and structure: A new parallel processing model. *Psychology of Learning and Motivation, 62*, 33–58.

Houdé, O., Zago, L., Mellet, E., Moutier, S., Pineau, A., Mazoyer, B., et al. (2000). Shifting from the perceptual brain to the logical brain: The neural impact of cognitive inhibition training. *Journal of Cognitive Neuroscience, 12*, 721–728.

Howarth, S., Handley, S. J., & Walsh, C. (2016). The logic-bias effect: The role of effortful processing in the resolution of belief – logic conflict. *Memory & Cognition, 44*, 330–349.

Johnson-Laird, P. N., & Byrne, R. M. J. (1991). *Deduction*. Hove: Erlbaum.

Klauer, K. C., & Kellen, D. (2011). Assessing the belief bias effect with ROCs: Reply to Dube, Rotello, and Heit (2010). *Psychological Review, 118*, 155–164.

Klauer, K. C., Musch, J., & Naumer, B. (2000). On belief bias in syllogistic reasoning. *Psychological Review, 107*, 852–884.

Klauer, K. C., & Singmann, H. (2013). Does logic feel good? Testing for intuitive detection of logicality in syllogistic reasoning. *Journal of Experimental Psychology: Learning, Memory, & Cognition, 39*, 1265–1273.

Luo, J., Liu, X., Stupple, E. J., Zhang, E., Xiao, X., Jia, L., et al. (2013). Cognitive control in belief-laden reasoning during conclusion processing: An ERP study. *International Journal of Psychology, 48*, 224–231.

Luo, J., Tang, X., Zhang, E., & Stupple, E. J. (2014). The neural correlates of belief-bias inhibition: The impact of logic training. *Biological Psychology, 103*, 276–282.

Macmillan, N. A., & Creelman, C. D. (2005). *Detection theory: A user's guide* (2nd ed.). Mahwah, NJ: Erlbaum.

Markovits, H., Forgues, H. L., & Brunet, M.-L. (2012). More evidence for a dual-process model of conditional reasoning. *Memory & Cognition, 40*, 736–747.

Morley, N. J., Evans, J. St. B. T., & Handley, S. J. (2004). Belief bias and figural bias in syllogistic reasoning. *Quarterly Journal of Experimental Psychology, 57A*, 666–692.

Morsanyi, K., & Handley, S. J. (2012). Logic feels so good – I like it! Evidence for intuitive detection of logicality in syllogistic reasoning. *Journal of Experimental Psychology: Learning, Memory, & Cognition, 38*, 596–616.

Newman, I. R., Gibb, M., & Thompson, V. A. (2017). Rule-based reasoning is fast and belief-based reasoning can be slow: Challenging current explanations of belief-bias and base-rate neglect. *Journal of Experimental Psychology: Learning, Memory, & Cognition, 43*, 1154–1170.

Newstead, S. E., Handley, S. J., & Buck, E. (1999). Falsifying mental models: Testing the predictions of theories of syllogistic reasoning. *Memory & Cognition, 27*, 344–354.

Prado, J., & Noveck, I. A. (2007). Overcoming perceptual features in logical reasoning: A parametric fMRI study. *Journal of Cognitive Neuroscience, 19*, 642–657.

Quayle, J. D., & Ball, L. J. (2000). Working memory, metacognitive uncertainty and belief bias in syllogistic reasoning. *Quarterly Journal of Experimental Psychology, 53A*, 1202–1223.

Ratcliff, R., Smith, P. L., & McKoon, G. (2015). Modeling regularities in response time and accuracy data with the diffusion model. *Current Directions in Psychological Science, 24*, 458–470.

Shynkaruk, J. M., & Thompson, V. A. (2006). Confidence and accuracy in deductive reasoning. *Memory & Cognition, 34*, 619–632.

Stanovich, K. E. (1999). *Who is rational? Studies of individual differences in reasoning*. Mahwah, NJ: Erlbaum.

Stanovich, K. E. (2012). On the distinction between rationality and intelligence: Implications for understanding individual differences in reasoning. In K. J. Holyoak & R. G. Morrison (Eds.), *The Oxford handbook of thinking and reasoning* (pp. 343–365). Oxford, UK: Oxford University Press.

Stanovich, K. E., & West, R. F. (1997). Reasoning independently of prior belief and individual differences in actively open-minded thinking. *Journal of Educational Psychology, 89*, 342.

Stanovich, K. E., & West, R. F. (2008). On the relative independence of thinking biases and cognitive ability. *Journal of Personality & Social Psychology, 94*, 672–695.

Stanovich, K. E., West, R. F., & Toplak, M. E. (2016). *The rationality quotient: Toward a test of rational thinking*. Cambridge, MA: MIT Press.

Stupple, E. J. N., & Ball, L. J. (2008). Belief – logic conflict resolution in syllogistic reasoning: Inspection-time evidence for a parallel process model. *Thinking & Reasoning, 14*, 168–189.

Stupple, E. J. N., Ball, L. J., Evans, J. St. B. T., & Kamal-Smith, E. (2011). When logic and belief collide: Individual differences in reasoning times support a selective processing model. *Journal of Cognitive Psychology, 23*, 931–941.

Thompson, V. A. (2013). Why it matters: The implications of autonomous processes for dual process theories: Commentary on Evans and Stanovich (2013). *Perspectives on Psychological Science, 8*, 253–256.

Thompson, V. A., & Evans, J. St. B. T. (2012). Belief bias in informal reasoning. *Thinking & Reasoning, 18*, 278–310.

Thompson, V. A., & Johnson, S. C. (2014). Conflict, metacognition, and analytic thinking. *Thinking & Reasoning, 20*, 215–244.

Thompson, V. A., Morley, N. J., & Newstead, S. E. (2011a). Methodological and theoretical issues in belief-bias: Implications for dual process theories. In K. I. Manktelow, D. E. Over, & S. Elqayam (Eds.), *The science of reason: A festschrift for Jonathan St. B. T. Evans* (pp. 309–338). Hove: Psychology Press.

Thompson, V. A., & Morsanyi, K. (2012). Analytic thinking: Do you feel like it? *Mind & Society, 11*, 93–105.

Thompson, V. A., Striemer, C. L., Reikoff, R., Gunter, R. W., & Campbell, J. D. (2003). Syllogistic reasoning time: Disconfirmation disconfirmed. *Psychonomic Bulletin & Review, 10*, 184–189.

Thompson, V. A., Turner, J. A. P., & Pennycook, G. (2011). Intuition, reason, and metacognition. *Cognitive Psychology, 63,* 107–140.

Thompson, V. A., Turner, J. A. P., Pennycook, G., Ball, L. J., Brack, H., Ophir, Y., & Ackerman, R. (2013). The role of answer fluency and perceptual fluency as metacognitive cues for initiating analytic thinking. *Cognition, 128,* 237–251.

Toplak, M. E., West, R. F., & Stanovich, K. E. (2011). The cognitive reflection test as a predictor of performance on heuristics-and-biases tasks. *Memory & Cognition, 39,* 1275–1289.

Trippas, D., Handley, S. J., & Verde, M. F. (2013). The SDT model of belief bias: Complexity, time, and cognitive ability mediate the effects of believability. *Journal of Experimental Psychology: Learning, Memory, & Cognition, 39,* 1393–1402.

Trippas, D., Handley, S. J., & Verde, M. F. (2014a). Fluency and belief bias in deductive reasoning: New indices for old effects. *Frontiers in Psychology, 5,* 631.

Trippas, D., Pennycook, G., Verde, M. F., & Handley, S. J. (2015). Better but still biased: Analytic cognitive style and belief bias. *Thinking & Reasoning, 21,* 431–445.

Trippas, D., Thompson, V. A., & Handley, S. J. (2017). When fast logic meets slow belief: Evidence for a parallel-processing model of belief bias. *Memory & Cognition, 45,* 539–552.

Trippas, D., Verde, M. F., & Handley, S. J. (2014b). Using forced choice to test belief bias in syllogistic reasoning. *Cognition, 133,* 586–600.

Tsujii, T., & Watanabee, S. (2009). Neural correlates of dual-task effect on belief-bias syllogistic reasoning: A near-infrared spectroscopy study. *Brain Research, 1287,* 118–125.

Verschueren, N., Schaeken, W., & d'Ydewalle, G. (2005). A dual process specification of causal conditional reasoning. *Thinking & Reasoning, 11,* 239–278.

Wilkins, M. C. (1929). The effect of changed material on ability to do formal syllogistic reasoning. *Archives of Psychology, 102,* 83.

8
LOGICAL INTUITIONS AND OTHER CONUNDRA FOR DUAL PROCESS THEORIES

Valerie A. Thompson and Ian R. Newman

Introduction

According to Dual process Theory (DPT; Evans & Stanovich, 2013), reasoning reflects the joint contribution of two qualitatively different sets of processes:

a. Type 1 processes are autonomous, and therefore usually faster.
b. Type 2 processes require working memory, and are therefore usually slower.

Although speed of processing is not a defining feature of DPT, it is nonetheless critical in explaining many reasoning phenomena: Type 1 processes are assumed to produce a default answer, which may or may not be overturned by Type 2 processes. Thus, the asymmetry in speed between Type 1 and Type 2 processes is crucial to the DPT explanation for many phenomena, including (but not limited to) belief bias (Evans & Curtis-Holmes, 2005), base-rate neglect (Pennycook & Thompson, 2012), the conjunction fallacy (De Neys, 2006), denominator neglect (Bonner & Newell, 2010), and performance on the cognitive-reflection task (Frederick, 2005). Two corollaries to the speed-asymmetry assumption are that processing is sequential (Type 1 precedes Type 2) and that the basis of the IQ-reasoning relationship is due to Type 2 processes (i.e., that high IQ reasoners have the capacity and/or disposition to inhibit the default response, reformulate the problem, and devise a new solution; Stanovich, 2011).

Thus, DPT provides an elegant explanation for several reasoning phenomena on the assumption that Type 1 processes are fast and first, whereas Type 2 processes are slower and require working-memory resources. The phenomena mentioned earlier are posited to occur when reasoners accept Type 1 responses instead of engaging Type 2 processing. Recently, the three pillars upon which this explanation rests have been called into question: *speed, sequence,* and *capacity*. In this chapter, we outline some of the evidence that challenges the core assumptions of DPT, discuss the implications of these findings for the DPT processing distinctions moving forward, and highlight some of the outstanding questions that remain for DPT.

Speed

An asymmetry in speed between Type 1 and Type 2 processes is a necessary part of the DPT explanation of reasoning outcomes. In order to provide the default response, Type 1 processes *must* be faster than Type 2 processes. Therefore, time pressure during reasoning should restrict Type 2 responses considerably and force reasoners to rely on default Type 1 responses. The classic case in favour of the DPT explanation is belief bias in reasoning. On this view, beliefs form a default Type 1 response, which must be overcome by logical Type 2 reasoning. From this interpretation, it follows that time pressure should increase the prevalence of belief-based (Type 1) responses by limiting the ability to perform logical (Type 2) reasoning. Consistent with this interpretation, accuracy on logical reasoning tasks is reduced when reasoning under time pressure (Shynkaruk & Thompson, 2006; Thompson, Prowse-Turner, & Pennycook, 2011), which can lead to an increase in belief bias (Evans & Curtis-Holmes, 2005). From this, it also follows that with enough time pressure, reasoners should be unable to discriminate valid from invalid inferences. In other words, reasoners should only be able to discriminate valid and invalid responses when given sufficient time to engage Type 2 processing.

Recent evidence challenges this straightforward interpretation. Newman, Gibb, and Thompson (2017) presented participants with base-rate and conditional reasoning tasks with a challenging deadline. On both tasks, there was evidence that participants used logical and probabilistic reasoning, even under a demanding time deadline. Notably, on the conditional reasoning task, participants discriminated valid from invalid inferences when given only 2 to 3 seconds to respond. Importantly, this effect was not limited to discrimination between the simple *Modus Ponens* (MP) inference and the invalid inferences: the valid (but more complex) *Modus Tollens* (MT) inference was also discriminated from the invalid inferences and accepted above chance performance. Moreover, 31% of responses failed to meet the deadline, which was considerably shorter than the typical amount of time required to read the problems, suggesting that this deadline allowed little time for Type 2 processing to occur. Bago and De Neys (2017) provided converging evidence for these findings. They also found that reasoners were able to quickly and confidently generate normatively correct responses under time pressure during base-rate and syllogistic reasoning tasks. Thus, responses that reflect logical and probabilistic rules were being produced rapidly, under strict time deadlines. Essentially, reasoners appeared to be able to provide logically sound responses on the basis of default Type 1 processes.

These data suggest that phenomena such as base-rate neglect and belief bias may not result from a processing speed asymmetry, because responses based on logic and probability can be generated quickly. However, we also note that the effects of validity and probability increased when participants were given more time to respond, supporting a role for Type 2 processes in generating logically and probabilistically sound responses. Nonetheless, it appears that at least part of the reason that people give responses that reflect the rules of logic and probability is because those answers were produced by Type 1 rather than Type 2 responses.

Sequence

Given that Type 1 responses are generated before Type 2 responses, Type 2 processes should not interfere with Type 1 processes. In the case of the belief-bias paradigm, beliefs are assumed to be processed prior to logic and probability. If this is the case, then the believability of a conclusion should interfere with the ability to judge conclusion validity, but not vice versa: Type 2 processing of validity should not interfere with Type 1 processing of believability that *preceded* it.

Handley, Newstead, and Trippas (2011) found evidence to the contrary using simple MP and disjunctive inferences. On each trial, participants were asked to judge either whether a conclusion was believable or whether it was valid. They found that the validity of the inferences interfered with believability judgments more than believability of the inferences interfered with validity judgments. which would not have been the case if believability was always processed first by default Type 1 processes. Instead, for these simple inferences, it appears that the validity is processed first. Furthermore, this pattern of interference was replicated by Pennycook, Trippas, Handley, and Thompson (2014) with a base-rate task. One interpretation is that these very simple inferences, such as MP, are a manifestation of Type 1 logical processing. In that case, the interference occurs between two Type 1 processes, not between Type 1 and Type 2 processes.

By that reasoning, for tasks that require more complex inferences, beliefs should interfere with validity, but not vice versa. That is, the complexity of the inference should preclude generating logical responses using Type 1 processes and instead necessitate Type 2 processing (which would also be slower than Type 1 processing by virtue of the complexity of the inferences required). To test this hypothesis, Trippas, Thompson, and Handley (2016) presented participants with MP and MT inferences, simple three-term syllogisms, and complex syllogisms; each trial contained instructions to respond either on the basis of beliefs or logic. Replicating Handley et al. (2011), for the MP inference, validity interfered with belief judgments more than the reverse. For MT and simple syllogisms, the interference was symmetrical. For the complex syllogisms, beliefs interfered more with validity than vice versa; this result is consistent with the DPT explanation. However, even for the challenging complex syllogisms, *there was still interference of validity on belief judgments*. There is scope to interpret this finding in a manner consistent with DPT: it is possible that reasoners were relying on heuristics such as *min* (Chater & Oaksford, 1999) on these complex problems, which allowed them to reach logical conclusions quickly. Nonetheless, the evidence again suggests that responses based on logic and probability are available quickly enough to interfere with judgments based on belief, which poses a challenge to the default interventionist theories.

Capacity

There is a robust relationship between IQ and reasoning performance (Stanovich & West, 2000). It has been argued that this relationship manifests at the level of Type 2 processing (Evans & Stanovich, 2013); high-IQ reasoners are more willing and able to inhibit default responses and deliberately engage Type 2 processing to compute new responses (at least when task demands are sufficiently high; Stanovich & West, 2008). Therefore, the IQ-reasoning relationship is a function of Type 2 processes that require time and working-memory capacity. As such, this relationship should emerge later in the time course of reasoning.

Thompson and Johnson (2014) used the two-response procedure (Thompson et al., 2011). Participants were instructed to respond quickly and intuitively for their first responses (Time 1) to four types of problems, then take their time and respond carefully for their second responses (Time 2). They also gathered standardized measures of IQ and found that the IQ-reasoning relationship emerged at Time 1, which suggests that Type 1 processes may also contribute to the IQ-reasoning relationship. Two additional studies provide substantiating evidence. Thompson (2017) found that IQ and correct responses on a denominator neglect task were correlated at Time 1, even when those responses were given under a very strict deadline (less than 2 seconds) that should have minimized Type 2 processes. These data suggest that Type 1 processes play a role in the IQ-reasoning relationship. Furthermore, she found that increases in accuracy between Time 1 and Time 2 were also correlated with IQ; this evidence is consistent with an additional role for Type 2 processes in generating normatively correct responses. In addition, Thompson, Pennycook, Trippas, and Evans (2017) used Handley et al.'s (2011) instructional manipulation and asked reasoners to respond to moderately difficult syllogisms and base-rate problems according to either beliefs or logic/probability. High-capacity reasoners showed *more* interference from logic/probability on their belief judgments than vice versa; this result suggests that for high-capacity reasoners, the logical response is the default one. Low-capacity reasoners showed the reverse pattern of interference. In sum, the evidence suggests that at least part of the IQ-reasoning relationship is due to differences in Type 1 processes, challenging the DPT assumption that the IQ-reasoning relationship is a function of Type 2 processing.

Unanswered questions for DPT: moving forward

To summarize, the DPT explanation for a number of reasoning phenomena rests upon an assumption regarding the relative speed, sequence, and capacity requirements of Type 1 and Type 2 processing. Evidence has been mounting that calls each of these three features into question. This and other evidence (see De Neys, 2012; Handley & Trippas, 2015) suggest that for a number of reasoning tasks, sequential models of DPT are more and more difficult to sustain. Instead, the data support the conclusion that several processing streams are initiated in parallel. There are currently four versions of these models, which differ mostly in terms of whether they posit that Type 2 processes are initiated along with Type 1 processes (Sloman, 1996), that multiple Type 1 processes are initiated at once and only intervened on by Type 2 processes in the case that these produce conflicting responses (De Neys, 2012; Pennycook, Fugelsang, & Koehler, 2015b), or that the crucial distinction is not between autonomy and WM, but the degree of complexity of the putative Type 1 and Type 2 processes (Handley & Trippas, 2015). Putting those distinctions aside, there are a number of other important unanswered questions for DPT:

Is there room for the traditional, serial version of DPT as an explanation for reasoning performance?

The answer is almost certainly "yes". Although the evidence is clear that for at least some tasks, multiple Type 1 processes are produced in parallel and that these Type 1 processes can produce outputs that are based on logic and probability, there are likely to be other tasks that demand a default-interventionist explanation. We hypothesize that this would depend on the relative speed of the underlying processes and the extent to which WM resources were necessary to compute a response based on logic and probability. We say speed even though autonomy is the defining feature of Type 1 processes because the default-interventionist logic works on relative speed, as argued earlier. A default-interventionist model would apply when one type of response (e.g., one based on beliefs) is generated relatively quickly and forms a default, whereas the other (e.g., one based on logic) was generated relatively slowly and required WM resources.

For instance, correct responses to simple inferences may require few working-memory resources. These correct responses could be produced by Type 1 processes (i.e., we concur with Elqayam & Evans, 2011, that the nature of the conclusion is not diagnostic of the processes that generated it) or Type 2 processes. Indeed, for some of the tasks that form the basis of our argument, the evidence is equivocal that they require working memory to complete. Although Franssens and De Neys (2009) showed that base-rate responses to a base-rate task were reduced under working-memory load, we have not been able to replicate that finding in our own lab. Moreover, Bago and De Neys' (2017) recent paper showed that even under a combination of WM load and time pressure, reasoners were able to produce base-rate–consistent answers as their first response. Thus, it is possible that responding on the basis of the base rates does not require WM. However, in the case of conditional reasoning and moderately complex syllogistic reasoning, there is evidence that a concurrent WM load disrupts performance (Klauer, Stegmaier, & Meiser, 1997; De Neys, Schaeken, & d'Ydewalle; 2005; De Neys, 2006). These data seem to raise a paradox: How do reasoners generate responses based on logic in conditions designed to limit the availability of WM resources, given that WM resources are needed to complete the task? We hypothesize that some reasoners, likely those high in capacity, can compute simple logical inferences with little capacity, and quickly enough to interfere with belief-based answers; these reasoners should also experience relatively little disruption from a concurrent load. Others require WM resources to compute the inferences, and this takes time. This conjecture is consistent with our observation that the proportion of logically correct inferences increases over time (Newman et al., 2017; Shynkaruk & Thompson, 2006).

For more complex inferences, such as syllogisms, more working-memory resources are required (Gilhooly, Logie, Wetherick, & Wynn, 1993; Gilhooly, Logie, & Wynn, 2002). In these instances, a default-interventionist model is probably fitting: evaluating believability is relatively easy and intuitive, but processing complex inferences takes time and working-memory resources. Essentially, dependent upon the task at hand, Type 1 processes can generate responses that are readily available to the reasoner, but to compute responses that are more demanding cognitively, Type 2 processing must be engaged. Thus, for some tasks (and for some reasoners), believability and logic/probability responses may be produced via Type 1 processes; for other tasks (and other reasoners), responses based on logic/probability will almost always necessitate Type 2 processes.

Isn't it costly to initiate multiple streams of processing at once?

The bulk of the evidence described here suggests that multiple Type 1 outputs are generated at once, but some theorists (Sloman, 1996; Handley & Trippas, 2015) suggest that Type 2 processes may also be initiated in parallel with Type 1 outputs. One of the main arguments against a parallel structure is that it is wasteful: Why begin a costly analysis (from the miserly processing perspective; Toplak, West, & Stanovich, 2011), only to have it pre-empted by a heuristic one (Evans, 2007b)? Certainly, there may be a cost when there are conflicting outputs (at least in terms of processing time), but, on the other hand, there are clear benefits when the outputs cohere. Redundancy gain refers to the enhanced performance that arises when responses are based on multiple stimuli that converge on a single response, as opposed to a response based on a single stimulus. Although most of the evidence for this phenomenon is derived from relatively simple tasks, there is recent evidence that this phenomenon also applies to complex tasks, such as semantic categorization (Shepherdson & Miller, 2014). Redundancy gain would allow more efficient processing of the non-conflict trials, wherein responses based on multiple stimuli (beliefs and logic) converged on a single response.

In fact, whereas the reasoning and decision-making literature has recently focussed on the costs associating with conflicting Type 1 outputs (see De Neys, 2014 for a review), some theorists have argued for the importance of coherence as a theoretical construct. In this context, congruity would be considered a subset of coherence, that is, having two processes lead to the same answer is one way to achieve coherence. Glöckner and Betsch (2012) showed that the time required to make a decision decreased with the coherence of the input, even when the coherent trials required more information to be processed than the incoherent ones. Moreover, these authors have proposed that the goal of Type 1 processes is to attempt to construct a coherent representation of the information available (Betsch & Glöckner, 2010). Similarly, Topolinski (2011) argues that the ability to detect incoherence and inconsistency is a basic cognitive skill and that intuitions of coherence play a critical role in this ability. On this view, intuitions of coherence arise from fluency of processing (produced by priming) that results in a positive affective experience (Topolinski & Strack, 2009a, b, c; Topolinski, Likowski, Weyers, & Strack, 2009). Finally, Koriat (2012) argued that coherence gives rise to confidence and is also the proximal cause of fluency effects. Specifically, confidence in a decision reflects the consistency with which the available information favours the chosen option, and that choices with a high degree of consistency are made fluently relative to less consistent ones.

How can the Type 1/Type 2 distinction continue to be useful as an explanation for reasoning phenomena?

That is, what reasoning phenomena can we explain using this terminology? For example, assuming a parallel structure in which answers based on both logic and belief can be attributed to either Type 1 or Type 2 processing, what is the DPT explanation for reasoning phenomena, such as belief bias, the conjunction fallacy, performance on the CRT, etc.? The traditional explanation is that the processing of beliefs and stereotypes form a default response that is not intervened upon by Type 2 processes. If we accept the current evidence, it seems like a logical/probabilistic Type 1 answer is also generated. How can we then tell whether a given answer was supported by Type 1 or Type 2 processes? One possibility is that for each reasoning task, we need to do a task analysis to sort out which Type 1 and Type 2 processes are operating. However, that seems like a daunting process and cedes a primary strength of DPT, which is the ability to predict and explain reasoning performance across a wide variety of tasks.

Pennycook (this volume) asserts that it is obvious that there are two modes of thinking and that they are qualitatively different (see also Sloman, 2014). Intuitively, that may be the case, but for this distinction to have theoretical traction, we must be able to identify, in the context of a task, which are the Type 1 and which are the Type 2 processes (and how they interact, of course). He suggests we use autonomy as the defining feature that distinguishes between Type 1 and Type 2 processes. This suggestion seems reasonable, but we still need to be able to show that in the context of a given task, some of the processes have been initiated autonomously, and we need to have an agreed-upon method to identify those processes. Here we suggest some possible methods for how to do this and suggest that researchers going forward take care to consider these methods before simply categorizing outputs as arising from Type 1 or Type 2 processes.

One possibility is the Stroop-like procedure that Handley and colleagues adapted for reasoning (Handley et al., 2011). This task asks reasoners to respond on the basis of one of two possible dimensions, such as logic or belief. The fact that people are slower to process incongruent than congruent items means that the underlying processes interfere with each other despite the explicit intention or goals of the reasoners and thus supports a Type 1 interpretation of those processes. Nonetheless, one cannot rule out the possibility that the observed conflict is due to Type 2 rather than

Type 1 processes. The simultaneous use of a WM load or speed instructions could reduce the potential contribution of Type 2 processes and increase the probability that the observed interference was generated by Type 1 processes.

Similarly, we would need to agree on a procedure for identifying Type 2 processes. Traditionally, researchers have used WM loads and speeded instructions as a way to reduce Type 2 processing. The key word here is *reduce* – one cannot actually eliminate all Type 2 processing (or the participant would be unable to articulate a response). Nonetheless, these are the most promising tools at our disposal to demonstrate that some processes *mostly* rely on Type 2 processes. A third possibility is to use an instructional manipulation. Evans, Handley, Neilens, and Over (2010) showed that high-capacity reasoners showed less belief bias than low-capacity reasoners, but only when instructed to reason logically. In other words, high-capacity reasoners were apparently able to overcome their disposition to belief-based reasoning when they intended to, but not otherwise.

Furthermore, if the articulation of a response necessarily requires Type 2 processing, how are we able to identify when Type 1 responses are autonomously generated? Indirect measures such as response times and confidence ratings have been used to make inferences about the cognitive processes that occurred before a response is entered. For example, when a reasoner is less confident and responds more slowly, it may be because they have generated more than one response to a problem and needed to resolve the conflict. In effect, these inferences are drawn about the cognitive processes underlying a response only after the response had been given, using the nature of the response as a guide. Ultimately, this presents an interpretational challenge: assessing the autonomy of the processes that led to the output from the output itself (i.e., classifying them as Type 1 or Type 2).

As an alternative, online measures, such as mouse tracking and eye tracking, may provide better insight into the cognitive processes that lead up to responses given by participants. Travers, Rolison, and Feeney (2016) used a mouse-tracking paradigm in which problems were displayed along with misleading lures and the correct answers. Even when participants ultimately clicked on the correct answer, they initially moved the mouse towards the misleading lure. These data provide insight into the time course of cognition and suggest that reasoners are initially drawn to the compelling lure.

Newman and Thompson (manuscript in preparation) recorded eye-gaze fixations during a base-rate task alongside self-reports of strategy applied to solve the problems. They found that reasoners spent more time attending to the base-rate ratios for incongruent problems than for congruent problems. Moreover, this pattern of visual attention was consistent regardless of participants' self-reported strategy use, that is, whether they reported relying mostly on the personality descriptions or the base-rate ratios to inform their responses. Crucially, these groups differed on their responses (the "ratios" group gave responses closer to the base-rate response for conflict problems) and their confidence ratings (the "descriptions" group was more confident than the "ratios" group for their hurried responses). In sum, the eye-gaze fixation data suggest that even if those in the "descriptions" group undervalue the base-rate ratio information and are less sensitive to the conflict than the "ratios" group (as indexed by confidence), their attention was nonetheless drawn to the base-rate ratios on those problems. Although preliminary, these data suggest that insight into the time course and relative autonomy of processes during reasoning could be gained through online measures taken prior to when a response is emitted.

Another possibility for sorting out the contributions of Type 1 and Type 2 processes may be to use the process dissociation procedure first developed by Jacoby (1991). Ferriera and colleagues (Ferreira, Garcia-Marques, Sherman, & Sherman, 2006; Ferreira, Mata, Donkin, Sherman & Ihmels, 2016; Mata, Ferreira, & Reis, 2013) have applied the process dissociation procedure to a variety of reasoning and decision-making tasks. For this, one needs to calculate two parameters: an index of controlled (i.e., Type 2) processing and an index of heuristic (Type 1) processing. This, in turn, requires that there be trials in which the two processes generate different answers (incongruent) and trials in which the two processes generate the same answer (congruent). One must also specify *a priori* which of the two possible responses is generated by heuristic and controlled processes. The control parameter, C, is computed as the difference in giving the heuristic response to congruent and incongruent trials [C = P(heuristic + congruent) − P(heuristic + incongruent)]; when this difference is large, it means that reasoners are giving the controlled rather than the heuristic response to the incongruent problems. The heuristic parameter, H, is computed as the ratio of P(heuristic + incongruent) to (1-C). The rationale is that giving the heuristic response requires controlled processes to fail (1-C) and for Heuristic processes (H) to succeed. In several studies, this group of researchers has shown that instructional manipulations, memory loads, processing goals, and other variables thought to promote Type 2 thinking primarily affect the C estimates, leaving H unaffected. Other variables such as priming affected estimates of H without changing C. Although the process dissociation procedure is controversial (see Payne & Bishara, 2009; Yonelinas & Jacoby, 2012 for reviews), the procedure offers another way to corroborate the assumed effects of manipulations intended to promote or reduce Type 1 and Type 2 processing.

Indeed, Payne and Bishara (2009) recommend that the process dissociation procedure be used to test the assumptions about the role of controlled and automatic processes in the context of a given task. The researcher should specify in advance what it means to exert control in any given task. Automatic processes are then defined empirically as those that influence behaviour when control fails. The researcher is then in a position to evaluate the contribution of the putative controlled and automatic processes to the task at hand.

Of course, the success of all of these manipulations requires that the person have the basic skills and knowledge to carry out the task. In Stanovich's terminology, people must have the mindware to succeed in the task, that is, that they understand the relevant rules of logic or probability, understand the difference between necessity and possibility, etc. An important lesson we should take to heart going forward is not to presume that reasoners understand these concepts and perhaps include a pre-test or a post-test with simple, non-tricky items to ensure that they do.

Similarly, the reasoner must also understand the instructions in the way that the experimenter intended (Henle, 1960); researchers should build in a manipulation check to ensure that the instructions are being followed. Another caution is that people must also have the motivation or disposition to do the mental work required to carry out the tasks in the manner that they are instructed to (Pennycook, Fugelsang, & Koehler, 2015a; West, Toplak, & Stanovich, 2008; Toplak et al., 2011). One may ascertain this either by measuring motivation using the AOT or CRT (Toplak et al., 2011) or by manipulating it, possibly by offering rewards. Behaviour that changes due to the reward structure is presumably under deliberate control and thus produced by Type 2 processes.

How do logical intuitions (Type 1) differ from logical reasoning (Type 2)?

The data outlined earlier clearly demonstrate the need to move beyond the "normative fallacy" that associates "biases" with Type 1 thinking and "accuracy" with Type 2 reasoning (Elqayam & Evans, 2011). It does, however, leave us with a difficult question to answer: How do logical intuitions (Type 1) differ from logical reasoning (Type 2; see also De Neys, this volume)? The data that we described earlier support the conclusion that the effects of logic/probability are observed in initial "intuitive" judgments and increase over an interval. Are the processes that give rise to a logical response at Time 1 the same as those that give rise to a logical response at Time 2, or can the same outcome be produced in different ways?

One possibility is that Type 1 logic might be produced by a heuristic such as *min* (Chater & Oaksford, 1999), whereas Type 2 logic might involve some more explicit reasoning about the structural relationships amongst variables (e.g., Johnson-Laird & Byrne, 2002). If so, we need to find a way to demonstrate that they are, in fact, different processes, for example, by showing that Type 1 and Type 2 logic are affected by different variables. As an example, Markovits and colleagues showed that when reasoning under time pressure in a conditional inference task, reasoners relied on probability information (i.e., the probability of the antecedent given the consequent), but switched to a counter-example strategy (i.e., rejected inferences that had even low-probability counter-examples) when given free time to reason (Markovits, Brunet, Thompson, & Brisson, 2013). This is evidence that fast and slow reasoning processes can be sensitive to different variables.

Can we continue to think about Type 1 and Type 2 processes as qualitatively different, or must we now think about them as lying on a continuum?

To accept them as different, we would need to be able to do a critical test of the hypothesis that there are two different kinds of processes operating in a given task rather than processes that differ along a continuum, such as complexity (Handley & Trippas, 2015). It has been argued elsewhere that the property of autonomy is important, given that autonomous processes unfold regardless of volition and therefore become an obligatory part of the problem space, with all of the implication that entails (Thompson, 2013). Conversely, some cognitive functions that require deliberation may not be completed because they are too taxing or perceived not to be worth the effort. Having said that, we are not convinced that we need to adhere to the claim that these are qualitatively different. What matters most, from the point of view of making predictions, is their *relative* autonomy; indeed, something like that construct will be needed to understand which of several Type 1 processes "wins" to produce the initial answer (De Neys, 2012; Pennycook et al., 2015b).

Indeed, this may be the most difficult question that is raised by the move to a parallel processing account: Given that Type 1 processes cue two different answers, why does one of them "prevail" to form a response? Again, for this new DPT to have traction, there needs to be an *a priori* basis to predict which answer forms the "default," at least for most people, most of the time. Pennycook (this volume) suggests that the relative fluency of the two processes might explain which one forms the basis of an answer, but once again, there needs to be a way to operationalize fluency that allows us to make predictions. Simple speed of response (the usual operational definition) may not be sufficient. For example, on a typical base-rate task, reasoners are able to process base rates very quickly, so quickly that removing them from a problem does not decrease the time required to give an answer (Pennycook & Thompson, 2012). Similarly, when instructed to respond either on the basis of the stereotype or the base rate, people are faster to make the latter response (Pennycook et al., 2014). And yet, when given free time to do the task, the modal response is to respond according to the stereotype. Thus, the fact that people can process base rates quickly does not mean that they form the modal response.

Complicating this picture is the fact that there are also likely to be individual differences in terms of which Type 1 process "wins." Our data seem to suggest that for high-capacity reasoners, answers based on logic/probability are produced quickly enough to interfere with answers based on belief, whereas the reverse is true for low-capacity reasoners. Skill, context (e.g., priming), and other variables are also likely to play a role in determining the outcome of this conflict.

Is it even possible, in principle, to dissociate Type 1 and Type 2 processes?

At the meta-theoretical level, the distinction between autonomy and deliberation may be a useful way to group phenomena together, but as argued earlier, at the level of experimental paradigms, it is challenging, although not impossible. Nonetheless, we are still left with the feeling that intuiting something is experientially different from what happens when we deliberate about something. For example, it feels like 4 + 2 is a fundamentally different problem to solve than 453 × 87. Despite the compelling nature of this example and our very strong feeling that intuition and deliberation are easy to tell apart, we conclude our chapter with an argument to the effect that they may be difficult to disentangle completely and that we must accept that every answer is produced by a combination of autonomous and controlled processes.

The starting point of this argument is that all processes require *some* WM or attentional resources. In order to form the basis of a response, a Type 1 output requires at least a minimal endorsement from working memory (Kahneman, 2003). Also, at a minimum, one needs to encode the cue that triggers the response. This cue may be one that is triggered by a fairly low-level act of deliberation (as, possibly, when one searches memory for the name of a childhood friend), and as such, requires some degree of intention. For example, the letter string "groane" may strike you as an odd looking non-word, until you know that it is an anagram, at which point the solution may "pop out."

Where does Type 2 thinking come into this? As noted earlier, one role may be as the initiator of Type 1 processing, as when one has an intention to search memory or solve an anagram. Another approach to this is to treat it as an essentially metacognitive question, which means that Type 2 processes are engaged to the extent that "something doesn't feel right" (Thompson, 2009). Incoherence may be one of many cues to a low Feeling of Rightness, but there are many others (Shynkaruk & Thompson, 2006; Thompson, 2009; Thompson et al., 2011) – to say nothing of the situations where a Type 1 answer is not produced. Type 2 thinking almost certainly exists on a continuum (Stanovich, 2011, Evans, this volume; Thompson, 2013). It may approve the initial response, justify it, question it, question it and leave it unchanged, or change it. In the case where the conflict between incoherent responses was strongly experienced, it may be engaged to choose between them. Deliberate thinking may be engaged to change a routine that is no longer appropriate (Betsch & Glöckner, 2010), to engage in hypothetical thinking about the consequences of a course of action (Evans, 2007a), or to change or re-organize some element of the problem space (Stanovich, 2011). Type 2 thinking may require a lot of WM resources or very few. Again, it seems laboured to try and make clear-cut distinctions based on whether or not WM resources are used and instead think about figuring out how to predict which of the Type 2 outcomes listed earlier are most likely to occur in a given context.

Finally, it seems likely that so much of what we study involves the back-and-forth of autonomous and deliberate processes (Betsch & Glöckner, 2010; Ferreira et al., 2006; Sloman, 2014). The anagram example illustrates this nicely. "Groane" may reorganize itself to the reader as "orange," but probably not unless you have the goal of looking for the anagram. "Orange" may pop out, or it may not. Staring at the letters for a few seconds may produce the answer, or it may not. If that fails, one might try re-arranging the letters, deliberately applying knowledge about English spelling, which also may produce a sudden insight: effort and autonomy interleaved. This illustrates another important point about the interplay between Type 1 and Type 2 processes: that they are continuously interactive so that few decisions will be purely Type 1 or Type 2 (Betsch & Glöckner, 2010). The point is that it is very hard to make firm distinctions between autonomous processes and processes that closely resemble them, and deliberate and intuitive processes likely work in tandem, rather than in strict sequence.

Conclusions

As experimentalists, DPTs have served us well and have generated a productive program of research. We hope the suggestions that we have made here will ensure that it continues to do so. It seems clear, however, that we have pushed the boundaries of DPT far enough that we need to regroup and think seriously about the conclusions that the data are pointing us towards. Where do we begin? As argued previously (Thompson, 2013), the fact that some processes unfold quickly and with little effort has profound theoretical implications: those fast answers will form the basis of the initial mental representation of the problem space, which means that they are also likely to shape the final representation. That is, although the final answer may move away from this initial one, it may be anchored in it, primed by it, a rejection of it, etc. Thus, understanding which answers are likely to be produced quickly is important, as is understanding how they are shaped by subsequent deliberation (or lack thereof). As we argue earlier, there are also several new and interesting questions to answer: What underlies "intuitive" and "deliberate" processes that produce similar outcomes (i.e., how do logical intuitions differ from logical reasoning)? If the same answer can result from fast and slow processes, it is an empirical question as to whether they are produced in the same way. How do we disentangle the Type 1 and Type 2 contributions to a given response? When two answers to a problem are primed, why is one chosen? What happens to the initial answer? When do people reflect on it, and what is the outcome of that reflection? Thus, although we start on uncertain footing, theoretically speaking, many profitable avenues for future research are opening up.

References

Bago, B., & De Neys, W. (2017). Fast logic? Examining the time course assumption of dual process theory. *Cognition, 158*, 90–109.

Betsch, T., & Glöckner, A. (2010). Intuition in judgment and decision making: Extensive thinking without effort. *Psychological Inquiry, 21*(4), 279–294.

Bonner, C., & Newell, B. R. (2010). In conflict with ourselves? An investigation of heuristic and analytic processes in decision making. *Memory & Cognition, 38*(2), 186–196.

Chater, N., & Oaksford, M. (1999). The probability heuristics model of syllogistic reasoning. *Cognitive Psychology, 38*(2), 191–258.

De Neys, W. (2006). Automatic – heuristic and executive – analytic processing during reasoning: Chronometric and dual-task considerations. *The Quarterly Journal of Experimental Psychology, 59*(6), 1070–1100.

De Neys, W. (2012). Bias and conflict: A case for logical intuitions. *Perspectives on Psychological Science, 7*(1), 28–38.

De Neys, W. (2014). Conflict detection, dual processes, and logical intuitions: Some clarifications. *Thinking & Reasoning, 20*(2), 169–187.

De Neys, W., Schaeken, W., & d'Ydewalle, G. (2005). Working memory and everyday conditional reasoning: Retrieval and inhibition of stored counterexamples. *Thinking & Reasoning, 11*(4), 349–381.

Elqayam, S., & Evans, J. S. B. (2011). Subtracting "ought" from "is": Descriptivism versus normativism in the study of human thinking. *Behavioral and Brain Sciences*, *34*(05), 233–248.

Evans, J. S. B. (2007a). *Hypothetical thinking: Dual processes in reasoning and judgement* (Vol. 3). Hove, UK: Psychology Press.

Evans, J. S. B. (2007b). On the resolution of conflict in dual process theories of reasoning. *Thinking & Reasoning*, *13*(4), 321–339.

Evans, J. S. B., & Curtis-Holmes, J. (2005). Rapid responding increases belief bias: Evidence for the dual-process theory of reasoning. *Thinking & Reasoning*, *11*(4), 382–389.

Evans, J. S. B., Handley, S. J., Neilens, H., & Over, D. (2010). The influence of cognitive ability and instructional set on causal conditional inference. *The Quarterly Journal of Experimental Psychology*, *63*(5), 892–909.

Evans, J. S. B., & Stanovich, K. E. (2013). Dual-process theories of higher cognition: Advancing the debate. *Perspectives on Psychological Science*, *8*(3), 223–241.

Ferreira, M. B., Garcia-Marques, L., Sherman, S. J., & Sherman, J. W. (2006). Automatic and controlled components of judgment and decision making. *Journal of Personality and Social Psychology*, *91*(5), 797.

Ferreira, M. B., Mata, A., Donkin, C., Sherman, S. J., & Ihmels, M. (2016). Analytic and heuristic processes in the detection and resolution of conflict. *Memory & Cognition*, *44*(7), 1050–1063.

Franssens, S., & De Neys, W. (2009). The effortless nature of conflict detection during thinking. *Thinking & Reasoning*, *15*(2), 105–128.

Frederick, S. (2005). Cognitive reflection and decision making. *The Journal of Economic Perspectives*, *19*(4), 25–42.

Gilhooly, K. J., Logie, R. H., Wetherick, N. E., & Wynn, V. (1993). Working memory and strategies in syllogistic-reasoning tasks. *Memory & Cognition*, *21*(1), 115–124.

Gilhooly, K. J., Logie, R. H., & Wynn, V. E. (2002). Syllogistic reasoning tasks and working memory: Evidence from sequential presentation of premises. *Current Psychology*, *21*(2), 111.

Glöckner, A., & Betsch, T. (2012). Decisions beyond boundaries: When more information is processed faster than less. *Acta Psychologica*, *139*(3), 532–542.

Handley, S. J., Newstead, S. E., & Trippas, D. (2011). Logic, beliefs, and instruction: A test of the default interventionist account of belief bias. *Journal of Experimental Psychology: Learning, Memory, and Cognition*, *37*(1), 28.

Handley, S. J., & Trippas, D. (2015). Chapter two-dual processes and the interplay between knowledge and structure: A new parallel processing model. *Psychology of Learning and Motivation*, *62*, 33–58.

Henle, M. (1960). On error in deductive reasoning. *Psychological Reports*, *7*, 80.

Jacoby, L. L. (1991). A process dissociation framework: Separating automatic from intentional uses of memory. *Journal of Memory and Language*, *30*(5), 513–541.

Johnson-Laird, P. N., & Byrne, R. M. (2002). Conditionals: A theory of meaning, pragmatics, and inference. *Psychological Review*, *109*(4), 646.

Kahneman, D. (2003). A perspective on judgment and choice: Mapping bounded rationality. *American psychologist*, *58*(9), 697.

Klauer, K. C., Stegmaier, R., & Meiser, T. (1997). Working memory involvement in propositional and spatial reasoning. *Thinking & Reasoning*, *3*(1), 9–47.

Koriat, A. (2012). The self-consistency model of subjective confidence. *Psychological Review*, *119*(1), 80.

Markovits, H., Brunet, M. L., Thompson, V., & Brisson, J. (2013). Direct evidence for a dual process model of deductive inference. *Journal of Experimental Psychology: Learning, Memory, and Cognition*, *39*(4), 1213.

Mata, A., Ferreira, M. B., & Reis, J. (2013). A process-dissociation analysis of semantic illusions. *Acta Psychologica*, *144*(2), 433–443.

Newman, I. R., Gibb, M., & Thompson, V. A. (2017). Rule-based reasoning is fast and belief-based reasoning can be slow: Challenging current explanations of belief-bias and base-rate neglect. *Journal of Experimental Psychology: Learning, Memory, and Cognition*, *43*(7):1154–1170. doi: 10.1037/xlm0000372

Newman, I. R., & Thompson, V. A. (2017). Base-rate consideration: Visual attention, conflict detection, and strategy selection. Manuscript in preparation.

Payne, B. K., & Bishara, A. J. (2009). An integrative review of process dissociation and related models in social cognition. *European Review of Social Psychology*, *20*(1), 272–314.

Pennycook, G., Fugelsang, J. A., & Koehler, D. J. (2015a). Everyday consequences of analytic thinking. *Current Directions in Psychological Science*, *24*(6), 425–432.

Pennycook, G., Fugelsang, J. A., & Koehler, D. J. (2015b). What makes us think? A three-stage dual-process model of analytic engagement. *Cognitive Psychology*, *80*, 34–72.

Pennycook, G., & Thompson, V. A. (2012). Reasoning with base rates is routine, relatively effortless, and context dependent. *Psychonomic Bulletin & Review*, *19*(3), 528–534.

Pennycook, G., Trippas, D., Handley, S. J., & Thompson, V. A. (2014). Base rates: Both neglected and intuitive. *Journal of Experimental Psychology: Learning, Memory, and Cognition*, *40*(2), 544.

Shepherdson, P., & Miller, J. (2014). Redundancy gain in semantic categorisation. *Acta Psychologica*, *148*, 96–106.

Shynkaruk, J. M., & Thompson, V. A. (2006). Confidence and accuracy in deductive reasoning. *Memory & Cognition*, *34*(3), 619–632.

Sloman, S. A. (1996). The empirical case for two systems of reasoning. *Psychological Bulletin*, *119*(1), 3.

Sloman, S. A. (2014). Two systems of reasoning, an update. In J.W. Sherman, B. Gawronski, & Y. Trope (Eds.), *Dual-process theories of the social mind* (pp. 69–79). Guildford Press.

Stanovich, K. E. (2011). *Rationality and the reflective mind*. Oxford: Oxford University Press.

Stanovich, K. E., & West, R. F. (2000). 24. Individual differences in reasoning: Implications for the rationality debate? *Behavioural and Brain Science*, *23*(5), 665–726.

Stanovich, K. E., & West, R. F. (2008). On the relative independence of thinking biases and cognitive ability. *Journal of Personality and Social Psychology*, *94*(4), 672.

Thompson, V. A. (2009). Dual process theories: A metacognitive perspective. In J. Evans & K. Frankish (Eds.), *In two minds: Dual processes and beyond* (pp. 171–195). Oxford: Oxford University Press.

Thompson, V.A. (2013). Why it matters: The implications of autonomous processes for dual process theories—Commentary on Evans & Stanovich (2013) *Perspectives on Psychological Science*, *8*(3), 253–256

Thompson, V. A. (2017). Metacognition and intuition in a denominator neglect task: Converging evidence from individual differences and gaze tracking analyses. Manuscript in preparation.

Thompson, V. A., & Johnson, S. C. (2014). Conflict, metacognition, and analytic thinking. *Thinking & Reasoning*, *20*(2), 215–244.

Thompson, V. A., Pennycook, G., Trippas, D., & Evans (2017). Do smart reasoners have better intuitions? Manuscript under review.

Thompson, V. A., Prowse-Turner, J. A., & Pennycook, G. (2011). Intuition, reason, and metacognition. *Cognitive Psychology*, *63*(3), 107–140.

Toplak, M. E., West, R. F., & Stanovich, K. E. (2011). The cognitive reflection test as a predictor of performance on heuristics-and-biases tasks. *Memory & Cognition*, *39*(7), 1275.

Topolinski, S. (2011). A process model of intuition. *European Review of Social Psychology*, *22*(1), 274–315.

Topolinski, S., & Strack, F. (2009a). The analysis of intuition: Processing fluency and affect in judgements of semantic coherence. *Cognition and Emotion, 23*(8), 1465–1503.

Topolinski, S., & Strack, F. (2009b). Scanning the "fringe" of consciousness: What is felt and what is not felt in intuitions about semantic coherence. *Consciousness and Cognition, 18*(3), 608–618.

Topolinski, S., & Strack, F. (2009c). The architecture of intuition: Fluency and affect determine intuitive judgments of semantic and visual coherence and judgments of grammaticality in artificial grammar learning. *Journal of Experimental Psychology: General, 138*(1), 39.

Topolinski, S., Likowski, K. U., Weyers, P., & Strack, F. (2009). The face of fluency: Semantic coherence automatically elicits a specific pattern of facial muscle reactions. *Cognition and Emotion, 23*(2), 260–271.

Travers, E., Rolison, J. J., & Feeney, A. (2016). The time course of conflict on the cognitive reflection test. *Cognition, 150,* 109–118.

Trippas, D., Thompson, V. A., & Handley, S. J. (2017). When fast logic meets slow belief: Evidence for a parallel-processing model of belief bias. *Memory & Cognition, 45*(4): 539–552.

West, R. F., Toplak, M. E., & Stanovich, K. E. (2008). Heuristics and biases as measures of critical thinking: Associations with cognitive ability and thinking dispositions. *Journal of Educational Psychology, 100*(4), 930.

Yonelinas, A. P., & Jacoby, L. L. (2012). The process-dissociation approach two decades later: Convergence, boundary conditions, and new directions. *Memory & Cognition, 40*(5), 663–680.

9
DUAL PROCESS THEORY
Perspectives and problems

Jonathan St B. T. Evans

Introduction

My love affair with dual process theory (DPT) began in the early 1970s, right at the beginning of my research career and has continued through many versions to the present day (see Evans, 2014). The theory is popular, judging by citation rates to recent review articles on the subject (e.g. Evans, 2008), but has also been subject to many recent criticisms. Some of these are hostile (Gigerenzer, 2011; Keren & Schul, 2009; Kruglanski & Gigerenzer, 2011; Osman, 2004) by which I mean that the authors concerned never liked DPT or had competing alternative accounts to promote. A response to these hostile criticisms was presented by Evans and Stanovich (2013). What has moved on apace in the few years since then, however, is the advent of *friendly* criticisms, especially of the form of DPT known as 'default interventionism' advocated by authors such as Stanovich, Kahneman and myself (Evans, 2007a; Kahneman & Frederick, 2002; Stanovich, 2011).

Apparent difficulties for the default-interventionist (DI) theory of dual processing have been exposed by several authors writing in this book, including Wim De Neys, Simon Handley and Valerie Thompson, as well as a number of their students and collaborators. All of these authors have been attracted by the theory but have nevertheless discovered recent experimental findings that they find increasingly difficult to reconcile with it. It is these friendly criticisms which give me more pause for thought about where the theory stands now and how it can take us into the future. In this chapter, I will explain what default interventionism is in some detail and deal with the issues about it that have been raised. First, however, I want to make some more general observations about the nature of dual processing.

The proposal that there are distinct types of thought that are intuitive and reflective has ancient philosophical roots and has manifested itself in psychology in many forms, often by authors who were ignorant of similar proposals by others (Frankish &

Evans, 2009). I agree with Pennycook (this volume) that the basic distinction is irrefutably present in the human mind, but I also agree with him that we have much more work to do to understand how these types of thought work. Following Stanovich (1999), the terms System 1 and System 2 became popular in describing sets of features attributed to intuitive and reflective thinking by various different authors. Although still used by some authors (most notably Kahneman, 2011) neither Stanovich nor I employ these terms any more, preferring to talk of Type 1 and Type 2 processes. It is likely that multiple cognitive and neural systems are involved, certainly for Type 1 processing. I will explain this in more detail shortly.

The received dual process theory and its fallacies

The *received* theory of dual processing (Evans & Stanovich, 2013) is a powerful meme. It is a culturally constructed generalised version of the theory which no particular author has proposed. Friends and enemies of the paradigm alike often call upon this cultural consensus in their discussions, without citing any specific source. A key feature of the received theory is that features typically associated with Type 1 (intuitive) processing, such as fast, associative, belief based and biased, are somehow assumed to be necessary and defining, as are their contrasts in Type 2 (reflective) processing, such as slow, rule-based, abstract and normative. Stanovich and I admit that our own past practice of listing typical features found in multiple dual process models (e.g. Evans, 2003; Stanovich, 1999) has inadvertently helped to create the myth that is the received theory. Nevertheless, it is a meme, and it has given rise to a number of fallacies. Evans and Stanovich mention some of these (2013, p. 226), and I will discuss a couple here relevant to recent criticisms of DPT:

> *The normative fallacy.* Type 1 processes lead to errors and biases; Type 2 processes lead to normatively correct answers.
> *The belief fallacy.* Type 1 processes are contextualised and belief based; Type 2 processes are abstract.

These fallacies arise because *in the experiments typically conducted by psychologists* (but not necessarily in the real world) these features are frequently correlated with Type 1 and 2 processing. However, they are not the necessary and defining features of the two types of processing to which I come later.

The normative fallacy

Although cognitive biases have often been attributed to Type 1 processes and correct answers to Type 2 processes in specific experiments, these cannot be defining features (see also De Neys, this volume). The *normative fallacy* is at its most dangerous when the correctness of an answer is somehow taken to be diagnostic of the type of processing. This simply cannot be true. A correct answer could, for example, reflect a lucky guess, a helpful heuristic or an association from relevant experiential learning, all of which classify as Type 1 responses. A wrong answer could also reflect quick and shallow Type 2 reasoning or the application of an explicit rule which lacks validity in the context in which it is applied. It is also well documented that fast, intuitive – 'Type 1' – responses can be the basis of much effective expert judgement and problem solving (Gigerenzer, 2007; Gladwell, 2005; Klein, 1998). I have discussed many examples of this in my own books.

The normative fallacy has arisen partly for historical reasons. In my own earlier work on cognitive biases (Evans, 1989), I placed great emphasis on heuristic (Type 1) processing in the explanation of cognitive biases, mostly by suggesting that preconscious processing directed attention towards irrelevant information, which was then used by subsequent analytic (Type 2) processing to infer the wrong answer. In Keith Stanovich's first major work on the theory (Stanovich, 1999), he strongly emphasised the correlation between cognitive ability measures (IQ and its correlates) and normatively correct performance on many cognitive tasks. As cognitive ability was strongly linked to Type 2 processing in his theory, the link between this and normative performance was reinforced. The idea that biases reflect quick and careless judgements in the absence of conscious reflection has also been encouraged by the more recent popularity of the Cognitive Reflection Test (Frederick, 2005). On the simple-looking three items of this test, even those of high IQ are prone to give an intuitively compelling but wrong answer that comes easily to mind.

In the literature on cognitive biases, psychologists typically present difficult and novel problems to their participants, to which relevant past experience is either hard to apply or provides unhelpful cues. Hence, finding the normative solutions usually requires explicit reasoning through working memory and sometimes suppression of prior beliefs. This gives rise to the typical correlation of Type 2 processing with normative success, although it may not be representative of good thinking outside of the laboratory. In more recent works, both Stanovich and I have recognised and critiqued the normative fallacy and worked hard to remove it from the literature. For example, in the revised version of my heuristic-analytic theory (Evans, 2006, 2007a), I placed equal emphasis on the role of Type 1 and 2 processing in the causes of cognitive biases. I offered the following definitions and discussed many applications of them:

> *Fundamental heuristic bias*: People focus selectively on information that is preconsciously cued as relevant.
> *Fundamental analytic bias*: People maintain the current mental model [supposition, hypothesis] with insufficient consideration or evaluation of alternatives.

Similarly, Stanovich (2011) in a major update of his theory, showed that application of Type 2 thinking was no guarantor of normative success. He discussed a form of explicit thinking which he called 'serial associative cognition' which was shallow and error prone. Moreover, he introduced other conditions for normative success. One was the presence of relevant 'mindware.' You cannot apply a rule in rule-based reasoning, for example, unless that rule is part of your explicit knowledge system (perhaps acquired by education). Moreover, such rules can be wrong. A factor in the perseveration of gambling, for example, is the false belief that later bets can compensate for earlier bets, when each individually has an expected loss (Wagenaar, 1988). Teaching compulsive gamblers probability theory – that is, correcting their mindware – has been shown to be an effective form of cognitive therapy (Raylu & Oci, 2002). To those conditions, Stanovich also adds that cognitive ability must be sufficient for the task in hand. Only those of higher ability can decouple their beliefs from the problem content in order to think hypothetically about more complex problems. Even among university student populations, instructions to reason logically and ignore beliefs are much less effective for those of lower cognitive ability (Evans, Handley, Neilens, Bacon, & Over, 2010).

The belief fallacy

Not only are Type 1 processes typically blamed for cognitive biases, but there are often in turn linked with belief-based processing, with the implication that Type 2 processing is somehow (necessarily) abstract and decontextualised. There is again much dual process writing which has encouraged this aspect of the received theory. For example, there is a clear linkage between associative and implicit forms of learning which appear to contrast with the acquisition and application of explicit rules (Reber, 1993; Sloman, 1996; Smith & DeCoster, 1999). The distinction between gist and verbatim representation in fuzzy-trace dual process theory (see Reyna et al. this volume) is similar. In one of the chapters of this volume, Trippas and Handley refer to 'the default-interventionist proposal that belief-based reasoning is predominantly driven by Type 1 processing' (for a similar claim, see Trippas, Thompson, & Handley, in press). This claim holds in some specific applications of the theory to particular paradigms, but not as a general statement.

Why is it a fallacy to equate belief with Type 1 processing? First of all, Type 1 processing need not be belief based. For example, it can be linguistic. My own dual process accounts, going back many years, have invoked the idea of Type 1 processing in accounting for phenomena such as matching bias, the tendency to focus on values named and disregarding the logical effects of negation. I have referred to 'if' and 'matching' heuristics, which direct attention and cue biases on *abstract* versions of the Wason selection task (e.g. Evans, 2007a, building on much earlier proposals). Type 1 processes are defined by their autonomous and preconscious nature, not by specific linkage to any memory or belief system. Second, the idea that Type 2 processing is abstract and decontextualised is also wrong. The rules and facts that are stored in our explicit memory systems may be retrieved by rapid Type 1 processes cued by the context, but they can certainly be applied in Type 2 reasoning. Take the example of medical diagnosis. In familiar cases, a doctor might be able to identify a disease by a simple pattern recognition process. However, when patterns of symptoms are unclear or alternative theories arise as to their cause, a doctor might well need to engage in slow, explicit effortful reasoning in order to infer the most likely explanation or the best course of action. Clearly, this Type 2 reasoning is belief based, in that it is only possible for someone with the relevant expert knowledge. It beggars belief that we could have evolved a system for Type 2 reasoning that was applied only in an abstract manner when the vast bulk of real-life thinking is contextualised.

I should acknowledge some difference between myself and Keith Stanovich on the belief fallacy, however. In his various writings he has consistently put more emphasis on decontextualisation in Type 2 reasoning than have I in mine. Evans and Stanovich (2013), in seeking common ground, linked my own defining feature of hypothetical thinking to his notion of 'cognitive decoupling'. Both require the idea that current beliefs about the world can be suspended or disregarded. In my case, the main application is in suppositional reasoning or thought experiments. For example, this is needed to evaluate counterfactual conditional statements (Evans & Over, 2004). Suppose I ask you to evaluate the claim, 'if Hillary Clinton had been elected president in 2016, then the world's climate would heat more slowly'. It is true that you need to decouple your actual belief that Donald Trump won the election. But the question requires comparisons of the perceived climate change beliefs and policies of the two candidates and their likely ability to put these policies into practical political effect. So the (Type 2) hypothetical reasoning involved in answering this question is still heavily belief based.

Type 2 processing and working memory

I completed my PhD in 1972 and decided to continue my research on reasoning, which was a Cinderella field of British cognitive psychology at the time. Far more fashionable was the study of memory and following the seminal work of Baddeley and Hitch (1974), particularly the research programme on working memory which has continued and flourished ever since (Baddeley, 2007). I remember receiving frequent advice in the 1970s that it would be greatly in my career interests to abandon work on reasoning and join this mainstream. In resisting this peer pressure, it certainly did not occur to me that my work had much relation at all to that of the Baddeley programme.

I see it now with a quite different perspective. If 'System 2' is in fact a singular system, it must be one and the same as the working memory system of Baddeley and Hitch. As Pennycook (this volume) rightly argues, the study of executive functioning and the study of Type 2 processing are essentially the same thing, differing only in the tradition of study, and particularly the level of cognitive process which has most attracted researchers. A lot of evidence supports this conclusion. From psychometrics we know that individual difference measures of reasoning, IQ and working memory capacity are all closely correlated (e.g. Colom, Rebollo, Palacios, Juan-Espinosa, & Kyllonen, 2004). From Stanovich and West's work, we know that measures of general intelligence correlate highly with the ability to reason out solutions to novel and difficult problems (see Stanovich, West, & Toplak, 2016, for their most recent work on this). Studies of reasoning and decision making which impose short time limits or concurrent working memory loads generally seem to interfere with responses attributed to Type 2 reasoning (see Evans, 2007a; Evans & Stanovich, 2013 for reviews of relevant studies). Also, the theoretical analyses in the dual process literature of Type 2 thinking as a singular resource, which can be applied effectively to only one thing at a time, resonates with the literatures on controlled attention and executive processing.

Working memory and executive function are not uniquely human, but they are uniquely *developed* in humans, allowing us to exhibit forms of thinking which are exclusive to human beings. This is one of the conditions, along with greatly enlarged frontal lobes and distinctively human cognitive modules for language and meta-representation, which allowed us to develop the 'new' mind that distinguishes our species from others (Evans, 2010, 2013). Although the great bulk of our cognitive processing is autonomous (or Type 1), it is the new mind which allows us to deal with novel problems and engage in complex problem solving that requires decoupling, supposition and explicit calculation.

Type 1 processing and intuition

If I am relatively sanguine about the definition of Type 2 processing offered by Evans and Stanovich (2013), I cannot really say the same about Type 1 processes. These are defined essentially by exclusion. Type 1 processes are autonomous, meaning that they are not consciously controlled or engaging working memory. The problem here is not that this definition is wrong, but that it is too broad for the practical purposes of dual process research on intuition and reflection. There are very many kinds of autonomous processes in the brain, including those which enable visual perception and language comprehension, for example. Basically, everything that does not involve working memory is autonomous. Do we really want a definition of Type 1 processing that includes the brain's control of our digestive system, for example? So the problem runs deeper than just rejecting the term 'System 1.'

It seems to me that we either need to define intuition as a subset of Type 1 processes (defined purely by autonomy) or to add something else to the definition of Type 1 processing as applied in dual process accounts of reasoning and decision making. I have an idea what this extra something might be, inspired by authors who have investigated the metacognitive feelings associated with intuitive judgements (Ackerman & Thompson, in press). I suggest that a feeling of knowing or correctness associated with such judgements is not just a determinant of whether more effort needs to be expended on learning, deciding or reasoning (Ackerman, 2014; Thompson, Prowse Turner, & Pennycook, 2011). The presence of such feelings is also a *defining feature* of intuitive processing. This certainly narrows the definition of Type 1 processing to exclude a number of autonomous processes in the brain. For example, the processes which deliver the visual representation of the world around us or present the meaning of a sentence post only their end product into consciousness without metacognitive feelings. So we could tentatively suggest that intuitive judgements are those supported only by some feeling of rightness, whereas reflective decisions are accompanied by some form of explicit reasoning or justification. With this idea in play, I now turn to the default-interventionist theory of reasoning which has been much discussed in the recent literature.

Default-interventionist dual process theory

A few years ago, I introduced the terms 'default-interventionist' and 'parallel-competitive' to distinguish two forms of dual process theory (Evans, 2007b). The former term has stuck particularly and is often described as the standard model of dual processing in the study of reasoning and decision making. Evans and Stanovich (2013) affirm their shared commitment to this form of the theory: 'Our joint view is that reasoning and decision making sometimes requires both (a) an override of the default intuition and (b) its replacement by effective Type 2 processing' (p. 236). It should be noted, however, that default-interventionist (DI) theory is a class of dual process theories which can differ in important details. For example, my heuristic-analytic theory, in both its original (Evans, 1989) and revised (Evans, 2006) forms, assumes that Type 1 processing precedes Type 2 processing. However, the theory makes no reference to a default intuitive *response*, but rather to mental representations. The theory postulates that Type 1 heuristic processes select information as *relevant* and that Type 2 analytic processes are always responsible for choosing a response. Matching bias, for example, arose because people's attention was drawn to matching cards on the Wason selection task whose choice was then rationalised by Type 2 reasoning (Ball, Lucas, Miles, & Gale, 2003; Evans, 1996). Unlike some authors (Kahneman & Frederick, 2002), I have also never suggested that 'System 2' is responsible for monitoring Type 1 processing and choosing to intervene. It seems odd to me that there should be a system which acts both as referee and one of the two competitors. Thus the problem of conflict detection and resolution is a thorny one.

Another issue with which I have grappled since my earliest work on dual processing (Wason & Evans, 1975) is that of the *rationalising* function of Type 2 processing. Very often it seems that we merely construct justifications for default intuitions. And yet there is much evidence that some of these problems are solved by the application of Type 2 reasoning: for example the correlation of solution rates with cognitive ability and the inhibitory effect of working memory loads and short time limits. In the case of the Wason selection task, it took me a long to time to find evidence that Type 2 reasoning did anything other than rationalise preconsciously cued card choices, but eventually I found some. Evans and Ball (2010) found that when matching cues attention to a card whose selection is hard to rationalise (the false-antecedent card), people may attend to it but *not* select it. Influenced also by the work of Valerie Thompson on how intervention can be influenced by metacognitive feelings (Thompson et al., 2011), I came up with a specific DI model which I discuss next.

The Evans (2011) default-interventionist model

To avoid any problems with received theory discussion, I am going to focus on a specific DI account, that of Evans (2011), illustrated in Figure 9.1. In this version, I do refer to a default response which is called A1. It makes little practical difference, as the model still assumes that Type 2 processing always follows before an answer is actually given. As one example consider the bat-and-ball problem which features in the Cognitive Reflection Test (Frederick, 2005):

> A bat and a ball cost $1.10 in total. The bat costs $1 more than the ball. How much does the ball cost?

The correct answer here is 5 cents, but many people give the 'intuitive' answer 10 cents, even those of high IQ. This seems to be a strong example of a default intuitive response that will be given unless there is intervention with reasoning. In the DI model (Figure 9.1), A1 would be 10 cents and A2 5 cents. As a second example, consider the Wason selection task with the following rule:

> If there is a P on one side of the card, then there is a 6 on the other side.

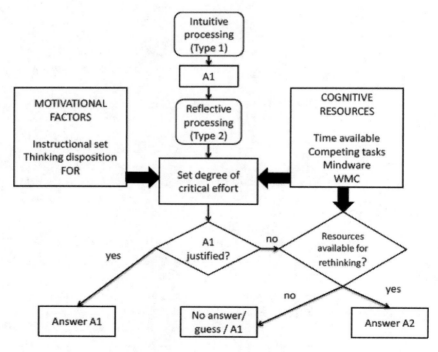

FIGURE 9.1 The Evans (2011) default-interventionist model
Adapted from Evans, 2011.

Participants know that each of four cards has a letter on one side and a number on the other. The visible sides are P, G, 6 and 4. Effectively, they have to make four decisions as to whether they need to turn over each card to test the truth of the rule. I will focus on just one of these: whether or not the 6 card should be turned over. The card is favoured by matching bias because it is present in the statement of the rule, so the default answer A1 is Yes, select it. Logical reasoning, if applied, will lead to the conclusion that whether or not there is a P on the back, we cannot tell if the rule is true or false. So A2 is No, do not select it.

The DI model shown in Figure 9.1 includes several specific processing assumptions that cannot be inferred from the received theory. First, it assumes that Type 2 reasoning is always applied, but with varying degrees of effort. This degree is affected by both motivational factors and cognitive resources, as shown in the diagram. Motivation can be intrinsic (holding a rational thinking disposition) or extrinsic (instructional set). Cognitive resources can also be a function of the individual – that is, it depends on their IQ or working memory capacity and on their education (mindware), but can also be a function of the environment when time limits or competing tasks are present. The influence of all these factors has, of course, been shown in many experiments.

The first task of Type 2 processing is to decide whether or not A1 is justified. So the default intuition is front and centre (unlike in parallel-competitive theories where Type 1 and 2 processes run side by side). The degree of effort which is expended on this depends on the factors described earlier. When people offer justifications that appear to do more than rationalise the default intuition (Lucas & Ball, 2005; Wason & Evans, 1975), these still require Type 2 reasoning, albeit lacking the accuracy and depth to reject the intuition. We know, however, that even when people accept cards on the selection task that are pragmatically cued, they still spend a fair amount of time thinking about them before committing to selection (Ball et al., 2003; Evans, 1996). Note that the choice of matching cards may (ultimately) be determined by Type 1 processing, but it is not fast, because time is expended justifying their choice with Type 2 reasoning. Thus the slowness of the response apparently conflicts with its heuristic nature. This is one reason why response times may not be a reliable indicator of the type of processing that determines our reasoning.

According to the model, if the default answer is rejected, then there may be an effort to reason out an alternative answer. This does not necessarily lead to A2, however – the intervention must also be successful. This depends upon having the relevant mindware and cognitive capacity to find the alternative answer. Failing that, people may revert to A1, give no response or simply guess. In the case of the bat-and-ball problem, originally presented by Frederick to Ivy League students, there seems little doubt that participants would have had the relevant mindware and cognitive capacity to find the correct answer. The reasoning is really quite simple. The only plausible explanation is that people choosing A1 made minimal effort to scrutinise it before accepting. This problem reflects a combination of two factors: (a) a very high feeling or rightness (Thompson & Johnson, 2014) in A1, making it a compelling intuition, and (b) low rational thinking disposition on the part of the participants accepting this intuition – meaning that they are not inclined to check intuitions with reasoning. On other tasks it is less clear. Consider the decision to choose or not choose the 6 card on the selection task problem described earlier. Rejecting this card requires specific logical insights. For example, people have to realise that the rule is not biconditional and that their purpose is to find falsifying rather than verifying cases.

Before leaving the case of the selection task, it is worth noting that the really hard decision is to choose the false consequent card – the 4 in the earlier example – which is not cued by the default intuition at all. Even a person who understands the importance of falsification may overlook this card because they never considered it in the first place. We know that a few people with high IQs, can make this choice (Stanovich & West, 1998). Is this because they are better reasoners, or because they are less captured by the default intuition? I return to this point later.

Logical intuitions and other problematic findings for default interventionism

Now I turn to the 'friendly' criticisms of the standard DI dual process theory. After many years of success and the resistance to hostile criticism (Evans & Stanovich, 2013), the paradigm seems in danger of imploding within the core reasoning research field. One of the first authors to come up with problematic findings was Wim De Neys, who has suggested the existence of 'logical intuitions'. Other mainstream researchers to present problems for the theory include Simon Handley and Valerie Thompson, as their own contributions to this volume indicate. Thompson and Newman, in particular, lay out a very clear summary of the problematic findings and a thoughtful discussion of the difficulties that they create for the standard theory. I will not repeat their full review here, but will briefly consider some of the findings and issues that need to be addressed.

Preconscious conflict detection

One of the fundamental ideas in dual process theory is that of conflict between Type 1 and 2 processes. In 1983 I first authored a paper on the belief bias effect in syllogistic reasoning entitled 'On the conflict between logic and belief in syllogistic reasoning' (Evans, Barston, & Pollard, 1983). I would not use that title now because it might be seen as promoting both the normative and belief fallacies! However, although this paper is often cited for developing the modern paradigm for studying belief bias and showing its key phenomena, it also advanced some basic questions for dual process theory. In particular, we showed that there was an apparent within-participant conflict on problems where logic and belief were incompatible. That is problems where the conclusion was either believable but invalid or unbelievable but valid. We did not find that some people go on logic and others on belief, but rather that the conflict might be resolved in different ways by the same individual on different occasions. Much later it was shown that different regions of the brain are activated according to which way the conflict is resolved (Goel & Dolan, 2003).

If conflict is between Type 1 processes – say supporting a belief-based response – and Type 2 processes – reasoning to the correct conclusion, then this has clear implications for default-interventionist DPT of the kind shown in Figure 9.1. It seems that conflict detection should be relatively slow, as we cannot be aware, say, that a belief-based answer to a syllogism is in conflict with one resulting from logical reasoning until we have had time to carry out the latter. However, it is in this regard that a number of recent experimental findings, using somewhat simpler logical tasks, have posed apparent problems with the standard theory. For example, it seems that in some cases conflict can be detected rapidly and preconsciously. De Neys has conducted a number of experiments on this (for reviews and discussions see De Neys, 2012, 2014; De Neys & Glumicic, 2008 and De Neys, this volume). Conflict may be detected in brain imaging or by slower responding, for example, even though the person makes a biased response and appears unaware of the logical solution. This evidence of preconscious conflict detection is clearly inconsistent with such conflict being between Type 1 and 2 processes in the standard DI model.

Many of De Neys' earlier studies on this depended on use of extreme base-rate tasks. For example, people might be asked to decide if Sam is a man or a woman given a description that stereotypically suggests a woman, but with base-rate information that indicates a 995 out of 1000 chance that Sam is male. Here the base-rate cue is extremely obvious, and there seems no reason why it should not operate intuitively to create a Type 1–Type 1 conflict. This is essentially De Neys' own explanation in what he calls a 'hybrid' model. According to this model, 'logical' intuitions as well as belief-based intuitions provide Type 1 cues (see De Neys, this volume). I am not quite sure why this is seen as an alternative to the standard DI theory, however. If we avoid any temptation to subscribe to the normative and belief fallacies described earlier, there is no necessary reason why a normative solution (assumed here to be the base-rate response) should reflect a Type 2 process, nor why a Type 1 cue need be belief based. I think certainly that results with this particular task can be accommodated by the standard DI model (or at least my version of it), especially because the findings do not replicate with non-extreme base rates (Pennycook, Fugelsang, & Koehler, 2012). De Neys (2014) has responded by pointing out that key findings of preconscious conflict detection have been replicated with other cognitive tasks, apparently more cognitively demanding, such as the conjunction fallacy (Tversky & Kahneman, 1983) or the bat-and-ball problem. These tasks are not all that complex, but it still is surprising that people giving the biased response (or at least their brains) have detected the conflict. For example, confidence ratings are lower for conflict problems (De Neys, Cromheeke, & Osman, 2011).

A similar problem has been posed by a different methodology adopted by Handley, Newstead and Trippas (2011) who appear to claim that their work refutes the default-interventionist theory and requires its replacement with a parallel processing model (see also Trippas and Handley, this volume). They introduced the innovation of asking people to decide the believability of conclusions as well as their validity. The result that they highlighted was that the logic of the problems interfered with these belief judgements. An example was:

> *If a child is crying, then it is happy.*
> *Suppose a child is crying.*
> *Does it follow that the child is happy?*

This is a modus ponens problem, which has a simple logical form (see Table 9.1). When given modus ponens with an abstract example, like the one shown in Table 9.1, the great majority of participants will correctly say that it is a valid inference. However, we have known for some years that modus ponens can be suppressed when the conditional statement is unbelievable, as in the earlier case. The believability of the conclusion interferes with the logical decision about its validity. But experimenters previously have only asked people to judge on the basis of logic. Handley et al. also asked people to judge whether or not the conclusion was believable and found that conflict effects still occurred. In the earlier example, the correct belief-based answer is No (the child is crying), but the logical answer is Yes, and this also interferes with the decision to judge belief. This is another kind of logical intuition.

Despite the claims made by these authors that these findings refute the DI theory, I am unconvinced, at least on the basis of the original paper. I think as in the De Neys experiments, we have a Type 1–Type 1 conflict. Recall the two fallacies discussed earlier. Just because modus ponens is logically valid, it does not mean that it requires Type 2 reasoning to achieve. This inference is almost universally made in

TABLE 9.1 Modus ponens and modus tollens

Modus Ponens

Logical form: If p then q, p, therefore q.

Example:

If a card has a G written on the front, then it has a 4 written on the back.

A card has a G written on the front

Therefore, it has a 4 written on the other side.

Modus Tollens

Logical form: If p then q, not-q therefore not-p.

Example:

If a card has a G written on the front, then it has a 4 written on the back.

A card does not have a 4 written on the back

Therefore, it does not have a G written on the front.

the absence of pragmatic conflicts and has been proposed to follow directly from our lexical entry for it (Braine & O'Brien, 1991). A person has to read through the problem presented, which gives plenty of time for the inference to be drawn automatically in this way, regardless of the instruction to disregard logic. It also seems evident to me that some degree of Type 2 processing is required to make the belief decision because people have to respond to an explicit instruction to process the information in a particular way.

The common elements in defending the DI theory against the findings of De Neys and those of Handley and colleagues are (a) the need to agree that some kind of 'logical intuitions' exist, in the sense that Type 1 processes cue the answer generally considered to be normatively correct, and (b) that conflict can be observed between rival Type 1 processes as opposed to the Type 1–Type 2 conflict proposed by Evans et al. (1983) and featured in many subsequent dual process accounts. There is no incoherence here, once the normative and belief fallacies are recognised and eliminated. But it does create problems for the explanatory power of the theory, as Thompson and Newman (this volume) note.

Other problem findings

One of the key assumptions in standard dual process accounts, such as that of Stanovich (2011), is that the correlation of normative accuracy with cognitive ability reflects the superior Type 2 reasoning ability of the higher-ability participants. There is, however, a complication pointed out by Evans (2007b). It could be that higher-ability people engage reasoning more often (the *quantity hypothesis*) or simply reason better when they do so (the *quality hypothesis*). This ambiguity is reflected in Figure 9.1, where cognitive resources have arrows both to influence the degree of processing effort engaged (quantity) and the likelihood of finding an alternative answer once it is engaged (quality).

What standard theories have not considered, however, is that cognitive ability also affects Type 1 processing. There is now evidence that it does so. One of the two tasks we considered that provides strong 'logical intuitions' is the extreme base-rate problem. Recently, Thompson, Pennycook, Evans and Trippas (2017) investigated this task with the conflict between beliefs and statistical information and the instruction to decide on the basis of beliefs or the numbers. Unlike previous studies, individual differences in cognitive ability were also measured. With lower-ability people, beliefs interfered with statistical judgements, just as the standard theory would predict. However, high-ability participants had great difficult in ignoring statistical information in order to make belief-based judgements. Thus it seems that higher-ability participants have stronger logical intuitions on this task (see also Thompson & Johnson, 2014).

The other strong logical intuition discussed is for modus ponens. Although not studied recently for this purpose, findings in existing studies are relevant. A puzzling result is that the tendency to make the rapid, automatic modus ponens is correlated with cognitive ability, whereas the endorsement of the complex and difficult modus tollens is not (Evans, Handley, Neilens, & Over, 2007; Newstead, Handley, Harley, Wright, & Farelly, 2004). Modus tollens is also a valid argument (see Table 9.1), but participants quite often fail to endorse its validity. Because modus tollens appears to require Type 2 reasoning, we would expect participants of higher ability to find it easier, but they seem not to do so. The fact that they find modus ponens easier is surprising given its very high endorsement rate and the fact that it does not seem to require Type 2 reasoning, with little, if any, load on working memory. So this inference seems to qualify as a logical intuition, but as with Thompson et al.'s recent finding on statistical reasoning, one that is stronger in people of higher cognitive ability.

Other relevant findings come from the two-choice task of Thompson and colleagues (Thompson et al., 2011) which was designed to measure intervention. Participants are asked to give quick intuitive answers and rate their Feeling of Rightness (FOR). Then they can reflect before giving a second answer, which can be different. The general finding is that when the initial answer has high FOR, people tend to spend less time rethinking it and are less inclined to change the answer. Thus Figure 9.1 includes FOR as a factor influencing the degree of processing effort applied. As an example, we recently showed that when responses on the Wason selection task comply with matching bias, they are made quicker, with higher FOR and are less likely to be changed (Thompson, Evans, & Campbell, 2013).

A key assumption in the standard DI account, however, is that intervention with Type 2 processes should improve reasoning performance on tasks *where Type 2 reasoning is required to solve them*. A difficulty is that at least on some tasks, such as syllogistic reasoning, feelings of confidence bear little relation to accuracy (Shynkarkuk & Thompson, 2006) and that people may be as inclined to change right answers to wrong ones as vice versa (Thompson et al., 2011). Moreover, Bago and De Neys (2016) also showed that those who are right on the second response tend to be right also on the first, having shown high FOR from the start. They used syllogisms as well as extreme base-rate tasks, albeit relatively simple ones (see later). Moreover, their findings held up in studies where speeded tasks and working memory loads were employed to interfere with Type 2 processing, defined as requiring working memory resources.

Implications for the current status and future value of default-interventionist dual process theory

The received theory, incorporating both normative and belief fallacies, is immediately falsified by these recent results. But the received theory belongs to no author and the fallacies are real, so we need to examine the issues more carefully. The finding of logical intuitions is undeniable, and if they are genuine intuitions, then they are Type 1 processes. On this approach we can attempt to retain a DI framework, but have to extend and refine it to deal with the problem of Type 1–Type 1 conflict.

I will start by considering the position adopted by De Neys (this volume) that on certain tasks, at least, cues to normative solutions are provided rapidly and intuitively and can conflict with cues prompting cognitive biases. This has the advantage of retaining the traditional DI framework which seems readily applicable to the more complex problem solving in the real world outside of the laboratory. However, the first question we have to answer is where could such intuitions come from? The approach I absolutely want to reject is that of unconscious thinking theory (Dijksterhuis, Bos, Nordgren, & von Baaren, 2006) which I have critiqued elsewhere (Evans, 2010). The idea that there is some alternative unconscious mechanism for complex reasoning seems nonsensical, given the mass of evidence for the importance of a central, capacity limited working memory system that supports, among many other things, complex reasoning. So if logical intuitions exist, as it seems they do, there must be heuristics supporting them. Although more complex problems have been used to a limited extent, most current research findings arise from the study of extreme base rates or modus ponens whose intuitive basis is fairly evident, as argued earlier.

Where more complex problems are used and some evidence of logical intuitions persists, we have to examine them carefully for cues to solutions that could be provided by simple heuristics, as Thompson and Newman (this volume) suggests. The simpler the reasoning task, the less strong can be the claims to challenge the DI model. For example, the syllogisms used by Bago and De Neys (2016), although involving three terms, appear to be 'one model' problems in the parlance of mental model theory (Johnson-Laird & Byrne, 1991). This means there is only one mental model that can be formed from which the conclusions are derived which could be achieved by rapid linguistic processing. In fact, the main way in which the mental model theory envisages Type 2 processing to occur is on problems where two or more models of the premises are available, not necessarily supporting the same conclusions. With such syllogisms, initial deductions may be subject to a search for counterexample models. So the intuitive logic finding of Bago and De Neys could simply reflect the fact that a model and implied conclusion forms simply by reading the premises. A recent study by Trippas et al. (in press) compared one-model and multiple-model syllogisms under instructions to choose conclusions by either logical validity or belief, with the method applied by (Handley et al., 2011). Their findings were consistent with the assumption that Type 2 reasoning is needed to solve the complex but not the simpler syllogisms. That is, belief interfered with logical judgements in both cases, but logical validity had little influence on belief judgements for the multiple model syllogisms.

The Trippas et al. (in press) study, referred to both by Trippas (this volume) and Thompson and Newman (this volume), has another problematic finding, however, in that they had evidence of logical intuition for modus tollens arguments, such as: If a child is happy then it cries; suppose a child laughs; Does it follow that the child is happy? In this case, the belief answer is Yes (the child laughs), but the logical inference No interferes with it. However, there are some unusual aspects to their findings with this task. Normally, modus tollens is much more difficult than modus ponens, but the success rate for the former under logic instructions (69%) was only marginally lower than the latter at 73%. It is possible that both inferences were being made in some rapid pragmatic manner. The evidence generally for modus tollens involving Type 2 reasoning is also questionable, because, as mentioned earlier, solution rates do not show the expected correlation with individual differences in cognitive ability.

Finally, we cannot rule out the possibility that when people reason under belief instructions they have nevertheless had time to complete some kind of Type 2 reasoning before answering the question. In these experiments participants are given several seconds to read the premises before the belief/logic instruction appears on the screen. Because they do not know if they will be required to reason logically or not, they might initiate a voluntary reasoning process during this interval. In short, although clearly challenging, none of these recent studies provides sufficiently clear evidence to refute the default-interventionist model. Parallel processing of initial cues certainly occurs; however, this may be within the Type 1 stage of generating initial intuitions and not evidence for parallel Type 1 and 2 processing of the kind discussed by Evans (2007b). More research is needed combining the study of individual differences with methods such as working memory loads or speeded responses, which can help to indicate whether or not Type 2 processing is involved in generating normative answers.

Summary and conclusions

The evidence of dual processing in the human mind is vast and convincing. More difficult is the application of specific dual processing models in explaining psychological experiments. The set of comfortable assumptions that constitute the 'received theory' of dual processing is wrong in some important respects and incorporates fallacies. In particular, typical explanations over the past 40 years or so have created the impression that Type 1 processing is belief based and prone to cognitive biases, whereas Type 2 processing is abstract and responsible for normatively correct answers. These explanations reflect the nature of the experiments and not that of dual processing, leading to dangerous fallacies.

Although there is much accumulated evidence for dual processing in the psychology of reasoning over the past 40 years or so, recent research has challenged a number of established assumptions, as contributions to this volume make clear. The most popular form of the theory which proposes that rapid intuitions are used for responding unless intervened upon by slower reflective processing is under particular challenge. It appears both that we have 'logical intuitions' on some of these tasks and that these may be stronger in those of higher cognitive ability. This certainly requires some re-thinking of the standard theory, but I feel that moving towards a parallel processing model is premature and may create as many problems as it solves. Critics must also be wary of the fallacies of the received theory when interpreting their findings.

Interesting and challenging though the recent findings are, they do not undo the previous 40 years of research on working memory and on dual processing in reasoning and decision making. People may have logical intuitions that become rapidly available on some relatively simple tasks, but that does not mean that all reasoning is done intuitively! There is a vast amount of research showing that working memory capacity is implicated in the performance of many cognitive tasks, including reasoning and decision making. There is the huge individual differences programme of Stanovich and West similarly showing that general intelligence measures and rational thinking dispositions predict performance on many reasoning and decision making tasks and clearly implicating Type 2 processing. So really what is at stake here is not the existence of dual process theory, but rather the serial or parallel nature of the cognitive architecture that underpins it. Although the serial default-interventionist model is being strongly questioned by several authors in the field, I have explained why I believe that further research is needed before we should abandon or radically revise this standard model.

Acknowledgements

I am grateful to Shira Elqayam, Valerie Thompson, Dries Trippas and Wim De Neys for their critical readings of an earlier draft of this chapter.

References

Ackerman, R. (2014). The diminishing criterion model for metacognitive regulation of time investment. *Journal of Experimental Psychology: General, 143*, 1349–1368.
Ackerman, R., & Thompson, V. A. (in press). Meta reasoning: Monitoring and control of thinking and reasoning. *Trends in Cognitive Sciences.*
Baddeley, A. D. (2007). *Working memory, thought and action.* Oxford: Oxford University Press.
Baddeley, A. D., & Hitch, G. J. (1974). Working memory. In G. A. Bower (Ed.), *The psychology of learning and motivation* (Vol. 8, pp. 47–90). New York: Academic Press.
Bago, B., & De Neys, W. (2016). Fast logic? Examining the time course assumption of dual process theory. *Cognition, 158*, 90–109.
Ball, L. J., Lucas, E. J., Miles, J. N. V., & Gale, A. G. (2003). Inspection times and the selection task: What do eye-movements reveal about relevance effects? *Quarterly Journal of Experimental Psychology, 56A*(6), 1053–1077.
Braine, M. D. S., & O'Brien, D. P. (1991). A theory of if: A lexical entry, reasoning program, and pragmatic principles. *Psychological Review, 98*, 182–203.
Colom, R., Rebollo, I., Palacios, A., Juan-Espinosa, M., & Kyllonen, P. C. (2004). Working memory is (almost) perfectly predicted by g. *Intelligence, 32*(3), 277–296.
De Neys, W. (2012). Bias and conflict: A case for logical intuitions. *Perspectives on Psychological Science, 7*, 28–38.
De Neys, W. (2014). Conflict detection, dual processes, and logical intuitions: Some clarifications. *Thinking & Reasoning, 20*(2), 169–187. doi:10.1080/13546783.2013.854725
De Neys, W., Cromheeke, S., & Osman, M. (2011). Biased but in doubt: Conflict and decision confidence. *PloS One, 6*, e15954.
De Neys, W., & Glumicic, T. (2008). Conflict monitoring in dual process theories of thinking. *Cognition, 106*, 1248–1299.
Dijksterhuis, A., Bos, M. W., Nordgren, L. F., & von Baaren, R. B. (2006). On making the right choice: The deliberation-without-attention effect. *Science, 311*, 1005–1007.

Evans, J. St B. T. (1989). *Bias in human reasoning: Causes and consequences*. Brighton: Erlbaum.
Evans, J. St B. T. (1996). Deciding before you think: Relevance and reasoning in the selection task. *British Journal of Psychology, 87*, 223–240.
Evans, J. St B. T. (2003). In two minds: Dual process accounts of reasoning. *Trends in Cognitive Sciences, 7*, 454–459.
Evans, J. St B. T. (2006). The heuristic-analytic theory of reasoning: Extension and evaluation. *Psychonomic Bulletin and Review, 13*(3), 378–395.
Evans, J. St B. T. (2007a). *Hypothetical thinking: Dual processes in reasoning and judgement*. Hove, UK: Psychology Press.
Evans, J. St B. T. (2007b). On the resolution of conflict in dual-process theories of reasoning. *Thinking & Reasoning, 13*, 321–329.
Evans, J. St B. T. (2008). Dual-processing accounts of reasoning, judgment and social cognition. *Annual Review of Psychology, 59*, 255–278.
Evans, J. St B. T. (2010). *Thinking twice: Two minds in one brain*. Oxford: Oxford University Press.
Evans, J. St B. T. (2011). Dual-process theories of reasoning: Contemporary issues and developmental applications. *Developmental Review, 31*, 86–102.
Evans, J. St B. T. (2013). Two minds rationality. *Thinking & Reasoning, 20*, 129–146.
Evans, J. St B. T. (Ed.). (2014). *Reasoning, rationality and dual processes: Selected works of Jonathan St B. T. Evans*. London: Taylor & Francis.
Evans, J. St B. T., & Ball, L. J. (2010). Do people reason on the Wason selection task: A new look at the data of Ball et al. (2003). *Quarterly Journal of Experimental Psychology, 63*(3), 434–441.
Evans, J. St B. T., Barston, J. L., & Pollard, P. (1983). On the conflict between logic and belief in syllogistic reasoning. *Memory & Cognition, 11*, 295–306.
Evans, J. St B. T., Handley, S., Neilens, H., Bacon, A. M., & Over, D. E. (2010). The influence of cognitive ability and instructional set on causal conditional inference. *Quarterly Journal of Experimental Psychology, 63*(5), 892–909.
Evans, J. St B. T., Handley, S., Neilens, H., & Over, D. E. (2007). Thinking about conditionals: A study of individual differences. *Memory & Cognition, 35*, 1772–1784.
Evans, J. St B. T., & Over, D. E. (2004). *If*. Oxford: Oxford University Press.
Evans, J. St B. T., & Stanovich, K. E. (2013). Dual process theories of higher cognition: Advancing the debate. *Perspectives on Psychological Science, 8*, 223–241.
Frankish, K., & Evans, J. St B. T. (2009). The duality of mind: An historical perspective. In J. St B. T. Evans & K. Frankish (Eds.), *In two minds: Dual processes and beyond* (pp. 1–30). Oxford: Oxford University Press.
Frederick, S. (2005). Cognitive reflection and decision making. *Journal of Economic Perspectives, 19*(4), 25–42.
Gigerenzer, G. (2007). *Gut feelings: The intelligence of the unconscious*. London: Penguin.
Gigerenzer, G. (2011). Personal reflections on theory and psychology. *Theory & Psychology, 20*(6), 733–743.
Gladwell, M. (2005). *Blink*. London: Penguin.
Goel, V., & Dolan, R. J. (2003). Explaining modulation of reasoning by belief. *Cognition, 87*, B11–B22.
Handley, S. J., Newstead, S. E., & Trippas, D. (2011). Logic, beliefs, and instruction: A test of the default interventionist account of belief bias. *Journal of Experimental Psychology-Learning Memory and Cognition, 37*(1), 28–43. doi:10.1037/a0021098
Johnson-Laird, P. N., & Byrne, R. M. J. (1991). *Deduction*. Hove & London: Erlbaum.
Kahneman, D. (2011). *Thinking, fast and slow*. New York: Farrar, Straus and Giroux.

Kahneman, D., & Frederick, S. (2002). Representativeness revisited: Attribute substitution in intuitive judgement. In T. Gilovich, D. Griffin, & D. Kahneman (Eds.), *Heuristics and biases: The psychology of intuitive judgment* (pp. 49–81). Cambridge: Cambridge University Press.

Keren, G., & Schul, Y. (2009). Two is not always better than one: A critical evaluation of two-system theories. *Perspectives on Psychological Science, 4*, 533–550.

Klein, G. (1998). *Sources of power.* Cambridge, MA: MIT Press.

Kruglanski, A. W., & Gigerenzer, G. (2011). Intuitive and deliberative judgements are based on common principles. *Psychological Review, 118*(1), 97–109.

Lucas, E. J., & Ball, L. J. (2005). Think-aloud protocols and the selection task: Evidence for relevance effects and rationalisation processes. *Thinking and Reasoning, 11*(1), 35–66.

Newstead, S. E., Handley, S. J., Harley, C., Wright, H., & Farelly, D. (2004). Individual differences in deductive reasoning. *Quarterly Journal of Experimental Psychology, 57A*, 33–60.

Osman, M. (2004). An evaluation of dual-process theories of reasoning. *Psychonomic Bulletin and Review, 11*(6), 988–1010.

Pennycook, G., Fugelsang, J. A., & Koehler, D. J. (2012). Are we good at detecting conflict during reasoning? *Cognition, 124*, 101–106.

Raylu, N., & Oei, T. P. S. (2002). Pathological gambling: A comprehensive review. *Clinical Psychology Review, 22*, 1009–1061.

Reber, A. S. (1993). *Implicit learning and tacit knowledge.* Oxford: Oxford University Press.

Shynkarkuk, J. M., & Thompson, V. A. (2006). Confidence and accuracy in deductive reasoning. *Memory & Cognition, 34*, 619–632.

Sloman, S. A. (1996). The empirical case for two systems of reasoning. *Psychological Bulletin, 119*, 3–22.

Smith, E., & DeCoster, J. (1999). Associative and rule-based processing: A connectionist interpretation of dual-process models. In S. Chaiken & Y. Trope (Eds.), *Dual-process theories in social psychology* (pp. 323–360). New York: The Guildford Press.

Stanovich, K. E. (1999). *Who is rational? Studies of individual differences in reasoning.* Mahway, NJ: Lawrence Elrbaum Associates.

Stanovich, K. E. (2011). *Rationality and the reflective mind.* New York: Oxford University Press.

Stanovich, K. E., West, C., & Toplak, M. E. (2016). *The rationality quotient: Towards a test of rational thinking.* Cambridge, MA: MIT Press.

Stanovich, K. E., & West, R. F. (1998). Cognitive ability and variation in selection task performance. *Thinking & Reasoning, 4*, 193–230.

Thompson, V. A., Evans, J. S. T., & Campbell, J. I. D. (2013). Matching bias on the selection task: It's fast and feels good. *Thinking & Reasoning, 19*(3–4), 431–452. doi:10.1080/13546783.2013.820220

Thompson, V. A., & Johnson, S. C. (2014). Conflict, metacognition, and analytic thinking. *Thinking & Reasoning, 20*(2), 215–244. doi:10.1080/13546783.2013.869763

Thompson, V. A. Pennycook, G., Trippas, D. & Evans, J. St B. T. (2017). Do smart people have better intuitions?'. Unpublished manuscript, University of Saskatchewan.

Thompson, V. A., Prowse Turner, J. A., & Pennycook, G. (2011). Intuition, reason, and metacognition. *Cognitive Psychology, 63*(3), 107–140.

Trippas, D., Thompson, V. A., & Handley, S. J. (2017). When fast logic meets slow belief: Evidence for a parallel-processing model of belief bias. *Memory & Cognition, 45*(4), 539–552.

Tversky, A., & Kahneman, D. (1983). Extensional vs intuitive reasoning: The conjunction fallacy in probability judgment. *Psychological Review, 90*, 293–315.

Wagenaar, W. A. (1988). *Pardoxes of gambling behaviour.* Hove, UK: Erlbaum.

Wason, P. C., & Evans, J. St B. T. (1975). Dual processes in reasoning? *Cognition, 3*, 141–154.

INDEX

activation strength 57
affective experience 127
Allais problem 84, 87
analytic cognitive style 36, 39
analytic processing 67, 76
answer fluency 19
anterior cingulate cortex 13, 53, 107
argument complexity 34
attentional control 77
automaticity 29, 54, 77
autonomous processes 20, 104, 115, 127, 142

base-rate neglect 13, 34, 53, 89, 121
base-rate task 14, 125, 147
bat-and-ball problem 10, 52, 147
belief-based responding 102
belief bias 30, 32, 66, 100, 111, 116, 140, 146
belief fallacy 140
belief instructions 74
belief-logic conflict 33, 35
bias blind spot 59
bias detection 53

categorical syllogisms 35, 101
class-inclusion error 88
cognitive ability 10, 30, 110, 139
cognitive biases 139
cognitive capacity 109; *see also* cognitive ability
cognitive control 12, 53, 71, 77
cognitive decoupling 7, 141
cognitive development 90

cognitive misers 48
cognitive output 9
Cognitive Reflection Test 9, 36, 144, 139
communicable arguments 61
concurrent load 54, 125
conditional reasoning 70, 122
conflict blind spot 53
conflict detection 15, 53–4, 57, 146
conflict monitoring hypothesis 14
conflict problems 32, 52, 102; *see also* incongruent problems
congruent problems 129
conjunction fallacy 92, 94, 121
controlled processing 12
corrective pattern 56
corrective time course assumption 55
correlated features 7, 51, 104, 138
counterexamples 40, 130

decision making 6, 28, 82, 86, 126
deduction 30
default-interventionist model 30, 67, 73, 105, 125, 137, 152
default system 48
defining features 7, 104, 138
deliberation 5, 48, 51, 57, 131
developmental reversal 91
disjunctive syllogisms 34
dorsolateral prefrontal cortex 13
dot memorization task 55
Dual Process 2.0 2
dual process theory 1, 100, 121, 137
Dube, C. 39, 109

158 Index

economic interactions 61
effortful processing 36
electro-encephalogram (EEG) 78
electrophysiology 66
encoding specificity 84
Epstein, S. 50
error monitoring 53
Evans, J. 42, 48, 61, 104
event related potentials (ERPs) 66, 70
evidence accumulation 32
executive control 107
executive functioning 51, 94, 141
eye-tracking 108, 128

false memories 93
false recognition 90
falsifiable nature 6
fast logic 58
Feeling of Rightness (FoR) 20, 113, 132, 143
feelings of affect 37
fluency effects 37, 127; *see also* answer fluency
framing effects 86
Freud, S. 28
functional labels 51
functional magnetic resonance imaging 13
fuzzy-trace theory 82, 140

gain-loss framing 91
gaze tracking 53
generic dual process theorizing 62
Gestalt theorists 85
gist representation 82, 86, 95
Gladwell, M. 1
gut feelings 58, 112

heuristic-analytic theory 143
heuristic intuition 56
heuristic processes 76
homunculus 14
human cooperation 61
hybrid model 53, 48, 62, 67, 76, 147

incongruent problems 129
individual differences 59, 106, 131
inhibition 86, 107, 121
inspection-time 109
instructional manipulation 73, 124, 128
instructional set 32, 145
intelligence 106
intentional control 75
introspection 55
intuition 6
IQ-reasoning relationship 124
irrefutable nature 6

Kahneman, D. 1, 48, 61
knowledge-based response 32

late positivity 68
liking task 37
load task 55, 106
logical intuition 54, 56, 130, 146
logical intuition model 16, 67, 112; *see also* hybrid model
logic/belief conflict 112
logic bias 73
logic-liking effect 37

matching bias 150
mathematics 50
metacognition 20, 86, 142
meta-reasoning 113
mindware 106, 109, 129, 145; *see also* mindware gap
mindware gap 107
misattribution paradigm 37
modal biased reasoner 59
modus ponens 33–4, 122, 148
modus tollens 34, 70, 122, 150
moral cognition 61
motivated reasoning 38–9, 105, 109
mouse tracking 128
mutual interference 34

N2 potential 68
need for cognition 86
neuroimaging 53
new mind 142
no-conflict problems 32, 52, 102, 112; *see also* congruent problems
non-detecting individuals 59
normative correctness 50
normative fallacy 138

override processing 54, 57; *see also* inhibition

P3 potential 68, 72
parallel model 29, 31, 48, 67, 124, 152, 176
Piaget, J. 88
probability theory 50
process dissociation procedure 129
processing architecture 51
psycholinguistics 82

rationalisation 107, 143
reasoning field 28, 52
recall/recognition dichotomy 58
received theory 138
recognition judgments 90

recognition memory 58
redundancy gain 126
reflection 6, 9, 138; *see also* deliberation
relative complexity 41
representativeness heuristic 14
response-bias 115
response time 12, 33, 109
risky choice 93

selective processing model 40, 104, 115
self-interest 61
sequential model 124; *see also* serial model
sequential sampling models 42
serial associative cognition 139
serial model 48, 125, 153
shallow analytic monitoring 15
signal detection theory 39, 42, 109
single-system account 91
Sloman, S. 50
Stanovich, K. 48, 139
stereotypical response 14
stimulus-response pairing 9, 18
Stroop deduction paradigm 41
Stroop task 12, 28
structure-based response 32, 41
suppositional reasoning 141

syllogisms 29, 53, 67, 151
System 1 47, 54; *see also* Type 1 processing
System 2 47, 54; *see also* Type 2 processing

thinking dispositions 10, 145
three-stage dual process model 17, 67, 76
time course 54, 66, 129
time pressure 54–5, 114, 122
transitive inferences 89
two-response paradigm 55, 107, 114, 124
Type 1 processing 7, 29, 66, 104, 111, 121, 127, 138
Type 2 processing 7, 40, 104, 111, 127, 138

unconscious processing 83

validation process 60
verbatim representation 82, 85

Wason selection task 140, 143
Wilkins, M. 116
working memory 7, 30, 35, 72, 93, 104, 124, 141
working memory load 125